TORTURE
IN BRAZIL

ILAS Special Publication

TORTURE IN BRAZIL

A SHOCKING REPORT ON THE PERVASIVE USE OF TORTURE BY BRAZILIAN MILITARY GOVERNMENTS, 1964–1979

SECRETLY PREPARED
BY THE ARCHDIOCESE OF SÃO PAULO

TRANSLATED
BY JAIME WRIGHT

EDITED WITH A NEW PREFACE
BY JOAN DASSIN

 University of Texas Press, Austin
Institute of Latin American Studies

Originally published as *Brasil: Nunca Mais* by Editora Vozes Ltda., Petrópolis, 1985. Copyright © 1985, 1986 by Archdiocese of São Paulo.

Published in the United States by Random House, Inc., New York, and simultaneously in Canada by Random House of Canada Limited, Toronto.

First Vintage Books Edition, August 1986

First University of Texas Press Edition, 1998

Requests for permission to reproduce material from this work should be sent to Permissions, University of Texas Press, P.O. Box 7819, Austin, Texas 78713-7819

♾ The paper used in this publication meets the minimum requirements of American National Standard for Information Sciences—Permanence of Paper for Printed Library Materials, ANSI Z39.48–1984.

Library of Congress Cataloging-in-Publication Data

Catholic Church. Archdiocese of São Paulo (Brazil)
    [Brasil, nunca mais. English]
    Torture in Brazil : a shocking report on the pervasive use of torture by Brazilian military governments, 1964–1979 / secretly prepared by the Archdiocese of São Paulo ; translated by Jaime Wright ; edited with a new preface by Joan Dassin.
    p.   cm. — (ILAS special publication)
    Originally published: New York : Vintage Books, 1986.
    ISBN 0-292-70484-4 (pbk. : alk. paper)
    1. Torture—Brazil. 2. Political persecution—Brazil. 3. Brazil—politics and government—1964–1985. I. Dassin, Joan. II. Title. III. Series: Special publication (University of Texas at Austin. Institute of Latin American Studies)
HV8599.B7C3813 1998
365'.644—dc21
                                             98-13511
                                               CIP

Write this as a memorial in a book.
Exodus 17:14

But recall the former days when,
After you were enlightened,
You endured a hard struggle with sufferings,
But were not overcome.
Sometimes you were publicly exposed to abuse and affliction,
And sometimes you were partners with those so treated.
For you had compassion for prisoners,
And you joyfully accepted the plundering of your property,
Since you knew that you yourselves had
A better possession and an abiding one.
Therefore do not lose your courage,
Which has a great reward.
Hebrews 10:32–35

CONTENTS

PREFACE TO THE NEW EDITION

by Joan Dassin

Little did I imagine that a casual conversation on the corner of 116th Street and Broadway would open so many worlds. I was waiting for the 104 bus when Al Stepan walked by and asked—as if having an inspiration at that moment—whether I would work with Jaime Wright on the English edition of *Brasil: Nunca Mais** (Brazil: Never Again), the wrenching account of human rights abuses that had just been published in Brazil. I was planning to go to Brazil a few weeks later to begin a Fulbright teaching and research fellowship, and hesitated only a moment before replying that I was deeply flattered by the proposal. My excitement grew as I realized what an extraordinary opportunity I had been offered.

In São Paulo a few weeks later, looking for Wright's unassuming house in the modest neighborhood of Brooklin Paulista—so different from its New York namesake—I wondered what I had taken on. When I got to the door, I desperately hoped that my credentials as a student of Brazil and human rights advocate would be sufficient to convince Wright of my suitability and trustworthiness for such a sensitive assignment. I remember his taking my measure with the same slow deliberation he directed to the project, and my own nervous need to be accepted. As it turned out, we forged a link that has lasted to this day. But my respect and awe have never diminished.

Jaime Wright and I worked hard over the next five months, revising the rough English translation of the original BNM text that he had done in Geneva some months before. He would give me sections of the text that I would then retype and rework on my Macintosh 128K computer—a real luxury in Brazil in those days. My most powerful memory of the process is the jarring contrast between the satisfaction I derived from improving the flow of the text by using good English style, which permits concision while the equivalent Portuguese demands elongation, and the often grisly content. I was always relieved to come to the analytical sections on the origins of the military regime or the social profile of groups targeted by the repression. The terrible passages with first-person accounts of torture were so chilling that I literally had to lie down or walk outside after working through them, and even so, I could edit only very small sections at a time.

We finished on schedule, and I was asked to write the preface for the English version, which we called *Torture in Brazil*. There was some discussion about the title. Would we lose too much of the sentiment implied in the Brazilian *"Nunca Mais"*? Also, how could the American reader be prepared for a plunge into such a different world, where the concepts of justice and punishment were distorted beyond recognition? Despite these emotional and moral concerns, I wrote a purposely dispassionate description of the project itself and the circumstances under which it was produced. My job, I thought, was to make clear how the project's use of the regime's own documents had irrefutably established that torture was an essential part of the military justice system in Brazil. Just as Cardinal Arns had asked Jaime Wright to "de-adjectivize" the Portuguese text, the facts in English would speak for themselves.

Even at the time, they spoke loudly indeed. With no guarantees except Cardinal Arns's personal prestige and the research team's staunch commitment to secrecy, the BNM project had challenged the political pact behind the 1979 amnesty law. Part of a reform of national security legislation that freed the few remaining political prisoners and allowed most exiles to return to Brazil, the amnesty technically benefited both former guerrillas and security agents. But its major effect was to take the human rights question off the public agenda as the country slowly returned to civilian rule.

During General Figueiredo's transitional government (1979–1985), both military and civilian leaders feared that investigations would trigger political instability and jeopardize the transition. Published just a few months after Figueiredo's successor, José Sarney, took office, the BNM project established that state agents had committed numerous politically motivated human rights violations in the 1964–1979 period. Yet the new civilian government made no attempt to assume responsibility or charge the perpetrators. On the contrary, the pact held, and even Sarney's many critics largely agreed that "let bygones be bygones" was the best strategy to keep the military at bay.

The flurry of press coverage provoked by the book's release showed how raw this nerve really was. Even today, the late Brazilian psychoanalyst Helio Pellegrino sounds remarkably prescient when he defended the

BNM project for taking on the "taboo" against so-called acts of revenge, as efforts to investigate human rights violations were often labeled. True to his vocation, Pellegrino worried whether a society constrained by fear—in this case, apprehension about a military crackdown—would be able to maintain its moral integrity. Hence he argued that the project drew on the noblest motives and humanistic tradition by denouncing the torturers on behalf of society.

The project organizers also took the moral high ground in defending their condemnation of torture as a crime against humanity. There was some irony in their disclaimer that it was "not the intention of the BNM project to prepare evidence [for] . . . a Brazilian Nuremberg trial." Painstakingly collected, sorted, and analyzed, the evidence of torture, abductions, disappearances, and other repressive practices was overwhelmingly detailed and incriminated specific individuals and the entire military justice system. Still, the intent of the project was not to prepare cases for prosecution, but rather to "ensure that the violence, the infamy, the injustice, and the persecution of Brazil's recent past should never again be repeated."

It would take a decade more for the Armed Forces to admit publicly—if indirectly—that 133 Brazilian and three Argentine political prisoners had been tortured to death and forcibly disappeared while in their custody. Hence their approval of a list of 136 names that was published with the Law of Disappeared Political Prisoners, passed in both houses of the Brazilian Congress and signed by President Fernando Henrique Cardoso on December 4, 1995, was tantamount to an admission of responsibility for the prisoners' fates.[1] The long-awaited law gives victims' families the right to obtain official death certificates and substantial financial restitution. It also permits the revision of the false death certificates of other political militants killed by the repressive apparatus, not included on the published list, who were said to have died by accident or suicide.[2] This was the case of journalist Wladimir Herzog, whose death in October 1975 while in the Second Army's infamous Information Operations Detachment–Center for Internal Defense Operations (DOI-CODI) in São Paulo mobilized domestic and international opinion against torture and repression in Brazil. In retrospect, Herzog's murder weakened support for the ultra-right in São Paulo, leading then-president Ernesto Geisel to sack the hardliner commander of the Second Army. The much-denounced death also fostered greater cooperation among religious leaders, the Brazilian Bar Association, the Brazilian Press Association and some unions, especially the Journalists' Union—groups that joined together to break the stranglehold imposed by the prevailing climate of fear and eventually formed the core of the "civil society" that would successfully press for redemocratization in Brazil.[3]

Right up until 1995, then, the BNM project was the closest Brazil would come to a "Truth Commission." It is deeply significant that the effort was private—even secret—and based in the moral authority of ecumenically minded religious leaders who would hold the state to account for however long it took to win government acknowledgment that torture, abductions, disappearances, and other repressive practices were embedded in the very structure of the military regime.

Undergirding this moral approach was a profound conviction that even skeptics would be convinced by the project's voluminous evidence and assiduous research. The comprehensiveness of the BNM materials is still astounding. *Torture in Brazil* was based on the Portuguese *Brasil: Nunca Mais*, a 312-page book summarizing the official proceedings of virtually all the cases tried in Brazilian military courts between April 1964 and March 1979. This larger universe contained more than one million pages of documents from 707 complete trials and fragmentary records for dozens of others. For safekeeping abroad, the entire archive was microfilmed in 538 rolls, which were subsequently donated to the Center for Research Libraries in Chicago. Through the Center's Latin American Microform Project (LAMP), the material is accessible to researchers at more than 100 North American universities.

All this material was analyzed in a 12-volume, 6,891-page encyclopedia, known as Project A. In Project A, the 35 BNM researchers analyzed the raw data, producing 111 statistical tables on topics from the types and frequency of torture to the sociological profile of the victims. Table 101, for example, is the famous list of 444 torturers that was produced by cross-checking the names cited by defendants in the project documents. Volume V was published as a separate book by Editora Vozes, BNM's Brazilian publisher, entitled *Perfil dos Atingidos* (Profile of the Victims). It is an extensive description of 47 Brazilian leftist organizations that were active before and during the 1964–1985 period. The volume barely scratches the surface of material included in 10,170 pages of pamphlets, mimeos, and publications produced by these organizations. These otherwise ephemeral documents were found attached to the trial documentation and were duly copied by the BNM team. Like the whole one-million-page archive, they are open to public consultation at the Edgard Leuenroth Archive of the Institute of Philosophy and Human Sciences at the University of Campinas in Brazil.

In effect, the audacity of the project was offset by its scrupulous attention to detail. Copying documents under the military's nose at the Brasília archives of the Supreme Military Court, the BNM team risked their own personal safety—for the five continuous years it took to complete the project. Never sure that the undertaking could be completed, the research team copied each document as if it were the last. Hence the meticulous single-mindedness that went into compiling an "encyclopedia" of torture became an antidote to this uncertainty. Politically, it was a daily act of resistance that countered the irrationality and horror of the abuses with reason and order. Likewise the patient didacticism of the interpretive sections in the BNM text compensated for the seemingly arbitrary nature of the repression. Arrest, detention, and torture were intentionally unpredictable, to heighten fear in the general population. But the project delved beneath the surface to find the rationale for the repression in the doctrine of national security, shattering the prevailing silence with the fine edge of consistent explanation.

All this failed to deter the critics who appeared in the aftermath of the book's Brazilian release. Aside from charges of revanchism, the most serious allegation was that BNM was one-sided. In focusing on torture and imprisonment, the project emphasized human rights violations committed and sanctioned by the state. This led to complaints that it failed to mention the terrorist acts committed by leftist organizations. In fact, BNM's emphasis was a way of contesting the prevailing view that the state-sanctioned torturers and the armed guerrilla groups committed equivalent excesses—the justification for the "reciprocal" amnesty. History would prove that equation false, and reveal that the military regime used the *pretext* of a major threat from internal subversion to justify the abrogation of all citizens' rights under national security legislation. The acquiescence of the justice system in the use of torture during preliminary inquests and in the admission of evidence produced under torture was an additional aberration—illegal even in the context of the already "exceptional" military justice system.

In the whirl of accusations, Brasil: Nunca Mais stood its ground. Cardinal Arns—along with Jaime Wright, the major spokesman for the project—agreed that *another* study should be done of persons killed by the subversive organizations. That, however, did not diminish the BNM achievement. Also, several books published in Brazil shortly after BNM attempted to defend the military point of view. Contending that occasional torture of political detainees was an unfortunate or even necessary weapon in the righteous war against subversion, they sought to discredit the BNM conclusion that torture was an essential part of Brazilian justice during the military dictatorship. But none of the books had any credibility; one was even written by a military officer whose name appeared on the BNM list of torturers. Meanwhile, *Brasil: Nunca Mais* conquered an enormous readership. Without any prior publicity, the book rocketed to number one on the Brazilian best-seller list within two weeks of publication. It remained on the list for 91 consecutive weeks, becoming one of the country's all-time best-selling nonfiction works.

From today's vantage point, the Brasil: Nunca Mais project appears not only to have marked the end of the military dictatorship in Brazil, but also to have become a milestone in the country's return to democracy. Concretely, the appeal made by Cardinal Arns at the end of his preface to the Brazilian edition of BNM led then-president Sarney to make Brazil a signatory of the Convention Against Torture and Other Cruel, Inhuman or Degrading Practices and Punishments while at the United Nations in September 1985. Several psychoanalytic and medical associations expelled doctors and other health professionals whose collaboration with the torturers was documented in the BNM project. Similarly, a number of implicated civil servants and even military officers were removed from their posts, although the latter have usually remained in the Armed Forces. Such removals have continued for years. In September 1995, for example, following denunciations by the British press and Amnesty International and a formal request for an investigation from the British Labour Party, the military attaché in the Brazilian Embassy in London was recalled to Brazil. The colonel in question had been cited twice in *Brasil: Nunca Mais* as having participated in torture when he served as a lieutenant in the First Battalion of the Military Police in Rio de Janeiro.

Despite its focus on past crimes, the project and its sequelae have cast a public spotlight on the endemic use of torture in police interrogations and imprisonment of so-called common prisoners, the vast majority of whom are African Brazilians, poor, and voiceless. They are condemned, as Jaime Wright has written, to languish where "they have always been: in prisons, police stations and penitentiaries, without specific charges, intimidated and humiliated by the barbarism of torture." Along with many Brazilian human rights organizations, Wright as spokesman for the BNM project has pressed tirelessly for the legal prohibition in Brazil of torture as a reprehensible instrument and crime against humanity *under any circumstances*. This was recognized in Article XLIII of Article 5 of the 1988 Federal Constitution, which specifies that "torture is an unbailable crime that cannot be pardoned or amnestied."[4] However, public indifference, legislative bottlenecks, a lack of political will on the part of the executive branch of government, and other factors have impeded the passage of the necessary implementing legislation by the National Congress. And regardless of the law, the practice of torture against poor and defenseless children, criminal suspects, and prisoners is still legion throughout the country. Its prevalence has led human rights advocates worldwide to denounce torture and execution by police of common crime offenders and suspects and gross violence against street children, along with substandard prison conditions and pervasive impunity for crimes committed in rural areas over land rights, as the leading items on the sorry list of human rights abuses in Brazil.[5]

Demonstrably, then, the Brasil: Nunca Mais project will have an enduring impact on the course of recent Brazilian history. The brainchild of a few audacious individuals, sustained by courageous outside funding and brought to fruition in unprecedented secrecy, the project more than fulfilled its original goals. These were to "preserve the memory of events that occurred during the period of military dictatorship, with an exclusive basis in the official documentation of the military justice system, and also to produce and multiply instruments of struggle in favor of justice."[6] In these lofty goals, it merits comparison with other truth commissions, defined as "official bodies set up to investigate a past period of human rights abuses or violations of international humanitarian law."[7] In Latin America, the National Commission on Truth and Reconciliation (Rettig Commission) created by President Aylwin in Chile and the United Nations Truth Commission in El Salvador are compelling examples of efforts—in the words of Chilean human rights lawyer José Zalaquett—"to overcome a legacy of dictatorial rule and massive human rights violations, even while the new government is subject to significant institutional and political constraints."[8]

Unlike these more recent examples, the BNM project had to operate within similar constraints with no government support and without overt backing from international organizations. In this regard it was more akin to human rights investigations in Argentina and Uruguay, both of which peaked in the mid-1980s and had significant pressure from and participation by nongovernmental human rights organizations. Nonetheless, in both the Argentine and Uruguayan cases, official commissions were appointed to investigate the recent past. In Argentina, then-president Raúl Alfonsín unilaterally created the National Commission on the Disappeared (Comisión Nacional sobre la Desaparición de Personas, or CONADEP). The commission comprised ten prestigious individuals and was chaired by the widely respected author Ernesto Sabato. Based on sources provided by nongovernmental human rights organizations and numerous victims' testimonies, the resulting report and book, *Nunca Más*, documented the cases of 8,961 persons who had disappeared during the infamous "dirty war." In Uruguay, the parliament established the Investigative Commission on the Situation of "Disappeared" People and Its Causes in April 1985. After seven months, the commission did secure evidence implicating the Uruguayan security forces in 164 disappearances that occurred during the years of military rule. By mandate, however, the commission was prevented from investigating illegal imprisonment or torture, which were much more common repressive methods in Uruguay. To compensate for the limited nature of the official commission's report, the Peace and Justice Service (SERPAJ), a leading nongovernmental national human rights organization, conducted its own unofficial investigation. The results were published in 1989 in a 442-page volume entitled *Uruguay: Nunca Más: Informe Sobre La Violación a Los Derechos Humanos (1972–1985)*.[9] Another strong nongovernmental project was carried out by the Centro de Estudios Paraguayos "Antonio Guasch," (CEPAG) which collected victims' testimonies in a 1991 volume called *El Precio de la Paz* (The Price of Peace). An emotional ceremony in Asunción marked the release of this effort to document human rights abuses in Paraguay under the notorious regime of Gen. Alfredo Stroessner, which ended in 1989 after thirty-four years with the dubious distinction of having been the longest surviving dictatorship in the Americas. Like BNM, this project was financed by the Geneva-based World Council of Churches (WCC).

Yet the Brazilian Nunca Mais project was able to achieve something that the neighboring groups did not—to establish official responsibility for politically motivated human rights abuses *on the basis of military records themselves*. A few military voices attempted to refute the evidence presented by the project. But for the most part, silence, and therefore a tacit admission of, at worst, guilt, or, at best, complicity, met the project's assertions. In Argentina, in contrast, it was not until more than a decade after the Sabato Commission had concluded its investigations that active military would come forward and begin to reveal their part in past crimes.

So Brasil: Nunca Mais continues to stand as a somewhat quixotic but deadly serious and ultimately galvanizing private endeavor. The project's greatest significance is symbolic. Like the Vietnam Memorial in Washington, D.C., which etched the names of those who died in the war into black stone and into our national conscience, the BNM project gave individual faces, particular circumstances, and, above all, names to both the victims and the perpetrators caught up in the net of violence and repression. Before the research and publication, it was possible not to know those specifics, and therefore to deny the extent of the repression and the degree to which it was central to government operations. Afterward, denial was impossible—although officially, at least, the government remained largely silent about the massive project and its revelations.

Given the project's moral force and inherent drama, it is not at all surprising that it has spawned not only historical analyses, but also investigative journalism, plays, and even a potential film. Lawrence Weschler's riveting book, *A Miracle, a Universe: Settling Accounts with Torturers*,[10] is a good example. Weschler cites Wright on how the Brazilian generals were "obsessed with keeping complete records as they went along. They never expected anyone to delve into those records . . . in any systematic fashion" (p. 15)—a partial answer, at least, to the baffling question of why the Brazilian generals kept such complete records of political trials, including defendants' denunciations of torture. Weschler also captures the flavor of the international, ecumenical cooperation that supported the project. He quotes Philip Potter, the World Council of Churches' general secretary who watched over one of the largest individual and per force *covert* grants in WCC history, telling potential contributors "that the world cannot really function except through trust—trusting that people will be truthful and circumspect" (p. 29). And, finally, Weschler elicits terrific answers to the most basic question of all—how did the team manage to keep the entire monumental endeavor secret for five years? Human rights advocate Paulo Sergio Pinheiro observes that the feat "was the true Brazilian miracle," while journalist Elio Gaspari agrees that the secrecy was "absolutely remarkable" and a reflection of the "seriousness of the people involved and the seriousness of the work." But the man who had run the photocopying operation had perhaps the best explanation: "Efficiency and luck," he said. "And divine protection" (pp. 78–79). Like the film *Shoah*, which focuses on the physical details and mechanical operations of the Nazi death camps, Weschler's book goes after the literal explanations of how the project was conceived and carried out, at the same time revealing the essence of the repressive regime.

The continuing fascination for the project can only be a reflection of the material's intrinsic power and hold on the minds and hearts of Brazilians and others who are moved by the country's history and long struggle for human rights. This new English-language edition makes the core of the project readily available to those who want to confront the excesses of the

Brazilian military regime, but should be interpreted in light of much subsequent scholarship and experience with transitions from dictatorship to democracy in various parts of the world. Hence the uniqueness of the BNM project is clearest when its achievements are compared to other "truth-seeking" enterprises, and when it is seen in the context of the necessary compromises and social tensions that are the inevitable legacy of systematic human rights violations. From that perspective, *Torture in Brazil* and the larger project from which it derives are windows into a formative national experience, told in the starkest individual and personal terms, but with great universal significance. For me, this multidimensionality continues to be BNM's most compelling feature. The personal risk incurred by those who conceived, carried out, and followed up on the project—and their constancy and faith in its unassailable moral power— is an added enhancement. Today, as when the Brasil: Nunca Mais project began over fifteen years ago, every means imaginable should be mobilized to create knowledge about the past and forge new instruments for justice so that torture will be eradicated in Brazil.

JOAN DASSIN
New York City
April 1996

Notes

* The Portuguese acronym BNM will be used throughout to refer to the project. In general, English names or Portuguese acronyms will be used as appropriate. All acronyms are identified in the glossary, Appendix I.

1. Jaime Wright, "Desaparecidos," *O São Paulo*, 27 September 1995.

2. "FH sanciona projeto dos desaparecidos," *Jornal do Brasil*, 5 December 1995.

3. See Fernando Pacheco Jordão, *Dossiê Herzog* (São Paulo: Global Editora e Distribuidora Ltda., 1979).

4. Jaime Wright, "Tortura, até quando?," *A Gazeta*, Vitória, (ES), 8 June 1994, p. 5.

5. Juan E. Mendez, Review of *A Miracle, a Universe: Settling Accounts with Torturers* by Lawrence Weschler, *Journal of Human Rights*, Vol. VIII, 1991, pp. 586–587.

6. Jaime Wright, "Dez Anos de 'Brasil: Nunca Mais,'" *Folha de S. Paulo*, 14 July 1995.

7. See Priscilla B. Hayner, "Fifteen Truth Commissions—1974 to 1994: A Comparative Study," *Human Rights Quarterly*, Vol. 16, No. 4, November 1994, pp. 597–675.

8. Introduction to the English Edition, *Report of the Chilean National Commission on Truth and Reconciliation*, trans. by Phillip E. Berryman (Notre Dame: University of Notre Dame Press, 1993), p. xxiii.

9. Hayner, pp. 614–617, 651–652.

10. New York: Penguin Books, 1991. Original edition by Pantheon Books, 1990.

FOREWORD

by PHILIP POTTER
General Secretary of the
World Council of Churches, 1972–1984

IT IS with deep gratitude and humility that I recommend this uniquely significant book: gratitude, that it has been possible for a courageous group of people legally to make use of records of Brazilian military courts dating from April 1964 to March 1979, to put before the public an account of the tragic practice of torture during a particularly eventful period of the history of the world and of Brazil; humility, because I, like all readers, share a common humanity with the tortured and the torturers, and, share too in the suffering and the guilt of those who were caught up in this degrading violation of our human nature.

I write as one who has been involved for nearly forty years in the ecumenical movement, which has always given prominence to the promotion of human rights and of the inviolable dignity of the human person. When the World Council of Churches (a fellowship of over three hundred Orthodox, Protestant, and Pentecostal churches in more than one hundred countries) was officially inaugurated in 1948, it made a clear declaration of human rights:

> We affirm that all men are equal in the sight of God and that the rights of men derive directly from their status as the children of God. It is presumptuous for the state to assume that it can grant or deny fundamental rights. It is for the state to embody these rights in its own legal system and to ensure their observance in practice. . . . We are profoundly concerned about evidence from many parts of the world of flagrant violations of human rights. Both individuals and groups are subjected to persecution and discrimination on grounds of race, colour, religion or political conviction. Against such actions, whether of governments, officials, or the general public, the churches must take a firm and vigorous stand, through local

action, in co-operation with churches in other lands, and through international institutions of legal order. They must work for an ever wider and deeper understanding of what are the essential human rights if men are to be free to do the will of God.

The inaugural assembly also called upon churches to press for the adoption by the United Nations of the Universal Declaration on Human Rights, which in fact was done on 10 December of that same year. Indeed, leaders of member churches of the World Council of Churches (WCC) participated in drafting this declaration. Article 5 of the Declaration categorically said: "No one shall be subjected to torture or to cruel, inhuman or degrading treatment or punishment."

In 1964 we hoped to hold the general committee meeting of the World Student Christian Federation, of which I was then president, in Brazil. Unhappily, the military coup that took place on 1 April 1964 forced us to meet in a neighboring country. We were and continued to be concerned about the fate of students, professors, and intellectuals who had been challenging the political, economic, and social system imposed by the new regime and who were subject to summary imprisonment and torture. During the years when I was director of the Commission on World Mission and Evangelism (1967–72) and general secretary (1972–84) of the WCC, I was deeply engaged in the issue of human rights. At our Fourth Assembly in 1968 we drew attention to the international character of human rights:

> Violations of human rights in one place may be quickly communicated to all, spreading an evil and destructive influence abroad. Nations should recognise that the protection of fundamental human rights and freedoms has now become a common concern of the whole international community, and should therefore not regard international concern for the implementation of these rights as an unwarranted interference.

It was in this spirit that appeals were made to the Brazilian authorities and to the world about what was happening in Brazil and elsewhere.

Of the many violations of human rights, why is torture singled out for attention by the international community, and why are Christians so concerned about it? First, torture is the most cruel and barbarous crime against the human person. Traditionally it has been argued—both by the ancient Greeks and Romans in relation to slaves and by the medieval Church in relation to what were called heretics—that torture was a means of forcing people to speak the truth. The reality today is that with the highly sophisticated instruments not only of physical but of mental tortures, it is possible to break the spirit of people and make them admit to whatever the torturer suggests. The intention is to reduce people to functional machines. The ultimate consequence of this is the phenomenon of our time: people disappear as though they had never existed. This is the very denial of our God-given human identity, contrary to the will and act of our creator. What is particularly intolerable today is that at a time when most peoples subscribe to the recognition and maintenance of human rights and the dignity of the human being, these rights are being most flagrantly suppressed and violated all over the world.

Second, because the torturers are willing agents in this degrading act, there must be overriding motives that drive them to act in this way to others. Invariably, it is in obedience to some tyrant or in the name of national security. In the pursuit of rapid economic development, a military regime assumes exceptional powers and dispenses with the constitutional rights of the citizen. These exceptional measures in fact bring greater hardship to the vast majority of the population. It is precisely those who raise their voices or act for the poor and oppressed who have been subject to torture and death. As Christians, we believe that the only national security worthy of its name lies in enabling people to participate fully in the life of their nation. It is only when there is real dialogue, a sharing of life with life in mutual trust and respect between people at all levels of society, that there can be true national security.

Third, the practice of torture is an indication of the inherited values that influence a society or nation. What has happened in Brazil has to be seen in the light of its long history since 1500 when the first colonists came. The treatment of Indians, the cruel institution of slavery that was abolished only in 1888, and the violent way in which Brazil was exploited over the centuries—all these have left their mark on the mentality of the people, and especially on the ruling classes. Unfortunately, the time of colonization was also the time of the Inquisition by the Church, which was therefore inhibited, in its evangelistic work, from disseminating the value of human dignity and justice for all. However, in the last thirty years or so, Christians have become aware of the need to awaken people's consciousness to promote respect for all persons and a more just society. This book is, therefore, an appeal to rethink traditional attitudes and values.

Fourth, torture is a concern for Christians and for all people of goodwill because it involves so many countries. That involvement takes many forms, beginning with the export of sinister instruments of torture and of police and prison hardware. Even more important is the economic and military involvement of countries where security is based on the control of the working population. This book is not only about one country, but about the whole community of nations. We are all responsible for what happened in Brazil.

It is in penitence and humility that we approach this book. It is not intended to be primarily an indictment, but rather an invitation to us all to discern our true being through the disfigured faces of the tortured and crucified so that we may have life in all its fullness. On the cross Jesus prayed for his torturers: "Father, forgive them, for they know not what they do." It was this Jesus who spoke to his disciples, as he does to us: "You will know the truth, and the truth will make you free." And that truth is known and done in being just and in affirming the dignity of every human being.

PHILIP POTTER
Geneva, Switzerland
5 June 1985

PREFACE:
A TESTIMONY AND AN APPEAL

by Paulo Evaristo, Cardinal Arns
Metropolitan Archbishop of São Paulo

THE anguish and hopes of the people should be shared by the Church. It is my hope that this book, written by experts, will strengthen our belief in the future.

Christ himself, who "went about doing good" (Acts 10:38), was persecuted, tortured, and killed. His legacy to us is the mission of working for the kingdom of God, which is justice, truth, freedom, and love.

The experiences that I wish to narrate in this preface are intended to reinforce the idea underlying all chapters of this book, i.e., that torture, apart from being inhuman, is the most ineffective way to lead us to discover the truth and to bring us peace.

I

During the period when the so-called subversives were being most intensively hunted down, I received in the archdiocesan offices twenty to fifty people every week, all trying to discover the whereabouts of their relatives.

One day two women came to me, a young one and an older one. The young one, as soon as she sat down in front of me, put a wedding ring on the table and said, "It's my husband's wedding ring. He disappeared ten days ago. This morning I found it on my doorstep. Father, what does its being returned to me mean? Is it a sign that he is dead or is it a sign that I should continue my search for him?"

To this day, neither of us has found the answer to that harrowing question.

The older woman repeated the question she had been asking for months: "Do you have any news about the whereabouts of my son?" Immediately after he was abducted she would come every week.

Later she came every month. For more than five years I followed the search for her son, through our Justice and Peace Committee and even through the president's personal assistant for civilian affairs. The body of that mother seemed to shrink from visit to visit. One day she also disappeared, but her imploring look will never be erased from my mind's eye.

No one on earth can describe the hurt of those who saw their dear ones disappear behind prison bars, without being able even to guess what had happened to them. The darkness deepens and the last glimmer of hope that the disappeared person is still alive flickers and dies.

For that mother and that wife, deep darkness covers the earth, as it did when Jesus died.

II

One unusual evening, a military judge came to my residence. He had studied in a Catholic school and showed understanding about the Church's work in São Paulo in defense of political prisoners.

At a certain point the conversation changed direction. The magistrate, apparently cool and objective, was overcome with emotion. He told me that he had just received two documents from different sources signed by different persons. Two political prisoners each stated that they had assassinated the *same* person, at an unlikely time and in altogether improbable circumstances. The judge concluded: "Imagine the psychological and maybe even physical condition of someone who reaches the point of declaring himself an assassin, even though he isn't!"

Interrogation under torture or the threat of torture, however, reaches even greater heights of absurdity and futility.

III

Before testifying to our Justice and Peace Committee, an engineer told me his tragic experience. He believed he had nothing to fear when he was detained. But since he had heard that torture was applied to those who did not confess at least something, he prepared to tell in detail everything about himself that could be interpreted in any way as opposition to the military regime. He would even tell more than he might in sacramental confession.

Yet, after taking down his personal data, the interrogators made him sit down—immediately—in the "dragon's chair."* From that moment, he said, "everything got mixed up. I no longer knew what I had done, nor what I had wanted to tell or even elaborate upon, in order to achieve credibility. I confused names, persons and dates, for it was no longer I who was speaking but rather the inquisitors who dominated and possessed me, in the most total and absolute meaning of the word."

After such degradation, how and when is such an innocent man to become a whole person again?

IV

What impressed me most during the years of vigil against torture, however, was how torturers themselves are degraded. This book, by its very nature, cannot provide full treatment of this issue. That is why I give the testimony.

Toward the end of January 1974, when the leaders of Catholic Workers' Action were detained, I spent four afternoons inside the Political and Social Police Department in the hope of seeing them. I had been called from the southern Brazilian city of Curitiba for this purpose, where I had been with all my brothers and sisters comforting our mother in the last days of her life.

During the long wait in the prison corridors, I was able to talk with police officers who conducted interrogations such as those described in this book. Five of them told me about their studies in Catholic schools. One of them had attended the Catholic University of São Paulo. They were all having serious problems with their families and in their private lives, problems which they themselves saw as a divine judgment on them. When I urged them to give up their horrific work, they answered, "It's impossible. You know why!"

Finally, late on Friday afternoon, in the presence of those police officers to whom I had spoken so bluntly, I was able to see two of our pastoral workers. They were in terrible shape. Months later, one of those same police officers was waiting alone to see me after mass in the church at Aclimação in São Paulo. With a cry of desperation he asked me, "Is there any hope that I will be forgiven?"

Only eleven years later, in March 1985, did I find out that, on

---

*See chapter 2, pages 18–19, for a description of the "dragon's chair."

the morning of 12 February 1974, a police officer had summoned the political prisoners up to his floor to announce to them, triumphantly and cynically, that my mother had died the day before. The prisoners lowered their eyes and said nothing.

I then remembered a warning given by a general, who was in fact against all torture: "Whoever tortures once, becomes changed as a result of the demoralization he has inflicted upon others. Whoever repeats torture four or more times becomes a beast. The torturer feels such physical and emotional pleasure that he is capable of torturing even the frailest members of his own family!"

The image of God, stamped upon the human person, is always unique. That image alone can save and preserve the image of Brazil and of the world.

That is why we appeal to the Brazilian government to sign and ratify the United Nations Convention against Torture and Other Cruel, Inhuman, or Degrading Treatment or Punishment.*

This entire book is written in blood and with much love for our country.

PAULO EVARISTO, CARDINAL ARNS
São Paulo, Brazil
3 May 1985

---

*On 23 September 1985, President José Sarney added Brazil's signature to this Convention.

TORTURE
IN BRAZIL

INTRODUCTION TO THE BRAZILIAN EDITION

BRAZIL is today experiencing a new page of hope in its history. With the election of the civilian Tancredo Neves to the presidency in January 1985 and the installation of his successor, José Sarney, following Neves' death just months later, twenty-one years of military rule have been overcome. The nation is dreaming of plans for reconstruction. Laws are beginning to be rethought. Those now in power have promised important policy changes to vast crowds gathered in public squares.

These same people, in earlier times, journeyed from hope to hope through similar new political beginnings that did not last very long. Years of greater tolerance of dissenting opinions and greater concern for social problems gave way, even before 1964 (the year of Brazil's most recent military coup), to fresh periods of intransigence, persecution, and even contempt for the demands of the marginalized.

This cannot now be repeated. The hope that is being born again today cannot be another transitory one. Decisions must be made and courageous measures taken to encourage the consolidation of democratic society. We must labor, tirelessly and constantly, to remove the vestiges of authoritarianism and to build a state based on the rule of law. That state must not only be firm in its foundations but also receptive to criticism. People must be allowed to participate, dissent, and challenge, and the cry of the poor, the cry of all the people, must be heard. Toward this end, we must learn the lessons that our recent past, our own history provides.

This book is the report on an investigation in the field of human rights. It is an unprecedented examination of the political repression that was directed against thousands of Brazilians considered by the military to be adversaries of the military regime that took power in April 1964. It is also an analysis of the resistance to that regime.

In March 1979, General João Baptista de Figueiredo was inaugurated as Brazil's president. He promised to broaden the political freedoms initiated during the previous administration of General Ernesto Geisel and to introduce democracy. A few months later, the research project "Brasil: Nunca Mais" ("Brazil: Never Again") began. Discretion and secrecy were essential to the success of the project. A small number of specialists dedicated themselves, for a period of more than five years, to produce the comprehensive study summarized in this book.

THE "BRAZIL: NEVER AGAIN" PROJECT

Everywhere in the world, the issue of political repression is almost always brought to public notice by the denunciations of victims or by reports written by organizations dedicated to the defense of human rights. Whether emotional or well balanced, these testimonies help reveal a hidden history. But at times they are accused of tendentiousness because they come from victims who are often politically motivated.

The "Brazil: Never Again" (BNM) research project was able to resolve this problem by studying the repression carried out by the military regime through the very documents produced by the authorities performing the controversial task. This was done by bringing together the official legal proceedings of practically all political cases tried in Brazilian military courts between April 1964 and March 1979, especially those that reached the Supreme Military Court.

By fixing 15 March 1979, the date of Figueiredo's inauguration, as the end of the period to be investigated, those responsible for the research project assured that the work could proceed with a degree of historical detachment from the political repression being studied.

In numerous ways, copies of the complete proceedings of 707 political trials and dozens of incomplete proceedings were obtained, amounting in total to more than one million pages. These pages were immediately microfilmed in duplicate so that one copy could be kept in safety outside Brazil. The BNM team studied these records for more than five years, producing a report (Project A) of approximately 7,000 pages. Copies of a limited edition of Project A will be distributed to universities, libraries, documentation centers, and organizations dedicated to the defense of human rights in Brazil and abroad. Project A is a full account of what this book contains in summary form.

There were numerous difficulties as well as substantial risks for those involved in the BNM project. On the one hand, the traumatic period from 1964–79—marked by routine torture, deaths, and disappearances—was still very much alive in people's minds, causing fear and making precautions necessary. There was never certainty that the project could be finished or that it would ever be possible to publish it.

On 30 April 1981, for instance, when the BNM project was well under way, a failed bomb attack on a Rio de Janeiro theater indicated that the repressive organizations studied in the project were still active. In the incident, two military police officers were injured, one of them fatally, when the bomb they were transporting exploded. It was widely assumed that the police bomb was intended for the thousands of young people attending a May Day celebration. In view of the fact that the repressive forces were still capable of attempting such crimes, those involved in the BNM project went through some alarming moments.

There was also the pressure of time. The investigation was necessarily slow, given the difficulty in bringing together the documentary sources and the necessity that each page of hundreds of military court proceedings be studied carefully. Nevertheless, there was a real urgency to complete the task before a change in the political situation could put an end to the study or before a "convenient" fire in government offices could destroy valuable documents. In 1945, at the end of Getúlio Vargas' authoritarian New State (Estado Novo), such a fire in Rio de Janeiro destroyed the documents of the political police headed by Felinto Müller.

That is why the BNM project was always racing against the clock. The publication of its results is therefore an encouraging victory over all those risks and difficulties.

Some further explanation is in order regarding our sources.

Why were official military court proceedings chosen as the basic documentary source? In his book *Surveiller et punir* (Surveillance and Punishment), the French thinker Michel Foucault demonstrates that it is possible to reconstruct a good portion of the history of a certain period through the penal proceedings kept in the archives of the judiciary of any given country. The real nature of the state is recorded there in the form of court sentences involving torture or the quartering of bodies in public and in rules for the surveillance of prisoners and for corporal and psychological punishment. We thought that if in Brazil we could reconstruct the history of torture, murders of political prisoners, police persecutions, and biased trials—using the government's own official documentation—then we would have irrefutable evidence that these practices were officially authorized.

It could be argued that, by dispensing with statements by the victims themselves and working instead with documents produced by the authorities of the military government, the BNM project would be doomed to confirming only a small proportion of the human rights violations committed during that period. The documentary sources could be compared to objects from which the agents of repression had removed the "fingerprints" of crimes committed during the investigation. There was, on the other hand, a compensation: whatever official documentation could be produced regarding judicial irregularities, illegal acts, unjust measures, and reports of torture and deaths would constitute incontrovertible conclusive evidence. In other words, confirmation that the facts of torture were presented before a military court, confirmed by witnesses, and even recorded officially by medical examiners, without resulting in any steps to eliminate such practices or to make their perpetrators criminally responsible, is as much of a direct challenge to government authorities as is the denunciation that a victim of torture makes before a human rights organization.

The challenge was thus accepted to work with the basic information contained only in military court proceedings. Only occasionally did the BNM project use complementary sources. These are cited in the endnotes.

THE BNM REPORT AND THE CONTENTS OF THIS BOOK

It is no simple task to produce an easily readable summary of thousands of pages containing the conclusions of an extended research project. It would be like trying to make a 28-minute TV program out of a 10-hour epic series.

Project A, the complete report on which this book is based, begins by describing the development of political institutions in Brazil between 1964 and 1979, starting with the origins of the military regime and ending with the building up of the repressive apparatus on the foundation of the Doctrine of National Security, the principal ideology of the regime.

Next, the methodology of the research project is explained, with military court proceedings classified according to the type of defendant charged (e.g., belonging to a particular leftist organization, social sector, etc.). An explanation regarding the collection of data, is also provided. In brief, it notes that two questionnaires were used to compile the information, which was then stored and processed on computers. Special computer programs were written for the project. The programs and the data generated, as well as microfilms of the actual documents, are stored safely outside of Brazil. In addition, a separate collection of 10,000 political documents appended to the military court proceedings also forms part of the project documentation. This entire archive will be of great value for future research into the Brazilian labor movement, the student struggle, and the history of clandestine leftist organizations, among other topics.

The third part of Project A is a detailed discussion of the results of research in the juridical field, through a comparison of what the laws—including those promulgated by the military regime—were intended to do and the actual practices of judicial inquests and proceedings. The dubious legitimacy of various national security laws and other legal codes decreed by the military regime is also discussed, followed by a study of the way these laws were routinely ignored in all cases where there was irregular treatment of persons being investigated.

In the fourth section there is a harrowing sequence of transcriptions of testimonies describing tortures, totaling approximately 2,700 typed pages. These denunciations, made in military courts, contain the names of torturers, torture centers, murdered political prisoners, the "disappeared," and countless other infamies. A list of all torturers named in military proceedings is provided, together with lists of all authorities connected with police and judicial acts of repression, as well as of all persons named as defendants or indicted.

The last section sets out the main conclusions that can be drawn from the study.

How was it possible to compress this vast amount of information into this book? A form had to be devised that could communicate the essence of those results without repeating the ungainly structure of a report or distressing readers with endless descriptions of the agonies of torture. Of course, it was not possible to extract a light or reassuring report from Project A. Only a strong and challenging book could emerge from a story of horrors.

In the following chapters, we have alternated the shocking denunciations with analytical passages that show the origins of the repressive apparatus, its structure, the uses of torture in the course of interrogation, and the collaboration of the judicial authorities in these abuses. In this fashion we have attempted to avoid the tedium of endless descriptions as well as the error of talking about those tortures and crimes as if they were unrelated to the political system installed in Brazil in 1964.

In the Portuguese edition, spelling and grammatical mistakes in original documents were preserved, although they will obviously not appear in the English edition. The only mistakes that have been corrected in both versions are those that might distort the meaning for the reader.

The objective of the research project "Brazil: Never Again," from its inception in August 1979 to its conclusion in March 1985, was to turn the wish expressed in its title into a reality, that is, to ensure that the violence, the infamy, the injustice, and the persecution of Brazil's recent past should never again be repeated.

It is not the intention of the BNM project to prepare evidence to be presented at a Brazilian Nuremberg trial. The project was not motivated by revenge. In their quest for justice, the Brazilian people have never been moved by such sentiments. What is intended is a work that will have an impact by revealing to the conscience of the nation, through the light shed by these denunciations, the dark reality of the political repression that grew unchecked after 1964. We thus observe the Gospel precept that counsels us to know the truth as a precondition for liberation ("You will know the truth, and the truth will make you free," John 8:32).

It is a happy coincidence that the results of this research project should be published at a time of national hope, when authoritarianism is being overcome, when new laws for the country are being promulgated, and when there is a new possibility of convening a constituent assembly to strengthen democratic institutions.

It is our hope that all who participate in that national debate will take note of the contents of this book, so that measures may be taken in order that these years of persecution and hatred may never again be repeated.

It is our hope that all who read this book will make a sacred vow to commit themselves to struggle ceaselessly to sweep from the face of the earth the practice of torture and eliminate from humanity the source of torture, of whatever type, for whatever offense, for whatever reason.

It is in this spirit that the project "Brazil: Never Again" was undertaken.

São Paulo, Brazil
March 1985

PART I

CRUEL, INHUMAN, AND DEGRADING PUNISHMENT

ONE

TORTURE CLASSES: GUINEA PIG PRISONERS

ÂNGELO Pezzuti da Silva, student, 23, detained in Belo Horizonte and tortured in Rio de Janeiro, told the Council of Military Justice of Juiz de Fora, in 1970:

> that, in the Army Police unit of GB [the former State of Guanabara, now Rio de Janeiro], the defendant and his companions confirmed that tortures are an institution, given the fact that the defendant was an instrument for practical demonstrations of this system, in a class in which more than 100 sergeants participated and whose teacher was an officer of the Army Police, called Lt. Ayton; that, in this room, while slides about torture were being shown, practical demonstrations were given using the defendant, MAURÍCIO PAIVA, AFONSO CELSO, MURILO PINTO, P. PAULO BRETAS, and other prisoners in the Army Police unit as guinea pigs . . .

The report was confirmed in the same military court proceedings by the testimonies of those listed above, such as Maurício Vieira de Paiva, student, 25:

> that the method of torture was institutionalized in our country, and that the proof of this is not simply the application of torture but the fact that classes were given on this subject, and that in one of them the defendant and some of his companions served as guinea pigs; this class took place in the Army Police unit of GB, was given to 100 military personnel from the Armed

Forces, and had Lt. HAYTON, from that military unit, as its instructor; that, while slides on tortures were being shown, practical demonstrations of them were given on the accused, such as the defendant and his companions, before the entire audience . . .

This episode was also reported in the 1970 court testimony of Júlio Antônio Bittencourt de Almeida, student, 24:

that, during the time the defendant was in the Army Police unit, a course on torture was given to between 80 and 100 members of that unit, for which prisoners served as guinea pigs; that the teachers and those attending the course were personnel of the Armed Forces . . .

Initially an abuse committed by interrogators upon prisoners, torture became a "scientific method" during the military regime in Brazil, and it was included in training curricula for military personnel. The teaching of this method for extracting confessions and information was not merely theoretical. It was practical, with persons used as guinea pigs, actually tortured in this gruesome learning process. One of the first officials to introduce this practice into Brazil was Dan Mitrione, an American police officer. As a police instructor in Belo Horizonte during the early years of the Brazilian military regime, Mitrione took beggars off the streets and tortured them in classrooms, so that the local police would learn the various ways of creating, in the prisoner, the supreme contradiction between the body and the mind by striking blows to vulnerable points of the body.[1] Although Mitrione was subsequently transferred to Uruguay and killed by local guerrillas, the practice of using live victims in torture classes continued in Brazil.

Dulce Chaves Pandolfi, student, 24, was also obliged to serve as a guinea pig in the barracks on Barão de Mesquita Street, in Rio, according to a statement attached to military court records dated 1970:

At the Military Police, the defendant was stripped naked and subjected to beatings and electric shocks and other torments such as the "parrot's perch." After being taken to her cell, the defendant was assisted by a doctor and, after a while, was again tortured with exquisite cruelty in a demonstration of how torture should be carried out . . .

In her testimony to the military court, she further stated:

> that, on 14 October, she was taken from her cell and taken to a place where more than 20 officers were present, and demonstrations of torture were performed on the defendant . . .

José Antônio Gonçalves Duarte, teacher, 24, was detained in Belo Horizonte. He revealed in his testimony to the military court in 1970 that he had even been tortured by a student of the military preparatory school:

> that he was tortured and beaten by the man in charge of the investigation, Captain João Alcântara Gomes; by Marcelo Araújo, rapporteur of the investigation; by Corporal Dirceu and by a student of the Colégio Militar whose name is unknown to the defendant; and also by a police officer from the Department of Thefts and Robberies, whose name is Pereira; that it was surprising to the defendant to see a student in training at the military preparatory school participating in such an infamous activity as inflicting torture on a human being.

The torturers not only bragged about their sophisticated technology of pain, but boasted that they were in a position to export it to repressive systems in other countries. This was stated in a letter from Haroldo Borges Rodrigues Lima, engineer, 37, dated 12 April 1977 and appended to military court records:

> Tortures continued systematically. They were accompanied by threats to subject me to new and harsher torments, which were described to me in detail. They said, with great pride, that in this matter they owed nothing to any foreign organization. On the contrary, they told me, they were already exporting know-how on the subject.

TWO

MODES AND INSTRUMENTS OF TORTURE

ARTICLE 5 of the Universal Declaration of Human Rights, of which Brazil is a signatory, states: *"No one shall be subjected to torture or to cruel, inhuman or degrading treatment or punishment."*

This principle was not observed by the Brazilian authorities during the twenty-one years of military rule, especially during the period covered by this study (1964–79). The study revealed almost one hundred different ways of torturing, by means of physical assault, psychological pressure, and the use of the most varied instruments on Brazilian political prisoners. The military court proceedings reveal full details of these criminal acts carried out under the auspices of the state. The testimonies from military court records, from which extracts are given in this chapter, describe the main modes and instruments of torture used in Brazil's repressive system.

The "parrot's perch"

> The parrot's perch consists of an iron bar wedged behind the victim's knees and to which his wrists are tied; the bar is then placed between two tables, causing the victim's body to hang some 20 or 30 centimeters from the ground. This method is hardly ever used by itself: its normal "complements" are electric shocks, the *palmatória* [a length of thick rubber attached to a wooden paddle], and drowning . . .
> [Augusto César Salles Galvão, student, 21, Belo Horizonte, 1970.]

. . . the parrot's perch was a collapsible metal structure
. . . which consisted of two triangles of galvanized tubing, of
which one of the corners had two half-moons cut out, on which
the victims were hung: the tubing was placed beneath their
knees and between their hands, which were tied and brought
up to their knees . . .
[José Milton Ferreira de Almeida, 31, engineer, Rio, 1976.]

Electric shock

Electric shocks are given by an Army field telephone that has
two long wires that are connected to the body, normally to the
sexual organs, in addition to ears, teeth, tongue and fingers.
[Augusto César Salles Galvão.]

that he was taken to DOI-CODI [Information Operations Detachment—Center for Internal Defense Operations], where
he was tortured naked, after taking a bath, while hanging on
the parrot's perch, where he received electric shocks from a
magneto,* to his genital organs and over his whole body . . . one
of the terminal wires of the magneto was tied to one of his toes
and to his penis, where he received successive discharges of
such intensity that he was thrown to the floor . . .
[José Milton Ferreira de Almeida.]

The "little pepper" and "doublers of tension"

There was a machine called "the little pepper," in the torturer's
language, which consisted of a wooden box; inside there was
a permanent magnet, in whose field a combined rotor turned,
and from its terminals a brush collected electrical current that
was transmitted through wires attached to the terminals already
described; this machine produced around 100 volts and a considerable electrical current, or something like 10 am-
peres . . . this machine was extremely dangerous because the
electric current increased with the speed of the rotor as it was
turned by the crank; that the machine was applied at a very
high speed, then suddenly stopped and turned in the opposite
direction, thereby creating a counter electromotive force that
doubled the original voltage of the machine . . .
[Ibid.]

---

*magneto: a small electric generator

. . . a magneto which produced low voltage and high amperage electricity; that, because it was a red box, it was called "the little pepper" . . .
[Gildásio Westin Cosenza, 28, radio technician, Rio, 1975.]

that there were two further machines that were known, in the technical language of electronics, as "doublers of tension," which means that starting with the feeding of an electronic circuit by simple radio batteries, you can achieve up to 500 or 1,000 volts but only with small electrical currents, like those in a television tube, and in automobile coils; that these machines had three buttons corresponding to three sections, weak, medium and strong; these buttons were pressed one by one or all of them at once; in this latter case, the resulting voltage was the sum of the three sections . . .
[José Milton Ferreira de Almeida.]

. . . doublers of tension fed by batteries which, unlike the magneto, produce high voltage and low amperage electricity, as in TV tubes; that this machine produced sparks which burned the skin and gave violent shocks . . .
[Gildásio Westin Cosenza.]

Drowning

Drowning is one of the "complements" of the parrot's perch. A small rubber tube is inserted into the mouth of the person being tortured, from which water begins to flow.
[Augusto César Salles Galvão.]

A hose with running water was inserted into his nostrils, and into his mouth, and he involuntarily breathed in every time he received an electric shock . . .
[José Milton Ferreira de Almeida.]

. . . drowning by means of a wet towel in the mouth: when your breathing has almost stopped, you receive a jet of water in your nostrils . . .
[Leonardo Valentini, 22, metal worker, Rio, 1973.]

The "dragon's chair," São Paulo

He sat down in a chair known as the dragon's chair, an extremely heavy chair, whose seat is a sheet of corrugated iron;

on the back part there is a protuberance where one of the wires of the shock machine can be inserted; that, in addition to this, the chair had a wooden bar that pushed your legs backwards, so that with each spasm produced by the electrical discharge your legs would hit against the wooden bar causing deep gashes . . .
[José Milton Ferreira de Almeida.]

He also received electric shocks in the dragon's chair, which is an electric chair of aluminum, all of this in order to extract declarations from him.
[Manoel Cyrillo de Oliveira Netto, 23, student, São Paulo, 1973.]

After being brutally undressed by policemen, I was made to sit in the dragon's chair, on a metal plate, with hands and feet tied and electric wires connected to my body touching my tongue, ears, eyes, wrists, breasts and genital organs.
[Marlene de Souza Soccas, 35, dentist, São Paulo, 1972.]

The "dragon's chair," Rio de Janeiro

The accused was obliged to sit in a chair, like one in a barber shop, to which he was tied with straps covered over with foam rubber, while other foam rubber strips covered his body; they tied his fingers with electric wires, and his toes also, and began administering a series of electric shocks; at the same time, another torturer with an electric stick gave him shocks between the legs and on the penis . . .
[José Augusto Dias Pires, 24, journalist, Rio, 1977.]

. . . a chair of heavy wood with its arms covered with sheets of corrugated iron, where there was a strip of wood used to push backwards the legs of the person being tortured . . .
[Gildásio Westin Cosenza.]

The "ice box"

For five days, she was put into an "ice box" at the barracks of the Army Police in Rio de Janeiro, on Barão de Mesquita Street . . .
[Jandira Andrade Gitirana Fiúza, 24, journalist, Rio, 1973.]

that he was placed naked in a very cold and very restricted space where he remained during most of the time he spent there; that in this same place there was excessive strident sound that seemed to come out of the ceiling, giving him the impression that his ears would burst . . .
[José Mendes Ribeiro, 24, medical student, Rio, 1977.]

that, being hooded once again, he was taken to a completely enclosed place where the walls were covered with black sound-proofing, and the temperature was extremely low; . . . that, in that room, he heard such strident deafening sounds as to drive him mad . . .
[José Augusto Dias Pires.]

. . . taken to a small room measuring approximately two by two meters, without windows, with thick walls, covered with sound-proofing, and in one of the walls there was a small observation hole covered with dark glass; . . . from that moment, he could only hear several different voices coming simultaneously from loudspeakers installed in the ceiling; they began to call him dirty names; that, he began to protest immediately with loud shouts against the unacceptable treatment to which he was being subjected; that the voices then stopped and were replaced by electronic noises so loud and so intense that he could no longer hear his own voice; . . . that there were moments when the electronic noises stopped and the walls of the cubicle were battered with great intensity for a long time with something like a hammer or a wooden shoe; and that on other occasions the ventilation system was disconnected and remained so for a long time, making the air very distressing to breathe, forcing him to breathe very slowly . . .
[José Miguel Camolez, 31, civil engineer and retired naval engineer, Rio, 1976.]

that he was thrown countless times into a cubicle called "the ice box," that had the following characteristics: its door was like a freezer door, measuring approximately two meters by one and a half meters; its walls were all painted black, with a partitioned opening connected to a system of cold air; that, on the ceiling of this room, there was a very strong light; that, when the door was closed, machines were turned on which produced noises varying from the noise of an airplane turbine to a strident factory siren . . .
[Gildásio Westin Cosenza.]

A cubicle similar to the "ice box" at the Army Police barracks, located on Barão de Mesquita Street in Rio's Tijuca suburb, was also found at the Navy Information Center in Rio:

> . . . placed in a cubicle, in an absolutely dark place, like a soundproof cell; that, in the above mentioned place, there was an electrical system that reproduced the most varied sounds, reminiscent of sirens, bombardments, etc., all this interspersed with periods of absolute silence . . .
> [José Ferreira Lopes, 30, worker, 1972.]

Insects and animals

> There was also, in his cubicle, to keep him company, a boa constrictor called "Miriam" . . .
> [Leonardo Valentini.]

> that at the Army Police headquarters there is a snake about two meters long, which was placed with the accused in a room two by two meters, for two nights . . .
> [Dalton Godinho Pires, 31, office assistant, Rio, 1973.]

> that, when returning to the torture room, she was placed on the floor with an alligator on her naked body . . .
> [Dulce Chaves Pandolfi, 23, student, Rio, 1971.]

> that, despite her being pregnant at the time and her torturers being aware of it . . . she was left without food for several days; . . . that the persons conducting the interrogations let dogs and snakes loose on the defendant . . .
> [Miriam de Almeida Leitão Netto, 20, journalist, Rio, 1973.]

> that she was transferred to the DOI of the Army Police on Barão de Mesquita Street, where she was submitted to tortures with electric shocks, drugs, sexual torments, and snakes and cockroaches; that these tortures were administered by the officials themselves.
> [Janete de Oliveira Carvalho, 23, secretary, Rio, 1973.]

> The defendant also wants to state that, during the first phase of her interrogation, cockroaches were placed over her body, and one of them into her anus.

[Lúcia Maria Murat Vasconcelos, 23, student, Rio and Salvador, 1972.]

Chemical products

that he also was given an injection of Pentotal [sic], a substance that makes a person talk, [and puts him] in a state of sleepiness . . .
[Olderico Campos Barreto, 31, farm worker, Salvador, 1979.]

. . . having a substance thrown in her face that she took to be some kind of acid, for it made her swell up . . .
[Jussara Lins Martins, 24, hairdresser, Minas Gerais, 1972.]

. . . constant tortures with electric shocks to various parts of the body, including genital organs; and the injection of ether, including squirting it into his eyes, . . . that, from the 14th to the 15th he was given a truth serum injection called "pentotal" . . .
[Alex Polari de Alverga, 21, student, Rio, 1972.]

Physical injury

that, on a certain occasion, police authorities inserted into his anus an object that looked like a bottle washer; that, on another occasion, these same authorities made the defendant stand on tops of cans, in which position he would be burnt with cigarettes and hit with closed fists; that to all this the authorities gave the name of Viet Nam; that the defendant showed to this Military Court a mark at the level of his abdomen where police authorities had cut him with a razor blade . . .
[Apio Costa Rosa, 28, bank worker, Belo Horizonte, 1970.]

The defendant suffered beatings with an aluminum club on his buttocks, until raw flesh was exposed, . . . they placed him on top of two open cans, which he remembered to have contained tomato paste; and made him balance on them with bare feet; every time he was about to lose his balance they connected the machine that produced electric shocks, which forced the defendant to recover his balance on the cans . . .
[José Afonso de Alencar, 28, lawyer, Juiz de Fora, 1970.]

They tied him to a stake with his hands behind him and began beating his whole body, after which they placed him, for two

hours, standing up with his feet on top of two cans of condensed milk and two live coals under his feet.
[José Genuíno Neto, 27, student, São Paulo, 1973.]

They forced the accused to place his testicles resting on the chair; that Miranda and the rapporteur Holanda tried to hit the testicles with the *palmatória;* . . . the accused underwent the punishment known as "the telephone," which consists of unexpectedly slapping both ears at the same time; that, as a result of this punishment, the accused was deaf for several days; that three days later the accused, while cleaning his ear, noticed that it had bled.
[Pedro Coutinho de Almeida, 20, student, Pernambuco, 1970.]

The accused was taken from the hospital, having been hung once again on a grid, with his arms above him; they put a hood over his head, his artificial leg having been taken from him; tied cord around his penis to prevent him urinating; . . . that, when the accused arrived at the interrogation room, they tied his testicles and dragged him across the room and then hung him from above by his testicles . . .
[Manoel da Conceição Santos, 35, farm worker, Ceará, 1972.]

Other modes and instruments of tortures

The hanging was carried out by a small rope that, tied to the victim's neck, suffocates him progressively until he faints.
[Augusto César Salles Galvão.]

that he spent two days in this torture room with nothing to drink, but having salt thrown in his eyes and mouth, and all over his body, so as to increase its conductivity . . .
[José Milton Ferreira de Almeida.]

that the stretching to which he referred, as an instrument of torture, is composed of two rectangular cement blocks, with rings to which hands and feet are tied with iron bracelets, where the accused was placed and where he underwent beatings for several days, from 12 to 17 May . . .
[Renato Oliveira da Motta, 59, newspaper vendor, São Paulo, 1975.]

Psychological tortures were interspersed with electric shocks and a position they called "Jesus Christ": unclothed, [the victim

is placed] standing up, arms stretched upward and tied to a wooden beam. The purpose [of the position] was to dislocate the muscles and the kidneys, they explained.
[Ibid.]

They continued to torture him with inhuman methods, such as the position of Christ the Redeemer, with four telephone books in each hand, on tiptoe, naked, with beatings on the stomach and on the chest, forcing him to stand erect again.
[Fernando Reis Salles Ferreira, 48, airline worker, Rio, 1970.]

that the accused's head was repeatedly put under water, with his mouth open, in a gasoline drum full of water; and that this method was known as "the Chinese bath" . . .
[José Machado Bezerra, 25, teacher, Fortaleza, 1973.]

"Chinese torture" was also the name used by agents from DOI-CODI in São Paulo to designate a torture to which another political prisoner was subjected toward the end of 1976:

With the application of these electrical discharges, my body would contract violently. The chair turned over on the floor several times and my head hit the wall. The contractions caused constant heavy banging against the chair. It was this that caused the bruises and injuries on my body that were confirmed by the medical report. Not satisfied with this kind of torture, my tormenters decided to submit me to the "Chinese torture." They made me lie down, naked and hooded, on a mattress, tied my legs and arms together and then tied them to my neck. So as not to leave any signs of shocks, they put small strips of gauze on my toes. They wet my body with water, several times, so that the electrical charge would have greater effect. The shocks followed one another until the end of the day. . . . During the electric discharges, the torturers taunted me about my state of health, stating that the shocks would drive me mad or cure my epilepsy.
[Aldo Silva Arantes, 38, lawyer, São Paulo, 1977.]

THREE

TORTURE OF CHILDREN AND WOMEN

IN Brazil, those suspected of subversive activities were indiscriminately tortured, regardless of their age or sex or moral, physical, and psychological condition. It was not only a matter of producing pain in the victims' bodies that would create inner conflicts for them, forcing them to reveal self-incriminating information that at the same time was useful to the repressive system. Officially justified by the urgency to obtain information, the objective of torture was to bring about the victim's moral destruction by breaking down emotional ties based upon kinship. Children were thus sacrificed before their parents' eyes, pregnant women had miscarriages, and wives were subjected to suffering to make them incriminate their husbands.

TORTURE OF CHILDREN

While giving her testimony in 1973 before the military court of Ceará, Maria José de Souza Barros, from the rural area of Japuara, declared that:

> they took her son to the woods and beat him so that he would tell about her husband; that the boy's name is Francisco de Souza Barros and [he] is nine years old; that the police took the boy at five o'clock in the afternoon and only brought him back around two o'clock in the morning . . .

Maria Madalena Prata Soares, teacher, 26, wife of José Carlos Novaes da Mata Machado, student, who was killed by security forces, declared in 1973 to the military court in Minas Gerais:

that she was detained on 21 October 1973, together with her son Eduardo, who was four years old; that the reason for her imprisonment was to make her reveal her husband's whereabouts; that for three days, in Belo Horizonte, pressure was exerted on her to tell where José Carlos was, in the following way: that, if she did not talk, her son would be thrown from the second floor, and this lasted three days . . . that, on the last night which her son spent with her, he was already very upset, for he could not understand why he was in prison, and asked her not to go to sleep, so she could see when the soldier came to get them; . . . he is unable to understand the reason for my disappearance and that of José Carlos; that the boy is traumatized, with a feeling of being abandoned . . .

While giving his testimony to the military court in Rio in 1969, Milton Gaia Leite, carpenter, 30, declared:

that he was imprisoned and tortured, with rape attempted against him, his children, and his wife, and that his children, five and seven years old, were also put in jail, not only in Paraná, but here also . . .

In São Paulo, Iára Ackselrud de Seixas, student, 23, saw her younger brother taken to their home by the police, bearing evident signs of torture, as stated in her testimony before the military court in 1972:

Several persons broke into the house and started to beat her and the others who were there, overturning everything, leaving her brother, who was only 16 years old, bloodied, limping, and handcuffed . . .

Children were questioned in an attempt to obtain information from them that would give their parents away. Former congressman Diógenes Arruda Câmara, in his testimony before the military court in 1970, reported what happened to the daughter of his fellow prisoner, Antônio Expedito Carvalho, a lawyer:

They threatened to torture his only daughter, Cristina, who was ten years old, in her father's presence; even so, they did not intimidate the lawyer but, in any case, they talked to the girl and she evidently had nothing to say, in spite of the threats made, which turned out to be entirely useless, since an innocent child would obviously not know anything.

When José Leão de Carvalho, advertising agent, was detained in São Paulo, on 24 June 1964, his children were not spared:

> . . . making threats to his younger children, which resulted in the boy Sérgio having to have medical-psychiatric treatment. He was three years old at that time . . .

In an effort to make César Augusto Teles, driver, 29, and his wife talk, the DOI-CODI agents went to their home and brought back their children to the military police department, where the children saw their parents bearing the marks of torture:

> On the afternoon of that day, around seven o'clock, my two children, Janaina de Almeida Teles, five years old, and Edson Luiz de Almeida Teles, four years old, were also abducted and brought to OBAN [Operation Bandeirantes—a special interrogation unit staffed by members of various security and police organizations]. We were then shown to them in our torn clothes, dirty, pale, covered with bruises. . . . Threats that our children would be molested continued for several hours.

César's wife, Maria Amélia de Almeida Teles, teacher, also gave her testimony before the military court in the same proceedings:

> that their two children were threatened with torture; that her husband was also tortured; that her husband was obliged to watch all the tortures she suffered; that her sister was also forced to be present when she was tortured . . .

Military court proceedings recorded other cases of torture involving relatives, such as the one reported by José Afonso de Alencar, lawyer, 28, as recorded by the military court of Minas Gerais, in 1970:

> that the wife of Carlos Melgaço was brought to see the beatings suffered by the accused, Melgaço, Ênio, Mário, and Ricardo; that, in the presence of such scenes, Melgaço's wife fainted several times . . .

The same thing happened with Luiz Artur Toribio, student, 22, when he was detained in São Paulo in 1972:

> As if this were not enough, he was tortured in front of his girl friend, Lúcia Maria Lopes de Miranda, and she in his presence.

In Fortaleza in 1972, José Calistrato Cardoso Filho, student, 29, gave the following testimony before the military court:

> that he was forced to sign said declarations because of the tortures and ill treatment that he suffered, applied not only to him, but also to his fiancée and sisters . . .

TORTURE OF WOMEN

The repressive system made no exceptions for women. The possibility that women could become pregnant, or the special risks they ran if they were already pregnant, made them especially vulnerable to sexual abuses.

Elsa Pereira Lianza, engineer, 25, detained in Rio in 1977, testified before the military court:

> that she was submitted to electric shocks on various parts of the body, including her arms, legs, and vagina; that her husband was forced to witness the administration of electric shocks, and the torturers amplified the screams of the accused so that they would be heard by her husband . . .

Inês Etienne Romeu, bank worker, 29, stated:

> that at any hour of the day or night I suffered physical and moral assault. "Márcio" invaded my cell to "examine" my anus and confirm whether "Camarão" had practiced sodomy with me. This same "Márcio" obliged me to hold his penis, while he contorted himself into obscene positions. During this period I was raped twice by "Camarão" and was forced to clean the kitchen completely naked, while listening to wisecracks and obscenities of the worst kind.[1]

Maria do Socorro Diógenes, 29, and another defendant suffered sexual abuse as a form of torture, according to the statement she made before the military court in Rio, in 1972:

On another occasion, the accused together with another defendant in this legal proceeding by name of Pedro, received electric shocks, applied by the police, who forced the accused to touch Pedro's genital organs so that, in this way, he might receive the electrical discharge . . .

Maria de Fátima Martins Pereira, medical student, 23, was violated in prison and told the medical court in Rio in 1977:

that, one day, five men broke into the "ice box," forced her to lie down, each one helping to hold her arms and legs open; that, while this was being done, another tried to insert a wooden object into her genital organ . . .

In Minas Gerais, the same thing happened to Maria Mendes Barbosa, teacher, 28, according to her testimony in 1970:

She was obliged to parade naked in front of them all, in this way or that way, while captain PORTELA pinched her nipples until they almost produced blood; that, in addition, they tried to violate her genital organ with a club; that, on this occasion still, her torturers bragged about their ability to satisfy a woman, and then made her choose one of them by lot.

In Rio, Maria Auxiliadora Lara Barcelos, civil servant, 25, testified in 1970 how she was forced into performing degrading acts with other political prisoners:

that in this room her clothes were taken off little by little; . . . that a police officer, while other police officers were uttering obscenities, stood in front of her imitating sexual acts that he would perform with the accused, while at the same time touching her body; this practice lasted two hours; that the police officer touched her breasts and, with scissors in hand, threatened to cut them off; . . . that at the Army Police headquarters, three prisoners were placed in a room, without any clothes on; that they first summoned Chael and made him kiss the accused all over, and then they called Antonio Roberto to repeat the same thing, . . . Corporal Nilson Pereira insisted that the accused look at him as a condition for receiving her meal . . .

In 1973, in Rio, the military court heard the testimony of Maria da Conceição Chaves Fernandes, proofreader, 19:

> that she was subjected to sexual violence in the presence and in the absence of her husband . . .

PREGNANCIES AND ABORTIONS

For the forces of repression, the necessities of state prevailed over the right to life. Many women who had their sexuality defiled in Brazilian military prisons and the fruit of their wombs ripped out preferred to keep silent so that the shame they had suffered did not become public knowledge. Today, in the anonymity of a recent past that has nonetheless left its marks, they keep secret the distress and violence they suffered. Others, however, chose to declare what they suffered to military courts, or had their cases related by husbands and companions.

José Ayres Lopes, administrative assistant, 27, detained in Rio, testified in military court in 1972:

> that the accused was blackmailed concerning his wife's pregnancy, so that he would admit to the declarations, under threat of [otherwise] causing his wife to have a miscarriage, thus endangering her life . . .

An identical situation faced José Luiz de Araújo Saboya, student, 23, in Rio in 1972:

> that during the period in which he was in DOPS and then in CODI, his wife was pregnant and she remained in prison as a means of moral coercion on the accused . . .

In Recife in 1970, the military court heard the testimony of Helena Moreira Serra Azul, student, 22:

> that the husband of the accused was in the room referred to, and she heard the sound of beatings outside; that, later, when she was taken again to the room where her husband was, his hands were swollen, his face reddish, his legs trembling, and his back so sensitive that he could not lean against the chair;

that Dr. Moacir Sales, addressing the accused, said that, if she didn't talk, the same would happen to her. . . . in the station, everybody already knew that the accused was pregnant . . .

In Recife, the same threat was made in 1972 to Helena Mota Quintela, salesperson, 28, according to her testimony:

that they threatened to have her child "wrenched out with the point of knife" . . .

In Brasília, Hecilda Mary Veiga Fonteles de Lima, student, 25, testified in 1972 that these threats affected the birth of her baby:

When they found out that she was pregnant, they said that a child of that race should not be born; . . . that on 17 October she was taken to testify at the CODI, but the session was suspended and, on the following day, because she wasn't feeling well, she was taken to the Brasília Hospital; that, when the nurse's attention was distracted, she was able to read her medical sheet, which said that she was hospitalized in a state of considerable distress and threat of premature childbirth; that the baby was born on 20 February 1972 and that, 24 hours later, she was told that she would be returned to the Criminal Investigations Squad . . .

Psychological pressure alone is enough to cause a miscarriage, as happened to Maria José da Conceição Doyle, medical student, 23, also in Brasília, in 1971:

that the accused was two months pregnant and lost her child in prison; although she was not tortured, she was threatened . . .

The same thing happened in São Paulo to Maria Madalena Prata Soares, teacher, 26, according to the testimony she gave in 1974:

that, during her imprisonment in Minas, it was discovered that she was pregnant and, on a date that she does not recall, she had a miscarriage in OBAN . . .

Other women had miscarriages as a result of the physical tortures they suffered, as was the case of Maria Cristina Uslenghi Rizzi, secretary, 27, who stated in military court in São Paulo in 1972:

that she suffered tortures, after which she had a miscarriage with considerable loss of blood . . .

Luiz Andréa Favero, teacher, 26, detained in Foz do Iguaçu, stated in 1970 to the military court of Curitiba what had happened to his wife:

> The accused heard the screams of his wife and, after asking the police not to ill-treat her in view of the fact that she was pregnant, they laughed at him; . . . that, on the same day, the accused received word that his wife had suffered a hemorrhage and that, later, it was ascertained that she had had a miscarriage.

Also in 1970, in her testimony before the military court in Rio, Regina Maria Toscano Farah, student, 23, declared:

> that they wet her body, after which they applied electric shocks to her whole body, including her vagina; that the accused had been operated on for anal fistula, which [consequently] hemorrhaged; that she was pregnant and that such tortures caused her to have a miscarriage . . .

FOUR

MEDICAL ASSISTANCE TO TORTURE

IT CAN be concluded from the study of military court proceedings that the use of torture as an interrogation method and as simple punishment was not random or accidental. On the contrary, torture was planned and even budgeted for by the police and military agencies charged with interrogating political prisoners. Its efficient execution, moreover, depended on a sophisticated investigative apparatus that included not only adequate sites for carrying out torture and technologically advanced equipment, but also the direct participation of nurses and doctors who advised the torturers in their grisly labors.

In 1972, student João Alves Gondim Neto, 25, testified as follows in the Fortaleza military court:

> that while he was at the barracks of the 23rd BC, he was visited by someone who was seeing all prisoners, and that he is sure that he was the medical officer of the 23rd BC; that the defendant was urinating blood at that time because of the beatings on his kidneys; that said person not only refused to medicate him, but also advised the torturers what parts of his body could be hit without leaving a trace . . .

Chauffeur César Augusto Teles, 29, also denounced the fact that doctors were abetting the practice of torture:

> As for me, I blanked out at dawn and learned later that I had been in a comatose state several hours because of the worsening

of my health as a result of tortures suffered. In the morning, when the shift of OBAN workers was changed, I was brought to [consciousness] by two doctors. . . . My wife [was also revived]; but the tortures against us proceeded with more intensity . . .

In Rio, teacher Maria Cecília Barbara Wetten, 29, went through the same kind of experience, as she testified in court in 1977:

that after being examined in the "ice box" by a doctor who took her pulse, she was taken to another room where they applied shocks so that she would declare that she belonged to a political organization . . .

Student Ottoni Guimarães Fernandes Júnior, 24, also testified:

that among the police officers there was a doctor whose function was to revive those who were being tortured so that the torture process would not be interrupted; that the defendant remained two and a half days on the parrot's perch where he fainted several times; and that on those occasions injections were applied in his veins by that same doctor; that the doctor gave him an injection that produced a violent contraction in the intestines, after which the torture method called tourniquet [a cloth, cord, plastic ornamental device applied to parts of the body, including the head, in order to stop the flow of blood and/or inflict pain] was used . . .

In 1970, in Rio, the navy's 1st Court recorded a similar denunciation made by economist Luiz Carlos de Souza Santos, 25:

that Dr. Coutinho, doctor at Flores Island, was in charge of applying stimulants whenever those who were being tortured fainted . . .

Other depositions taken in various Brazilian military courts report similar situations, recording instances of doctors who facilitated the practice of torture, tried to revive victims, and treated political prisoners:

that he was hung twice during this period on the parrot's perch, and while there he had a heart and respiratory stoppage; and

that a diagnosis was given by the male nurse who accompanied the torturing that it was aerophagia or the blocking of respiratory channels as a result of the electric shocks; that his blood pressure reached 18 and 20 by 14, and that he received massive doses of Cepasol in 25 milligrams and also muscular tranquilizers so that his body could once again become sensitive to the pain of the beatings to which he had been submitted, for after a certain moment he became insensitive to all pain . . .
[José Miltom Ferreira Almeida, 32, engineer, São Paulo, 1976.]

that after the application of scientific methods that the defendant classifies as being torture he blanked out for a period of approximately five hours; that when the defendant came to he saw that he was in the Armed Forces Hospital in Brasília; that when he came to they were giving him an electrocardiogram; . . . that after his recuperation he was taken back to the barracks of the Military Police of Brasília, after fifteen days of treatment . . .
[José Duarte, 66, railroad worker, São Paulo, 1973.]

When I was put on the parrot's perch for about half an hour, I was beaten by three individuals, one of whom was in charge of the electric shock machine, the wire of which was attached to my genital organ and the other was grounded and placed inside my anus (they were all commanded by a fourth individual who appeared to be writing). When I could no longer stand the torture, I proposed to them that I would tell everything. From that moment I don't remember anything else because I passed out. I came to while I was being treated by a doctor who was taking my blood pressure.
[1st Sergeant Antônio Martins Fonseca, 50, of the military police, São Paulo, 1975.]

I saw a medical officer apply injections to the young man who was unconscious, after which they threatened him once again; that the defendant would also go through the same kind of torture that had been applied to that young man, and if he did not resist, they would apply injections so that he would regain consciousness and be tortured again and again until he would tell them what they wanted or until he died; that he entered into a state of shock and lost his voice while remaining in a state of half-consciousness; that he does remember rather vaguely that he was surrounded by several officers, a typing

machine in a room whose location he was unable to determine; that for several days he evacuated blood while being medicated by the medical officer . . .
[Antônio Rogério Garcia Silveira, 25, student, Rio, 1970.]

that Major JOÃO VICENTE TEIXEIRA threatened to kill the defendant, always showing the photograph of a dead person and saying that he would do to him the same thing he had done to BETO, a dangerous person, in that photograph; that Major TEIXEIRA sent him to a doctor whose name he remembers as MEIRELES; that this MEIRELES, according to what the major himself had told the defendant, was the man who signed the death certificates of dead subversives; that the doctor told him after examining him that that was nothing and that he must resist bravely . . .
[Apio Costa Rosa, 28, bank worker, Juiz de Fora, 1970.]

that the defendant received blows upon his abdomen and also electric shocks on his scrotal zone; that he was also hit in that zone; that he had to remain in a kneeling position for a long period during interrogations; that the defendant still has scars on his knees from those sufferings; that there was a doctor ready to treat the defendant and to massage him during those ill treatments . . .
[Pedro Gomes das Neves, 37, merchant, Fortaleza, 1974.]

I had suffered three heart attacks during the dozens of times in which I was on the parrot's perch. After the last attack they brought two doctors to examine me. They declared me to be "well" although one of them returned the following day to tell me that he was going to propose my removal for humanitarian reasons . . .
[Renato Oliveira da Motta, 59, newspaper salesman, São Paulo, 1975.]

These transcripts clearly indicate that doctors and nurses witnessed and even participated directly in the practice of torture. On occasion, these tortures resulted in the death of the victims.

It can be concluded as well that doctors who frequently furnished the authorities with false reports to cover up the evidence of torture also disguised the real causes of death in those cases when the tortures were fatal. These fraudulent medical reports listed a prisoner's cause of death in a manner generally consistent with the "official version" of events. Causes of death mentioned most often were "running over," "suicide," and "death by gunfire." Torture was never mentioned. Surviving prisoners who witnessed deaths under torture inside the security agencies often contradicted or denied the conclusions of these falsified medical reports in their own depositions. Medical examiners, usually connected with the state departments of public security, also participated in concealing corpses. This was to keep relatives from seeing the marks of torture on the victims' bodies.

From the study of military court proceedings, it was possible for the BNM project to identify names of medical examiners implicated in the practice of writing reports to cover up deaths by torture, including the following: Harry Shibata, Arnaldo Siqueira, Abeylard de Queiroz Orsini, Orlando José Batos Brandão, and Isaac Abramovitc, in São Paulo; Rubens Pedro Macuco Janini, and Olympio Pereira da Silva, in Rio de Janeiro; Djezzar Gonçalves Leite, in Minas Gerais; Ednaldo Paz de Vasconcelos, in Pernambuco.

The necroscopic reports, in particular, furnish other names. Student Alexandre Vannuchi Leme, for instance, was killed on the premises of the Second Army's DOI-CODI in São Paulo, 17 March 1973. His necroscopic report, however, signed by coroners Isaac Abramovitc and Orlando José Bastos Brandão, indicates that he "had thrown himself under a vehicle, thereby suffering a contusion on his head." The death of Carlos Nicolau Danielli, killed under torture on the premises of the Second Army's DOI-CODI in São Paulo, in January 1973, was "verified" in an autopsy report signed by Isaac Abramovitc and Paulo Augusto de Queiroz Rocha as having occurred in an exchange of gunfire with security agents.

Even fanciful versions of "suicide" were given in autopsy reports to cover up assassinations by torture. An example was the report on the death of Military Police Lieutenant José Ferreira de Almeida on 12 August 1975 in the Second Army's DOI-CODI. Medical examiners Harry Shibata and Marcos Almeida declared that death was the result of "asphyxiation by constriction of the neck." Shibata would repeat the same report in the death under torture in October 1975 of journalist Wladimir Herzog, a case which mobilized civilian opposition to the regime.

PART II

THE REPRESSIVE SYSTEM

FIVE

THE ORIGINS OF
THE MILITARY REGIME

WHAT happened in Brazil to produce so many acts of grim cruelty?
Were these acts of inhuman hate simply the handiwork of a few
insane individuals who by chance worked in the official agencies
charged with carrying out political repression?

Some historical explanation is necessary to answer this question.
Torture, of course, is a very old institution throughout the world.
In Brazil, as elsewhere, it has been used routinely during inquiries
into the activities of political dissenters. After the 1964 military coup,
however, torture was administered to members of the political opposition on a systematic basis. Moreover, the practice was an essential component of the semiautonomous repressive system that
eventually grew out of all proportion even to the authoritarian state
itself. Torture became a daily fact of Brazilian life because those
sectors within the military that justified all measures in the maintenance of internal security held sway within the state apparatus.
At the same time, the political regime closed down, eventually
excluding even segments of the traditional elite from political participation. In brief, by 1968 a powerful system of repression and
control was entrenched in Brazil.

This system, however, cannot be understood in isolation from the
broad sweep of Brazilian history. The armed forces that assumed
power by overthrowing President João Goulart in April 1964 were
following a long tradition of military intervention in Brazil. This
tradition goes back to the monarchist period (1822–89) and continued during the so-called Old Republic (1889–1930). Most often, the

military would be called upon by the central government—whether monarchist or republican—to repress popular uprisings. Indeed, the success of these repressive actions has resulted in a historically erroneous image of Brazilians as conformist, accommodating, and submissive. In reality, popular uprisings were frequent.

The monarchist period, for example, witnessed the so-called Equator Confederation, a movement for social change in the northeastern states of Pernambuco, Paraíba, Rio Grande do Norte, and Ceará from 1824 to 1825. The Confederation was led by the Carmelite Father Joaquim do Amor Divino Rabelo Caneca, who was later executed. Other revolts occurred in Ceará in 1831 and 1832. In the northern state of Pará, the "Cabanagem," named after the huts ("cabanas") of rebels who lived on the edge of rivers, erupted from 1835 to 1840 and ended with the military killing half the state's population. From 1838 to 1841, the basket-maker Manuel Francisco dos Anjos Ferreira led cowpunchers, artisans, peasants, slaves, and ex-soldiers in a popular uprising (called the "Balaiada," referring to "balaio" or "big basket") in what is today the northern state of Maranhão. In 1835, the Farrapos War began in the southern states of Santa Catarina and Rio Grande do Sul. It was settled only ten years later. The "Sabinada," named after the movement's main ideologue, medical doctor Francisco Sabino Alvares da Rocha Vieira, took place in Salvador, Bahia, Brazil's first capital, between 1837 and 1838. The Liberal Revolt, in the center-south states of São Paulo and Minas Gerais, took place in 1842; and the Praieira Revolution, in Pernambuco, in 1848.

In 1831 the National Guard was established to deal with such uprisings. It was officially an auxiliary force of the army, responsible for controlling internal opposition to the central government while the army remained in charge of defense against external aggression. In practice, the National Guard defended the interests of the rural oligarchy. Toward the end of the nineteenth century, when the influence of the rural landowners began to decline as a consequence of the growing importance of the new industrial bourgeoisie, the influence of the National Guard also declined. The war against Paraguay from 1864 to 1870 brought the regular army decisively to the fore. From that time on the army also began openly to intervene in political matters. The fact that it competed with the National Guard, which had come to be identified with the rural oligarchy, gave the army for a time a reputation for defending progressive causes.

The most important event for the army in this regard was its participation in the overthrow of Emperor Pedro II in 1889, which resulted in the establishment of a republican system in Brazil. The armed forces were in fact the main instigators of the plot, and the first two presidents of the newly established republic were military men, General Deodoro da Fonseca and General Floriano Peixoto. Nonetheless, despite its identification with progressive republicanism in Brazil and its active role in the overthrow of the monarchy, the army was also a repressive force, containing uprisings among the poorer classes when they sought to resist the authority of the republican government. These two apparently contradictory functions existed side by side.

During the first phase of republican life, the two most significant episodes involving army repression took place at Canudos, Bahia, in 1897 and in Santa Catarina in the so-called Contestado of 1912. Motivated by harsh living conditions and spurred on by messianic leaders, the peasant population in these hinterland areas rose up against the central state, only to be beaten down by the armed forces.

After 1922, the army was weakened by internal divisions. The lower military ranks, led by lieutenants, opposed the generals and other high-ranking officers implicated in the corrupt practices of big landowners. In 1924 and 1927, the lieutenants led revolts against their superiors. The epic march of the Prestes Column, a band of rebels led by Communist Party leader Luís Carlos Prestes who from 1924 to 1927 made their way through 8,000 miles of the Brazilian backlands in an effort to gain adherents for a revolt against the central government, also contributed to the agitation of the period. The common purpose of the uprisings was a call for morality in public life, universal suffrage, and greater nationalism—causes supported by the emergent urban middle classes. Although the lieutenants' movement did not seek an alliance with the workers' movement (which had grown significantly in the first two decades of the twentieth century), it did spearhead the push for political change that resulted in the 1930 revolution.

In 1930, dissident sectors of the rural oligarchy closed ranks with the rebellious lieutenants to create the Liberal Alliance. The Alliance presented Getúlio Vargas as its presidential candidate. Despite accusations of electoral fraud, and with the help of the armed forces, Vargas was inaugurated. Appearances notwithstanding, there was no deep change in the system of power. The new government was in fact formed by an alliance between the old rural oligarchy and the emerging industrial sectors. The military apparatus, now united around Getúlio Vargas, became the main instrument for consolidating the new pact between the two most powerful interests in Brazil.

The alliance between the revolutionaries who supported Vargas and the traditional oligarchy against which the revolution had ostensibly been directed caused an irreconcilable breach between Vargas and the original members of the lieutenants' movement. Their opposition to the new regime led to the formation of the National Liberation Alliance (Aliança Nacional Libertadora—ANL) in January 1935. The ANL brought together communists, whose number had grown during the 1920s, and many nationalist politicians seeking land reform and a fairer distribution of income. For a few months the ANL grew at a rapid rate, holding forth in the street and barracks. It was then banned by the Vargas government.

The army had its baptism of fire as an anticommunist force in November 1935, when the Communist Party instigated an insurrection. The rebellion was limited to army barracks and promptly suppressed, but to this day the episode is remembered by the armed forces in annual celebrations reaffirming the sacred ideals of the fight against communism. As would be the case in 1964, the violent and extended repression that followed the 1935 insurrection revealed that the objective of those in power was not simply to punish the rebels behind the so-called communist plot. Rather, the elite group represented in the cabinet felt that the time had come to strike at the democratic demands advocated by the original lieutenants' movement and legitimated, at least in part, by the 1930 revolution. The detection of the supposed "communist plot"—in reality the reassertion of these demands—provided an ideal pretext to repudiate decisively the pressures for democratization. Riding the wave of repression, the upper ranks of the armed forces united around Vargas in 1937 to introduce an undisguised dictatorship, which came to be called the "New State."

With the outbreak of World War II, the competition of the great powers for allies was intensified, and Brazil, as a strategically important part of the South Atlantic, became a focal point. The international situation was also reflected in internal Brazilian politics, with the armed forces divided in their sympathies. The early Nazi victories were celebrated by the leadership of the Brazilian armed forces, but those elements favoring the Allies gained influence as the war situation shifted.

At the same time, the nationalist gains achieved by the New State struck at American interests inside Brazil. Sectors linked to the United States began to plot Vargas' overthrow. In October 1945, soon after the end of the war, a coup d'état commanded by General Góis Monteiro deposed the former dictator.

The succeeding period in Brazilian history, 1946–64, was a time of economic development and social change that created profound modifications in the Brazilian social structure. These changes were nationalist and democratic, but also authoritarian in character. Fascist elements were strengthened within the Brazilian military.

After a brief period of democratic freedoms, President Marshal Eurico Gaspar Dutra took a sharp turn toward the political right in 1947. The Dutra government was strongly pro-American, uninterested in the needs and opinions of the people, and rigidly authoritarian in character. Particularly important in determining its course was the ideological influence of the American military on the Brazilian armed forces. Nonetheless, growing discontent with Dutra led to Vargas' reelection to the presidency in 1950 on a nationalist platform. Despite the Vargas victory, however, it proved difficult to expel American interests from Brazil. Both economically and politically, those interests were already firmly rooted.

By this time, the play of forces that would result in the April 1964 coup was beginning to take shape. The delicate balance between the interests of the foreign monopolies on which the Brazilian economy was increasingly dependent and the popular pressures for national control of development was difficult for Vargas to sustain. Once again, rightist sectors in the military planned to depose him, but their plans were preempted by Vargas' suicide on 24 August 1954. This unexpected event set off passionate popular demonstrations throughout the country directed against symbols of the presence of American capital in Brazil. Frightened by this demonstration of the popular will, the military was forced to postpone its takeover attempt.

From Vargas' suicide in 1954 to January 1956, when Juscelino Kubitschek, the newly elected president, took office, the country experienced more unrest caused by the same rightist sectors. During this period, however, the right encountered resistance from nationalist elements within the armed forces. Those officers planning a coup d'état had once again to retreat. Prevented from assuming power, they concentrated their efforts in the Superior War College and in the elaboration of the ideology that came to be known as the "National Security Doctrine."

Kubitschek finished his term in office in 1960 and was replaced by Jânio Quadros, who was elected on a wave of populist sentiment. Nonetheless, Quadros' administration was authoritarian in its approach to internal affairs, even though it maintained an open international policy. The Quadros administration was cut short by the president's resignation on 25 August 1961, a surprising gesture that historians have still not satisfactorily explained.

Quadros' vice-president, João Goulart, considered the principal heir to Vargas' nationalism of the 1950s and branded a radical by those in the higher ranks of the armed forces, was nearly impeded from succeeding Quadros by the veto of three military members of the cabinet. The veto evoked a strong popular protest, particularly in Goulart's home state, where then governor Leonel Brizola—himself Goulart's brother-in-law and political ally—led massive street demonstrations in favor of Goulart's inauguration. Fearing that the country was on the brink of civil war, the military once again withdrew. They did manage, however, to impose a parliamentary system of government that removed power from the president.

The period between 1962 and 1964 was marked by popular influence on the political system. A national plebiscite gave Goulart a landslide victory and enabled him to abolish the parliamentary system imposed by the military. This in turn allowed him to increase the pace of broad structural reforms. Goulart's program for sweeping social change, known as "basic reforms," drew on substantial support from unionized workers. In spite of the organizational weaknesses of the labor unions at the local level, they had developed an ample capacity for mobilization. The number of unions that supported Goulart's "basic reforms" increased steadily.

In addition, workers began to organize an all-encompassing structure called the General Workers' Command (CGT). Created in violation of labor legislation from the Vargas period that had been modeled on Mussolini's labor code, the CGT was seen by forces opposed to the Goulart government as a warning sign that a communist revolution was imminent in Brazil.

The period was one of high inflation, but workers generally achieved salary readjustments that kept pace with the rising cost of living. In rural areas, peasant organizations, known as Peasant Leagues, were created. By 1964, a total of 2,181 leagues had been formed in twenty states. Overt class conflicts developed in rural areas just as they had in the cities. The rural conflicts, in particular, led to panic among conservative landowners, who were determined to avoid land reform at all costs.

In the cities, students, artists, and numerous sectors of the urban middle classes joined the ranks of those committed to implementing Goulart's nationalist program, particularly a new educational structure, land reform, and legislation to control the expatriation of profits. A nationalist front was formed in the Brazilian congress, which also exerted pressure for reform.

Before this mobilization could effectively challenge the powers of the traditional elites, the proponents of a coup d'état, openly supported by representatives of the United States government, made their final preparations for a military takeover. The high inflation then manifest and the instability of the political scene favored the message of the right to the middle classes, that only a strong government could control the situation. In fact, inflation had risen from 30% in 1960 to 74% in 1963. In addition, strong opposition to Goulart's economic policies in the Brazilian congress had prevented him from implementing a three-year plan designed to spur the growth rate and reduce inflation to 10%.

Further complicating the economic situation was the problem of outflow of capital: during the first months of 1964 alone, more than two billion dollars were sent to foreign banks. The balance of payments problem was aggravated by the suspension of all U.S. government aid to Brazil, with the exception of funds sent directly to state governors opposed to Goulart, in particular those from the political and economic heart of Brazil: Carlos Lacerda from Rio de Janeiro, Adhemar de Barros from São Paulo, and Magalhães Pinto from Minas Gerais.

The readiness of the United States to collaborate in the planned coup was the final signal that spurred to action those generals interested in overthrowing President Goulart. Lieutenant Colonel Vernon Walters, at the time the military attaché to the U.S. embassy in Brazil, offered arms to General Carlos Guedes, one of the officers who would finally set the coup in motion. The United States also financed organizations such as the Brazilian Institute for Democratic Action and the Institute for Research and Social Studies, both of which were involved in massive antigovernment campaigns throughout the country.

The political crisis reached its climax during the early months of 1964, when the movement for basic reforms finally elicited support among the lower ranks of the military. In September 1963, the so-called Sergeants' Revolt had taken place in Brasília, by then the capital of the country. The Association of Navy and Marine Personnel of Brazil, also sympathetic to the reforms and to the Goulart government, had been formed in 1962. These insurgent organizations allowed the generals to invoke the need for military discipline, forcing Goulart into at least a temporary retreat. Goulart's position, like that of Getúlio Vargas in 1954, became untenable. He was unable to halt the advance of the right by calling on the Brazilian people to defend the law and incapable of placating the irritated military commanders.

While the country was in the midst of these successive crises, a huge public rally was convened. On 13 March 1964, more than 200,000 people gathered in front of Rio's Central Brazil Railroad station. Goulart, flanked by members of his cabinet and several state governors, addressed the crowd and signed the basic reform bills then and there. The rally was intended as a demonstration of power to halt the sedition, which was already being publicly carried out. Despite the symbolic force of the act, the government and those forces sympathetic to it could not demobilize the opposition. The generals, for their part, were moved to set a date for their takeover.

Unfortunately for Goulart, practically the entire middle class as well as important sectors of the rural and urban working classes had been convinced by the anticommunist propaganda of the anti-Goulart forces. They included the Social Democratic Party and the National Democratic Union, both financed by the United States. The Roman Catholic Church, particularly the hierarchy, also joined in the campaign against the Goulart government. They were supported by the major newspapers, which helped mobilize vast numbers of government critics in demonstrations that became famous as "marches of the family, with God, for freedom."

In the closing days of March 1964, marine personnel meeting in the Metalworkers' Union in Rio de Janeiro rebelled against the military authorities. This set the stage for the actual coup, which occurred on April 1. There was virtually no resistance. The nationally supported popular reform movement, based on the legal structures of a constitutionally elected government, could not resist the force of arms. With the coup, the long period of instability came to an end. Brazil entered a new phase, one which would bring about profound changes in the country's political, economic, and social structure.

SIX

THE CONSOLIDATION OF THE AUTHORITARIAN STATE

THE APRIL 1964 takeover resulted in the shelving of nationalist proposals of development. Despite periodic minor adjustments, the economic policy imposed by the military depended upon two major strategies: the concentration of income and the denationalization of the economy.

The orientation of the military's economic plan was evident in its policies on income and taxation, land distribution and ownership, and investment. Denationalization of the economy, in particular, meant opening up all doors to foreign capital through measures such as easy credit and fiscal incentives for the estabishment of multinational corporations in Brazil and the removal of obstacles to the repatriation of profits. The official tolerance of frauds designed to bypass legal controls on economic activity and the routine granting of permission for land purchases to foreign groups also contributed to the flow of foreign capital both into and out of the country. The major consequence of these policies was increasing foreign indebtedness. In order to impose these policies, moreover, it was necessary for the military to introduce a whole series of authoritarian and repressive measures. These were adopted by successive governments after 1964.

The policy of income concentration had particularly serious social consequences. The policy sought, above all, to provide attractive conditions for foreign and large-scale national investors by increasing profitability on investments. For most Brazilians, however, the encouragement of capitalist growth meant the unprecedented reduction of personal income. This was most evident during the years of the "Economic Miracle," 1969–73, when the growth rate in Brazil was among the world's highest. At the same time, there was a marked deterioration in living conditions for large numbers of Brazilians. Signs of poverty such as hunger, slums, and disease increased alarmingly.

Since the economic policy was extremely unpopular among the most numerous sectors of the population, it had to be implemented by force. In order to forestall any dissent, the military changed the country's juridical structure, built up the security apparatus responsible for internal repression and political control, and radically modified the relations among the executive, legislative, and judicial branches of the government. This was done by strengthening the executive branch to the point where it became an all-powerful state.

In the early years of the military regime, however, from 1964 to 1968, some semblance of democratic normality was maintained. When President Goulart was deposed in 1964, for example, efforts were made to present the takeover as an "indirect election" carried out by the legislative branch of the government, rather than as a coup d'état that replaced the constitutionally elected civilian president with a general nominated by the armed forces.

The new government was "legitimated" by the so-called Institutional Act of 9 April 1964, promulgated just days before the inauguration of Marshal Humberto de Alencar Castello Branco as the first military president. The act, soon to be followed by other "institutional acts" that would change the entire juridical structure of Brazil, clearly proclaimed: "The victorious Revolution, as the Constituent Power, confers its own legitimacy upon itself." By the time the act expired on 11 June 1964, it had been invoked to remove 378 persons from office and deprive them of their political privileges for ten years. Among those affected were three former presidents (Juscelino Kubitschek, Jânio Quadros, and João Goulart), six state governors, two senators, sixty-three federal deputies, and more than three hundred state deputies and city council members. Seventy-seven army officers were put on the retirement list, together with fourteen navy officers and thirty-one from the air force. Approximately 10,000 civil servants were fired; 5,000 investigations affecting 40,000 persons were initiated. Castello Branco created the General Committee for Investigations to coordinate the military police investigations that were begun throughout the country. In June, the

National Information Service—the Brazilian intelligence organization—was created. Its power would grow in the years to come.

The dictatorship was taking shape. In October 1965, after government candidates were defeated in state elections in Minas Gerais and Rio de Janeiro, Institutional Act. No. 2 (AI-2) was promulgated. This decree abolished all political parties and allowed the executive to disband the legislative branch at will. It made presidential elections indirect and extended the jurisdiction of military courts over the civilian population. The introduction to AI-2 stated: "It was not said that the Revolution was, but that it is and will continue."

From that point forward, only two political parties were permitted: a government party, the National Alliance for Renewal (Aliança Renovadora Nacional—ARENA), and an official opposition party, the Brazilian Democratic Movement (Movimento Democrático Brasileiro—MDB). The latter was not free to challenge the military regime. In February 1966, Institutional Act No. 3 established indirect elections for state governors.

In 1966 disputes regarding the successor to Castello Branco developed within the armed forces, which had become the de facto electoral college. The "hard line" was victorious, and imposed its presidential candidate, General Artur da Costa e Silva, the minister of war, as the nominee. Costa e Silva would be rubber-stamped by an intimidated Congress the following year. Also in 1966, six more members of Congress were removed from office. The executive branch of the government decreed arbitrary congressional recesses, and military troops were deployed around the congressional chambers. When Costa e Silva was finally inaugurated in March 1967, a new constitution as well as new national security and press laws were decreed. In effect, these laws gave total license to the president of the republic and several high government officials.

Despite increasing repression, opposition to the regime slowly began to gain strength in the streets, factories, and schools. With the urban middle classes in the forefront of the protest movement, confrontations with the military regime increased. After the police attacked a student demonstration in March 1968 in Rio, killing 18-year-old high school student Edson Luís, protest demonstrations spread like wildfire throughout the country. Workers' movements also appeared with some vigor.

The armed forces further escalated the repression by decreeing Institutional Act No. 5 on 13 December 1968. Three reasons were given as pretexts for the crackdown: the increase of criticism from within the officially permitted opposition party, the Brazilian Democratic Movement; the proliferation of street demonstrations; and the appearance of armed opposition groups, which justified their activities with the argument that no resistance to the dictatorship was possible through legal channels. The final provocation that led to the decree of AI-5 was a speech by federal congressman Márcio Moreira Alves that was considered insulting to the armed forces.

Unlike the previous institutional acts, AI-5 had no expiration date. It was barefaced dictatorship. The national congress, six state legislative assemblies, and dozens of city councils were disbanded. Sixty-nine additional members of Congress as well as Carlos Lacerda, the former governor of the state of Rio de Janeiro and one of the three main civilian architects of the coup, were removed from office. One of Lacerda's civilian co-conspirators, former São Paulo governor Adhemar de Barros, had already lost his post in 1966. The third civilian power behind the coup, Minas Gerais governor Magalhães Pinto, survived these political purges.

This whole arsenal of acts, decrees, prohibitions, and forcible removals from political office put an almost complete stop to the denunciations of the regime, mass protests, and demands by popular movements. Many were convinced that clandestine activities were the only viable form of opposition. In August 1969, when Costa e Silva suffered a stroke and had to relinquish the presidency, the ministers of the three military services seized power in order to prevent Pedro Aleixo, Costa e Silva's civilian vice-president, from assuming office. During this period, a vicious circle was established: the armed resistance intensified its actions and carried out abductions of foreign diplomats (including the American ambassador Charles Elbrick, who was kidnapped in Rio in 1969), demanding in exchange for their release the release of political prisoners; the ruling military junta, in turn, introduced the death sentence and banishment for political crimes, increasing the penalties already contained in the National Security Law. In addition, the junta imposed by decree an even more authoritarian constitution, appended to the 1967 constitution as Constitutional Amendment No. 1. Congress, which had been closed down at the end of 1968, was reopened only to rubber-stamp the selection of General Emílio Garrastazu Médici to the presidency of the republic. The struggle within the military regarding the choice of Médici remained secret.

When Médici took office on 30 October 1969 with the motto "Security and Development," he ushered in the most repressive and violent period since Brazil had become a republic. A number of virtually independent "security organs" were created to carry out the suppression of civil liberties. In the following years thousands of Brazilians were sent to prisons, and torture and killing by the state became routine.

At the same time, the country experienced a period of economic expansion and growth that came to be known as the "Economic Miracle." Large-scale projects were undertaken, especially massive public works like the bridge from Rio de Janeiro to Niterói, its sister city across the Guanabara Bay, and the Transamazonian highway, which would link the remote interior of the country with the more populated central cities. Such ventures were carried out in a climate of jingoism stimulated by official propaganda, glorifying the state on the one hand, and unchecked by the censored media, on the other. Although elections were held during this period, the prohibition of legal political party activity resulted in a lack of popular interest in voting. In the November 1970 congressional elections, for example, the total of abstentions, blank, and voided ballots amounted to 46% of all registered voters. During the Médici administration, which lasted from 1969 to 1974, Brazil developed an increasingly negative image abroad. It became known as a country where people were tortured, persecuted, sent into exile, and deprived of their political rights.

The Church, which had supported the overthrow of João Goulart, began to change its stance as it encountered increasing difficulties in its relations with the state. The Church itself became a victim of acts of repression: priests and nuns were imprisoned, tortured, or killed, churches raided and bishops placed under surveillance.

Willing to use even inhumane means to achieve their ends, security forces gained important victories in their fight against underground political organizations. All data collected by the BNM project confirm the reports made during the Médici period by human rights organizations on tortures, killings of political opponents, disappearances, raids on private homes, the complete lack of respect for the rights of citizens, and failure to observe the legislation enacted by the regime itself. The BNM study revealed that the highest level of tortures and deaths occurred during this period.

Toward the second half of 1973, weakened by the international oil crisis, the "Economic Miracle" began to show signs of imminent collapse. In an effort to recover the legitimacy that had eroded during the Médici period, the military changed tack and chose General Ernesto Geisel as Médici's successor. In the five years of his administration (1974–79), Geisel implemented policies designed to strengthen the military regime by acceding, at least in part, to civilian demands. The hallmarks of the Geisel period were the reopening of political life, the reinitiation of dialogue with those sectors of the political elite that had been excluded from power, and the easing of repression against civilian opponents of the regime. By providing these sectors with some negotiating space, Geisel's policies actually confined the opposition to the regime within limits that did not immediately threaten its stability. By 1974, moreover, the armed resistance groups had been virtually obliterated. Despite harsh but sporadic repression, the Geisel period was characterized overall by conciliatory gestures toward the government's critics. In the final analysis, however, the military's objective during Geisel's administration was to maintain the system installed by the 1964 coup.

Most significantly, the Geisel period was marked by carefully calculated policy shifts that alternated permissive and repressive attitudes toward the regime's opponents. These shifts revealed the limited nature of the democratic opening in Brazil during this time, but they did permit opposition forces to gather strength. As part of this official strategy, Geisel and General Golbery do Couto e Silva, who occupied a number of cabinet positions and was generally considered the architect of the regime's policies, relaxed press censorship. They also tried to channel the growing popular unrest toward Congress and the official parties and away from the government.

As a result of this controlled liberalization, thirteen of the twenty-two vacancies in the Brazilian Senate were won by the opposition party, the MDB, in the November 1974 elections. In the lower house, the Chamber of Deputies, the number of MDB representatives increased from 87 to 165 seats, while the number of seats held by ARENA, the government party, decreased from 223 to 199. The armed forces grudgingly accepted the defeat, allowing the results to stand. Fearing a repetition of these losses in subsequent elections, however, the regime arbitrarily altered the electoral rules in a manner designed to tip the scales in ARENA's favor.

In regard to human rights questions, the early months of the

Geisel administration witnessed a tactical shift in the methods of the repressive forces. Because of greater press freedom, official reports of people being "run over," "committing suicide," and "being killed while attempting to escape"—when in reality they had been killed, often under torture, after capture and imprisonment—lost credibility. As a result, the repressive forces sought to conceal such cases by claiming the victims had disappeared. During this period, "disappearances" became more common than before.

Security organizations apparently sought to make a "clean sweep" of all groups on the left, annihilating those who had resisted previous repression. Although they sporadically indicated some concern for improving the human rights situation, the "security community"—those agencies charged with carrying out internal repression and under direct military command—did not on the whole change the pattern of repression that had been established during the Médici years, which was based on abduction, torture, and extrajudicial killings. Despite proof of their abduction, approximately twenty citizens detained by the security organizations at the time of Geisel's inauguration were never seen again.

Members of Congress opposed to the regime denounced the situation daily. Their outspokenness provoked government reprisals intended to establish clearly the acceptable limits for protesting human rights violations. In the short period between January and April 1974, politicians who crossed this line were summarily removed from office. In this way, even the softer-line Geisel government wanted to make clear that its new openness did not imply tolerance of forces it considered to be on the left.

In November 1976 municipal elections were held. The tenor of the campaign was radically different from that of the 1974 elections. The so-called Falcão Law, named after its author Armando Falcão, then Geisel's justice minister, drastically limited the use of radio and television in campaigning. The measure also restricted political meetings and public assemblies. In spite of these arbitrary restrictions on political information, the election results demonstrated that the opposition MDB party was maintaining its upward trend while ARENA decreased in strength. Although ARENA retained comfortable majorities in municipal councils and city governments, regime strategists were sufficiently concerned by the election results to examine the possibility of reorganizing the two-party system in effect since 1966.

On 1 April 1977, when government pressure on the MDB failed to make it approve the reorganization of the Brazilian judiciary system—which, in brief, would have increased executive branch power—Geisel disbanded the Congress and decreed the "April Package." This was a new set of constitutional changes intended to perpetuate the regime and halt the opposition's growth. Among other measures, these changes reorganized the selection of the electoral college to favor the government, invented the post of appointed senator, and extended the term of the president of the republic to six years.

The April Package was a bitter blow to opposition sectors that had responded enthusiastically to the promise of liberalization. Significantly, though, the campaign for the restoration of human rights and the denunciation of abuses in this area was not affected, in particular because the press, by then largely free from censorship, chose to pursue the issue.

An episode that indicated the government's posture with regard to these denunciations was the visit paid by the archbishop of São Paulo, Cardinal Paulo Evaristo Arns, to General Golbery. The archbishop was accompanied by a committee of relatives of the disappeared political prisoners. Initially, Golbery promised to provide information within thirty days regarding the prisoner's whereabouts. He subsequently reneged on that promise. Justice Minister Falcão went so far as to inform the press that those listed as "disappeared" had never been detained.

Nonetheless, the security organizations were forced to change with the times and adapt to the new opposition pressures. This became evident when two deaths under torture occurred in the Information Operations Detachment–Center for Internal Defense Operations (DOI-CODI) in São Paulo in October 1975 and January 1976. The first victim was journalist Wladimir Herzog; the second, a metalworker named Manoel Fiel Filho. Both murders evoked a very strong reaction from broad sectors of the public. After the second killing, Geisel dismissed the commander of the São Paulo–based Second Army, General Ednardo D'Ávila Mello. The sacking was widely interpreted as a blow to the autonomy of the security forces, and it had a serious impact on military circles.

In December 1976, faithfully copying the methods of the Médici period, DOI-CODI agents raided a house in the São Paulo suburb of Lapa, where leaders of the underground Communist Party of

Brazil were meeting. Party activists Pedro Pomar and Angelo Arroyo were killed on the spot, and the death of one of those detained, João Batista Franco Drummond, was announced shortly afterward. it was stated that he had been run over "while trying to escape."

No further deaths under interrogation were recorded after 1977, although reports of torture continued to be made in the few military court proceedings that were initiated that year. By 1977, the tensions that led to factionalism within the armed forces were becoming known to the general public. At the same time, rightist groups regularly carried out terrorist acts. Responsibility for these acts was claimed by groups that in reality were fronts for the former agents of torture organizations. Because of liberalization in the overt political order, the so-called information community—those military and police groups connected with internal intelligence-gathering activities and responsible for the repression—was forced to carry out its actions in greater secrecy. This "secret arm of repression" continued to function even as the regime opened more and more space for the opposition.

In the 1976–77 period, the first major incident perpetrated by rightist terrorists was an attack on Monseigneur Adriano Hipólito, bishop of Nova Iguaçu, a major diocese in the state of Rio de Janeiro. On 22 September 1976, the bishop was abducted by hooded men who took him to a wooded area, beat him up, and left him naked, while his car was driven away and blown up by a heavy charge of explosives in front of the office of the Brazilian National Bishops' Conference. It was evident that the bishop was singled out in order to express the hostility of the government to the Conference, which had frequently expressed concern over the human rights situation.

The impunity with which these first attacks were carried out ensured that they would continue. Despite formal statements condemning the incidents, the military regime gave the terrorists a virtual carte blanche. In August of 1976, bombs exploded in the offices of many important organizations identified with progressive forces, including the headquarters in Rio de Janeiro of the Brazilian Bar Association and the Brazilian Press Association. The São Paulo office of the Brazilian Center for Analysis and Planning was bombed the following month. In the state of Minas Gerais, also, twenty-four separate incidents, including eleven bomb attacks and various threats, raids, and assaults, were recorded by October 1978.

Despite the frequency of these terrorist attacks from the right and other measures indicating that Geisel's "slow, gradual, and guaranteed" loosening of the political scene could easily swing back toward more repression, a new national situation did begin to emerge, catalyzed by the growth of urban social movements and Church-sponsored "ecclesial base communities." Despite its will to maintain power, the military regime was becoming increasingly isolated. Economic deterioration added to its woes.

Beginning in February 1978, Brazilian Committees for Amnesty began to be formed throughout the country. The committees spearheaded a campaign for unrestricted amnesty for those who were charged with political crimes. They defended political prisoners who went on hunger strikes to protest harsh prison conditions and organized public denunciations of tortures, killings, and disappearances.

Afraid of an impending crisis, the generals, as had been the case since 1964, sought to resolve their internal dispute by coming to an agreement over which of their number would succeed General Geisel. Factions in disagreement with Geisel's liberalization strategy supported General Sílvio Frota, minister of the army, who became a candidate despite Geisel's opposition. The ensuing conflict provoked a crisis, nearly producing a clash between the military factions. Such an outcome was forestalled because of the clear superiority of those forces loyal to Geisel. Geisel's chosen candidate, General João Baptista de Oliveira Figueiredo, head of the National Information Service (SNI), prevailed instead. Frota was dismissed from the army ministry and sent into early retirement.

In November 1978, the government suffered another electoral defeat: in races for the national senate, the opposition MDB obtained 18.5 million votes, compared to 13.6 million for ARENA. Finally ceding to the clear mandate for change, the government revoked Institutional Act No. 5. During the previous ten years, AI-5 had been the most visible face of the dictatorship, and had imposed a *de facto* state of siege in Brazil. Despite the revocation, some of the exceptional measures permitted under AI-5, such as the power of the executive to declare a state of emergency and to suspend civil rights for a period of up to 120 days, were incorporated into the constitution then in effect.

By the end of the Geisel administration, the post-1964 military regime had produced approximately 10,000 political exiles; 4,682 persons had been removed from office and deprived of their political rights; and 245 students were expelled from universities. Thousands of citizens had passed through the political prisons of the regime. The list of dead and disappeared was close to 300.

The inauguration of General Figueiredo as the fifth military president to serve since the 1964 military takeover took place on 15 March 1979. This date was chosen to end the period researched by the BNM project.

What kind of situation did Figueiredo inherit? In brief, he faced the challenges of a worsening economic situation and an opposition newly strengthened by the reform of national security legislation. Political prisons gradually emptied after Figueiredo took office. Exiles began to return, and the opposition was united in the campaign for an unrestricted amnesty. Nonetheless, the military regime survived. Working-class leaders were persecuted and killed in rural areas and in the cities. In fact, there was considerable government interference in labor union affairs, particularly in major strikes called by automobile workers in the industrial belt surrounding the city of São Paulo. This authoritarian stance demonstrated that the "democratic opening" in Brazil was directed more to the nation's political elite and to sectors of the middle class than to the working classes.

SEVEN

THE HISTORY AND LEGAL STRUCTURE OF THE REPRESSIVE SYSTEM

WHEN President João Goulart was deposed on 2 April 1964, there was an initial moment of indecision. Since the armed forces were not in total accord, it was not immediately clear which group would assume the most direct command of the state apparatus.

The group headed by Marshal Humberto de Alencar Castello Branco prevailed, not because it had the most important military role in the coup, but because it was the only faction to present an overall plan for Brazilian society. This plan had been maturing since the 1950s in the Higher War College (Escola Superior de Guerra—ESG); it was to become known as the Doctrine of National Security.

Founded on 20 August 1949, the ESG was the inspiration of Marshal César Obino, then chief of staff of the armed forces. To this day, it is housed in the Fortress of St. John in Rio de Janeiro. The origins of the school are in the period when the Brazilian Expeditionary Force (Força Expedicionária Brasileira—FEB) fought in Italy under American command during World War II. The close relationship that resulted between American military officers and their Brazilian counterparts, including Castello Branco and Golbery do Couto e Silva, led the latter to believe that the war might continue—or a third one begin—pitting the Western allies against the Soviet Union. Although the Brazilian officers entered the war on the Allied side, their antifascist spirit—which, in theory, had led them to fight in the war in the first place—was actually less developed than their anticommunist convictions. Indeed, Góis Monteiro, minister of war during Vargas' New State, had defended Brazil's alignment with Germany. Nonetheless, the Brazilian officers developed strong ties with their American fellow officers.

After the war, that generation of Brazilian officers began to attend American military courses in considerable numbers. General Golbery do Couto e Silva later stated: "The FEB was not only important because of our going to Italy. Possibly more important still was the FEB's visit to the United States. . . . I went, and my stay had a great impact on me."[1] When these officers returned to Brazil, they had been profoundly influenced by a new concept of national defense. They had learned in American war colleges that strengthening the national system against possible external attack was in fact less important than shoring up institutions against an "internal enemy" that might be trying to undermine them.

In 1949, three years after the National War College was founded in the United States, the ESG was founded in Brazil and placed under the jurisdiction of the high command of the armed forces. From 1954 to 1964, the Brazilian ESG developed an elaborate theory for intervention in the political life of the nation. From 1964 onward, it also trained personnel to occupy political posts in the national government.

In addition to elaborating the official ideology of the military regime, the ESG established the national intelligence service, known as the National Information Service (SNI). The SNI was designed by General Golbery, who was to have a central role in the establishment of the political system introduced by the new military regime. It is perhaps in Golbery's own book, *Geopolítica do Brasil*, that the most concise statement of the Doctrine of National Security is to be found. This text became the official manual of the generals in power. Golbery wrote:

> There is thus a new dilemma, that of well-being versus security. This was pointed out by Goering in the past, in an imprecise but highly suggestive and well-known slogan: "More guns, less butter." And, in truth, there is no way to escape the need to sacrifice well-being for security, once the latter is truly threatened. The peoples who refuse to admit this learned the lesson they deserved in the dust of defeat."[2]

In other words, if "national security" is theatened, the sacrifice of well-being is justified. In practice this means the loss of freedom, constitutional guarantees, and the rights of the human person. While Goering was referring to peoples threatened by an external enemy, Golbery extended the notion to include a threat posed by an enemy among the Brazilian people themselves.

It was not until 1968, one year after the imposition of the National Security Law, that the first systematic criticisms of this new state ideology appeared. A pioneer commentary came from within the Catholic Church. It struck at one of the pillars of the Doctrine of National Security: the defense of the "Christian West." The claim of such a doctrine to call itself Christian was vehemently rejected by Monseigneur Cândido Padim, bishop of Bauru, in the state of São Paulo:

> The ideological group that has come out of the ESG holds absolute power and is mostly made up of military personnel; the notion of Western Christian civilization, as it is preached by the DSN [Doctrine of National Security], is a catchphrase that will not stand up to a cold confrontation with the message of the Gospel; democracy is merely a name that disguises the reality of military totalitarianism; . . . and national sovereignty is restricted to the point where it has disappeared. The anti-History that was let loose in the world through the policy which erupted into the reality of active Nazism is also evident, to a certain and very comparable extent, in Brazilian national politics. [3]

The concept of "national power" fundamental to this ideology was questioned by theologian Joseph Comblin, a Belgian priest who wrote important works on the effects of military dictatorship on the lives of the peoples of Latin America:

> It is always accepted in any society that a small proportion of the national resources and income should be reserved for collective defense and for the security of the state as well. But, since such expenditures yield no return or satisfaction of a personal nature, they are reduced to the necessary minimum. In a National Security System, on the contrary, the minimun becomes the maximum. All energies of citizens must be channeled to security and become power [for the state]. The National Security System produces, as a matter of fact, a human situation which is worse than slavery. In slavery, human energy

is transformed into material energy so as to produce economic results. Such results are innocent in themselves. The slave has at least the satisfaction of producing useful goods, even though he may not receive anything for himself. But a citizen subordinated to national security is called upon to build up power that will be used to dominate people, to break their will and destroy their personalities.[4]

The official ideology that permitted the hunting down of the "internal enemy" was also used to justify profound changes in the structures charged with maintaining state security. One change was the unchecked growth of security organs; another, the proliferation of restrictive legislation. The security organs operated with virtual autonomy. By the beginning of the 1970s, they formed a veritable state within the state, protected by institutional acts that stripped citizens of the guarantees inherent in a society subject to the rule of law. In the final analysis, the agents of repression were also protected by the absolute authority of military commanders.

Civilians also collaborated. The Permanent Group for Industrial Mobilization, initiated before the coup in contacts between the insurgent military officers and businessmen, was founded in April 1964. This was the first of a number of groups created to help channel the fighting power of the armed forces to the new doctrine of maintaining internal security and guarding against "revolutionary war" waged by dissidents from within the country. Businessmen also laid the foundations of a national Brazilian armaments industry, which would continue to grow in the years following the coup. Eventually, arms production would be directed to the export market, and Brazil would become the fifth largest exporter of arms in the world. The generals' success in this area is notable, in view of the failure of the other fundamental aspects of the military's economic policies.

After seizing power, the armed forces seriously prepared to combat any form of popular revolt against the regime they had imposed by force. More important than preparation for open warfare, however, was their preparation for a secret war to be waged in the form of interrogations, surreptitious investigations, telephone taps, and the storing and processing of information about supposed opposition activities. A broad range of activities were considered to constitute opposition to the government, including protests in various forms, campaigns for higher wages, and pressure for democratic reforms, as well as the activities of clandestine organizations dedicated to overthrowing the regime.

While information about the activities of the security organs and the repressive forces which operated through them was largely censored, the Brazilian press did frequently refer to the intelligence unit, SNI, often simply calling it the "System." The SNI was established on 13 June 1964 "to oversee and coordinate intelligence activities throughout national territory, in particular those that pertained to National Security." This "System" had a pyramidal structure. The various interrogation chambers run by the security organs were at the base. At the apex was the National Security Council. The granting of ministerial rank to the SNI chief, plus the fact that he was one of four cabinet members who met with the president of the republic in the first working meeting of each day, indicates the importance of the SNI in the national political system. Both Médici and Figueiredo, the third and fifth military presidents, respectively, served as heads of the SNI. Finally, the SNI was a sizable structure. In addition to its central agency in Brasília, there were eight regional agencies, covering Brazil from the city of Manaus in the north to the city of Porto Alegre in the south. From 1964 to 1981, the budget for maintaining these agencies alone increased 3,500 times.

To improve the efficiency of the repression it was also necessary to integrate the repressive institutions connected with the army, navy, air force, and the federal and state police. In mid-1969, when sectors of the opposition in São Paulo resorted to illegal forms of political action, including urban guerrilla warfare, in the wake of Institutional Act No. 5, Operation Bandeirantes (OBAN) was created. Only semiofficially under the auspices of the military authorities, OBAN was funded by contributions from various multinational corporations, including Ford and General Motors. While it was not formally connected with the Second Army headquarters in the city of São Paulo, the Second Army's commanding officer, General Canavarro Pereira, was a regular visitor to OBAN headquarters. The headquarters was in fact a police precinct, and the OBAN staff was made up of regular members of the army, navy, and air force, as well as the political state police, the federal police, the civil police, the military state police, and the civil guard—in short, representatives of all types of security and police organizations.

The fact that OBAN was extralegal gave it flexibility and impunity with regard to methods of interrogation, which in turn enabled it to score important victories in the "fight against subversion." Won over by this success, the high-ranking officers responsible for national security approved the experiment. The OBAN structure was thus used as a model for the creation, on a national scale, of official organs for repression that were known by the acronym DOI-CODI.

The DOI-CODI units (Information Operations Detachment–Center for Internal Defense Operations) were formed in January 1970. Responsibility for them was centralized in the army, though personnel from the two other armed services also participated. In each territorial unit of Brazil the DOI-CODIs took over effective command of all security organisms existing in the area, whether they were staffed by the armed forces or by the federal and state police.

Strengthened by their legal underpinning and their army commanders, and provided with a regularly budgeted income, the DOI-CODIs were the most important organs of political repression. They were also responsible for the greatest number of human rights violations. The State Departments for Political and Social Order (DEOPS), which operated at the state rather than the national level, and the regional offices of the Federal Police Department also continued to carry out repression in their own spheres of jurisdiction. They too were responsible for political investigations, abductions, interrogations, and, according to abundant reports, torture and murder of political prisoners.

In the state of São Paulo, the DEOPS was in virtual competition with the DOI-CODIs as to which organ could more effectively pursue repression. Led by the notorious Sérgio Paranhos Fleury, the São Paulo DEOPS tortured and killed numerous political dissenters. It also formed a mob known as the Death Squad. Ostensibly created to eliminate common criminals, the Death Squad in fact assassinated hundreds of Brazilian citizens, many of whom had no criminal record at all.

In July 1969 the state military police units were reorganized throughout the country so that they could carry out new directives for internal security. The control of these units was transferred from the state governors directly to the army's high command and regional military commanders.

It is important to note that the activities of this complicated repressive apparatus were not limited to Brazil. Statements made by Brazilian exiles referred to the fact that they were interrogated and even tortured after the military coups d'état in Bolivia in 1972, in

Chile in 1973, and in Argentina in 1976. These acts were carried out by Brazilians who did not conceal their military or police affiliation. There were also cases where interrogations were conducted by military personnel of the countries in question. Brazilian agents were often present in the torture chambers.

It is worth repeating that the Doctrine of National Security was the ideological umbrella that justified such practices. Aside from the semiclandestine repressive apparatus, the doctrine was the basis of numerous laws and regulations that applied to all aspects of national life. In accordance with the objectives articulated by the National Security Council, numerous decrees and decree-laws were proclaimed; new bills and constitutional amendments were presented for rubber-stamping by the emasculated Congress; and, whenever necessary, secret decrees were issued. The Doctrine of National Security was institutionalized not only in the National Security Law, but in a vast web of legislation and institutional structures.

The National Security Law (LSN), first promulgated in 1967, was modified several times. In 1969, for example, the penalties prescribed for political crimes were increased in order to carry out more effectively the intensification of repression that followed the declaration of AI-5 in December 1968. The LSN was modified again in 1978, this time in response to broad-based pressures for redemocratization. Specific aspects of the law that had been the targets of systematic criticism by international democratic bodies were changed. The death penalty and life imprisonment for political crimes were abolished; the right to certify the physical and mental health of detainees was granted; the time during which prisoners could be held in solitary confinement was reduced. Other minor changes were made as well. Nonetheless, the repressive spirit of the law remained intact.

The documents collected by the BNM project demonstrate conclusively that the LSN guaranteed security only for the military regime itself, while subjecting citizens to the insecurities of rule by force. The LSN, moreover, superseded all other laws, including the federal constitution. Once the regime established that internal opposition could not be tolerated if security were to be maintained, all democratic principles were abolished. Indeed, the vague language of the LSN embodied concepts that were in direct contradiction to constitutional principles. Most importantly, any kind of opposition to the regime became a punishable crime.

The LSN had a broad reach. It circumscribed the freedom of the press, for newspapers and broadcasting were supposed to play a "positive" role in strengthening "permanent national objectives" as they were officially defined. Criticism that might "indispose" public opinion against the authorities or create "animosity" toward the armed forces was prohibited. Even routine news stories about social conditions in Brazil fell into the proscribed category. Other fields were also affected, such as labor law and the criminal code. The Strike Law, for example, regulated the right to strike and included extra sanctions for strikes that were continued even after they had been declared illegal by the courts. Punishment for these offenses was also prescribed in the LSN, which increased the penalties sixfold over those established by the labor legislation.

In brief, the National Security Law was intended to perpetuate the authoritarian state, to the permanent exclusion of the rule of law and the establishment of a democratic order. It should also be observed, finally, that those who implemented the LSN lived in a world untouched by the constraints they applied to others. The authorities responsible for political interrogations, in particular, had unlimited power over those whom they questioned. This enabled them to carry out numerous violent and coercive acts. Even after it was modified in 1978, the LSN permitted the political police an immense scope of arbitrary action. The LSN thus served as an instrument for the repression of any and all opponents to the military regime. It exposed Brazilian citizens to the arbitrary exercise of power, foisting upon the nation an imported ideology which, when applied to Brazil, produced a prolonged period of unjust social policies. In the final analysis, these policies sought to perpetuate long-standing social inequalities.

EIGHT

HOW SUSPECTS WERE DETAINED

THE WAYS in which those suspected of political activities against the government were detained was symptomatic of the repressive system created by the Brazilian military regime. Although the generals claimed to respect all individual rights of citizens guaranteed by the constitution, detention by abduction was systematically practiced with no legal basis.

Lara de Lemos, civil servant, 50, testified to the military court magistrate, in 1973, how she was detained in Rio:

> The accused was surprised at the way in which she was detained, for it was carried out late at night, by three individuals of untidy appearance, without a court order, who ordered her to go with them; in the vehicle to which they took her they put a hood over her head and forced her to lie down on the floor of the car so that she would not be seen; she found later that the place of her imprisonment had been the PE . . .

Detentions were surrounded by an atmosphere of terror. Even persons who were not suspects were not spared intimidations, as can be seen from a letter attached to military court proceedings in Rio in 1970, written by Adail Ivan de Lemos, medical student, 22:

> When I entered the dining room, my mother, sitting at the typewriter, was weeping silently. A little while before, around 3:20 P.M., my brother had been detained while studying. Min-

utes later, he was physically attacked, in my mother's room, suffering, in his own words: "a violent beating." The beating and pushing was nothing compared with what took place later. But even there, separated from his mother by only a few feet, he had his head banged against the wall.

Paulo César Farah, journalist, 24, had a similar experience, also in Rio, according to his declaration in a military court that same year:

> that in the residence of his parents the said group practiced extreme moral torture, forcing his mother to undress in the presence of the other members of the group; that, immediately afterward, his wife was taken to the CODI and tortured until she declared where she lived; that, soon afterward, on the 7th, his residence was raided by officers of said unit, without any legal warrant, accompanied by his wife who was bearing signs of torture . . .

The suspicion of subversion spread to include the relatives and friends of persons being sought by the military police forces. In the light of the ideology of national security, the enemy was not only the individual person, but a network of relationships seen as the potential nucleus of an organization or revolutionary party. Therefore, those who happened to be close to the wanted person, by ties of profession, affection, or kinship, were themselves indiscriminately and relentlessly pursued by agents embodying the power of the state. This is demonstrated by the case of Luiz Andréa Fávero, teacher, 26, detained in Foz do Iguaçu in 1970:

> The accused was taken by surprise in the home of his parents by a veritable swarm of police; that said individuals invaded the house, handcuffed his parents and, initially, took the accused to one of the rooms of the house; in said room, the police tore off the clothes of the accused and placed his feet in a basin of water, and, using wires from an electrical apparatus, proceeded to apply shocks; . . . that the accused was then taken to the door of the room where his wife was and there he saw that the same process of torture was being administered to her; that the accused was, immediately afterward, taken outside the house, where he saw his parents tied-up inside a vehicle . . .

People were tortured first and interrogated afterward. In this way a psychological climate of terror was created, which was favorable for extracting confessions that would catch the greatest number of persons in the net of repression. Torture was practiced before the detainee was taken to a police precinct or military headquarters, with no concern for the presence of neighbors or bystanders. That is what happened to José Afonso de Alencar, lawyer, 28, and to his friends, when the house in which they lived in Belo Horizonte was raided in 1969:

> that the accused began to be beaten on the day when he was detained, which beating was done with a meat mallet, a hammer, and an aluminum truncheon, after [he and his companions] had been stripped naked; that one of his torturers hit him with the mallet on the shoulder until he drew blood, which left a mark on him; that, with the aluminum truncheon, the torturers mainly hit them all on their joints, this taking place until approximately 11:00 P.M.; because the neighborhood, somewhat alarmed, forced the police to transfer the accused and his companions to the 12th RI . . .

At times the police would arrive shooting at random, as Júlio Bittencourt Almeida, student, 24, also detained in Belo Horizonte, testified in a letter he wrote to the military court, which is included as part of the legal proceedings:

> On 28 January 1969, we were taken by surprise, at dawn, by the action of a police convoy commanded by the torturer Luiz Soares da Rocha. What I saw was the following: I was sleeping when I was awakened by the sound of gun shots. Then I saw the door of the pantry being broken down and a person entered firing many shots; then I heard, to my right, a burst of machine-gun fire. On my left, I saw my companion Maurício staggering, wounded in the back. The police invaded the house. . . . We were, on this occasion, severely beaten by the police convoy, who wanted to execute us.

Although injured, some prisoners were taken directly to be tortured. This was the case of José Calistrato Cardoso Filho, businessman, 29, detained in Recife and interrogated in 1972, as he wrote in a letter to his lawyer.

> I was detained and shot, receiving four bullets in my leg, and even so I was given electric shocks, immersion, parrot's perch,

"telephone," burnings, violent beatings; they would put pressure on my neck and, when I fainted, they would give me injections to revive me and would let me rest before continuing the tortures.

A similar incident took place with João Manoel Fernandes, accountant, 22, according to the testimony he gave to the military court in 1970.

> . . . in the Paraná DOPS, where he was subjected to beating on the face and abdomen, kicks on his legs, and the *palmatória;* he was not put on the parrot's perch because he was convalescing from a bullet wound suffered at the time he was detained; . . . that he now wants to clarify how he was detained: that, on the occasion of his detention, he was in the apartment on Presidente Farias Lima Street, . . . number 1,305, in Curitiba. It was approximately 8:00 P.M., when the livingroom door was beaten down, and several police personnel rushed into the room with guns in hand, firing; that one of the bullets hit the accused in the throat and came out of the left shoulder blade; that, from that point, he was taken and kicked all the way to the Cajuru Hospital, in Curitiba, where he received first aid . . .

There were instances of persons wanted by the security forces who, of their own volition, went to a police station or military installation to clear themselves of suspicion. The records of the military courts demonstrate that, even in such cases, the repressive system did not respect the fundamental rights of persons. An example was the testimony given in 1973 in Rio, by Lúcia Regina Florentino Souto, student, 23:

> that she reported voluntarily to the First Army in order to make a statement, and was taken from there to another place with a hood over her head, where she was beaten and subjected to various types of maltreatment, and was also left without food; that she had her arm in a plaster cast at the time, and ended up having to be taken to the Army's Central Hospital for treatment . . .

A similar reception was accorded to Jandira Andrade Gitirana Praia Fiuza, journalist, 24, in Rio, according to her response to questioning in a military court, in 1973:

She was not detained, but reported voluntarily to the authorities, accompanied by her husband, co-defendant in these proceedings, and was held in prison 22 days; that she was put into the "ice box" of the Army Police, on Barão de Mesquita street, for five days, where she suffered physical, moral, and psychological torture . . .

A similar situation occurred in the questioning of Rosane Reznik, secretary, 20, in Rio in 1970:

that the first time she went to the Flores Island was to visit her sister who was in prison there; on that occasion, the Commander said that she should make a statement and, as she was already there, she offered to make it: . . . that, one week later, a [illegible] came to her house with the request that she go to the island, as the Commander needed to talk with her; and so, in this fashion, she accepted the invitation and went, and was then put in prison; that, on the following day, she made the statement, which was elicited through electric shocks to her breasts, beating with a *palmatória,* attempts to hang her, slaps on her face, besides telling her that her sister would be assassinated . . .

The most notorious episode of voluntary reporting to the security forces was the tragic case of the journalist Wladimir Herzog, who was killed in São Paulo's DOI-CODI on 25 October 1975, ten hours after going to that unit to make a statement to clear himself. [See chapter 17.]

The legal proceedings of political trials in military courts also contain reports by defendants that their belongings were stolen by agents of the security forces. As a rule, this happened at the time persons being sought were detained and their home was broken into by police or military forces.

The testimony of Milton Tavares Campos, mechanic, 20, given in 1971 in Juiz de Fora, in the state of Minas Gerais, records:

that, when he was detained in São Paulo, by the OBAN, a number of his belongings were taken, including a radio, a wrist watch and an alarm clock, a suitcase with personal effects, and 200 cruzeiros in cash, 50 cruzeiros of which were given to the interrogating officer . . .

Maria Aparecida Santos, accountant, 23, in her testimony in São Paulo in 1970, stated:

> that she was detained by Operation Bandeirantes which took from her a purse containing 215 cruzeiros in cash, glasses, and a gold ring with a precious stone, in addition to her accountant's ring, none of which were returned to her . . .

Gildásio Westin Cosenza, radio technician, 28, stated in the First Military Court of São Paulo in 1976:

> . . . that among the electronic equipment there was an "AF-105 multi tester," around 50 electronic tubes, two television sets, and various spare parts and tools; that he was left with only the clothes he was dressed in, for they also took the 200 cruzeiros that were in the pocket of his pants . . .

Jodat Nicolas Kury, businessman, 56, detained in Curitiba in the state of Paraná in 1975, described, in a letter included in his legal military court proceedings, an extortion attempt made while he was being tortured:

> He answered that my life was in his hands and that, if I paid him 5,000 cruzeiros he would save me. I answered him by saying that, even if I had wanted to comply with his proposal, I would not be able to do so. But he replied right away by saying that the keys to my house and to my business, including the key to the safe, were there with him and that he could go at night to the store to get the money and a checkbook.

PART III

AGAINST EVERYTHING AND EVERYBODY

NINE

A PROFILE OF REPRESSION

ONE of the tasks of the BNM project was to transfer the data from complex legal proceedings into a computer in such a way that a comprehensive statistical survey could be compiled. This chapter includes data extracted from 695 of the total number of 707 legal proceedings examined to provide a profile of political repression between 1964 and 1979 and of those affected by it.

There were 7,367 defendants charged in these 695 trials; some individuals were defendants in more than one proceeding. On the average, ten individuals are named as defendants in each trial; in one inquest, however, initiated to investigate the participation of navy and marine personnel in political campaigns, an astounding 284 defendants were named.

Approximately 88% of the defendants were male and only 12% were female; 38.9% were 25 years old or less, a fact which reveals the courage of young people in facing the risks of resistance. Among 2,868 youths under the age of 25, moreover, 91 were not yet 18 years old when the military court proceedings were initiated against them.

Of the 4,476 whose educational level was recorded in the military court proceeding, 2,491 had a university degree, and only 91 declared themselves illiterate. This is striking in a country where little more than 1% of the population is university-educated, and where more than 20 million people over 18 years of age are classified as illiterate. This educational level indicates that most of the defendants were of middle-class origins.

The geographical origins of the defendants indicate that resistance to the regime was a predominantly urban phenomenon. Although the greater part of the defendants were born in rural areas, most lived in state capitals at the beginning of their trials: 1,872 were concentrated in Rio de Janeiro, and 1,517 in São Paulo.

The army was the main agent of repression, responsible for 1,043 detentions. An additional 884 detentions were carried out by agents of the DOI-CODIs, which were also commanded by army officers. In 3,754 cases, representing 51% of the total, there are no records as to which agency carried out the detention.

The date and time of detention are recorded in only 3,975 cases, an irregularity which suggests that the law was repeatedly disregarded. This lack of respect for the legal rights of the defendants is even more evident when it is noted that, of these 3,975 defendants, no fewer than 1,997 were detained even before formal inquests were initiated. These extralegal detentions prove that the security forces largely ignored even the huge arsenal of laws at their disposal that sanctioned increased control over the citizenry.

The military also regularly failed to observe even their own legal procedures. Of the cases studied, for example, 6,256, or 85%, were characterized by no notification of the detention to a judge. In 816 cases, or 11%, notification of the detention to a judge was made only after the legal time limit had passed. In only 259 cases, or 4%, was a judge notified within the stipulated legal period.

The accusation most frequently brought against defendants was militancy in a banned political party organization. This was the charge in 4,935 cases. The second most frequent charge was participation in violent or armed actions, with 1,464 so accused. Other reasons for indictment included having held office in the Goulart government or even simple associations with the deposed regime. This charge was made in 484 cases. In 145 cases, the simple expression of ideas considered objectionable by the military, even if through normal legal channels, such as in the press, in classrooms, in sermons, etc., was sufficient reason for indictment. This charge, it should be added, was notoriously anticonstitutional, even according to the constitution written by the military regime itself in 1967 and amended in 1969. Equally unconstitutional was the indictment of 18 persons for the expression of presumably objectionable ideas through artistic means.

The distribution of these charges over the period studied reveals the pattern of repression that drove those who dissented from the regime's policies to increasingly extreme acts. The repression was concentrated in two phases: the first, from 1964 to 1966, coinciding with the Castello Branco administration and the immediate aftermath of the coup; the second corresponding almost exactly to the period of the Médici administration—1969–1974—when 4,660 defendants were tried following the declaration of Institutional Act No. 5. In the proceedings that directly followed the coup, and until the promulgation of AI-5, the most frequent charge was participation in social movements and organizations. In the 1964–1968 period, the military concentrated its investigations into the activities of the labor movement, the nationalist movements among military personnel, student activities, and organizations representing various sectors of civilian society. Beginning in 1969, however, the primary accusation levied against those questioned was militancy in banned political party organizations. Accusations of participation in armed actions increased considerably during the period as well. It is clear that as the military regime closed down legal channels of opposition through its initial acts of repression, it also drove those groups who were dissatisfied with the political and socioeconomic model into clandestinity and violent action.

One of the most impressive statistics regards the number of times that reports were made in the military courts of torture during imprisonment. Aside from the immense number of defendants who may have been victims of torture *without reporting it* to the military courts, no fewer than 1,918 citizens testified that they had been tortured during interrogation. Significantly, 1,558 or 81% of these reports of torture refer to the 1969–1974 period, that is, the years of the Médici administration and of the "Economic Miracle."

It should be noted, moreover, that the data cited up to this point refer to individuals cited as defendants, that is, the 7,367 names contained in 695 military court proceedings. These were persons whose political activities were investigated and who were brought to trial. The BNM research also collected the names of an additional 10,034 individuals who appeared in the documentation in connection with interrogations only. Of this total, 6,385 were orginally accused in inquests that resulted in military trials, but their names did not appear in the list of those actually indicted when the trials began. The remaining 3,649 individuals were called as witnesses during the initial investigations. They should not be excluded from the list of those directly affected by political repression, especially given the fact that numerous episodes were recorded in which witnesses were not only detained during the interrogation period, but tortured as well. There were at least 100 instances recorded in the legal proceedings of torture administered to indicted persons who were not brought to trial. Many more than those 100 must have been tortured without that fact being recorded in legal proceedings.

The average number of those named in an inquest who did not stand for trial in a military court is close to 14 per proceeding. In some cases, many more citizens were questioned. The well-known military police inquest headed by Colonel Ferdinando de Carvalho, ostensibly to investigate the activities of the Brazilian Communist Party, investigated 889 individuals in Rio de Janeiro in 1964. Of these, a mere 16 were brought to trial. The list of those investigated included former president Juscelino Kubitschek, who was forced to submit to disrespectful interrogations by the colonel for days on end.

Approximately two-thirds of the 6,385 indicted persons who were never tried were nonetheless detained in prison. In only 89 of these cases was there regular notification to the legal authorities, a figure that once again proves that the constitutional rights of individuals and the laws created by the military regime itself were regularly disregarded when the organs of repression required absolute power in order to conduct their investigations. The figure also confirms that in the case of most of the individuals detained, there was an element of abduction.

TEN

AGAINST LEFTIST ORGANIZATIONS

ALMOST two-thirds of the 707 legal proceedings studied by the BNM project refer to political organizations prohibited by legislation in effect before the April 1964 military coup. After the coup, however, these organizations were harshly persecuted by security organs dedicated to the elimination of the "internal enemy."

Although it is beyond the scope of this book to discuss in detail each of the some fifty leftist organizations that are mentioned in the proceedings, some basic information about their principal characteristics will help to illuminate the pattern of repression that developed. This profile indicates, for example, that despite the argument of security forces that their violence was a response to the violence perpetrated by groups on the left, many of the banned organizations did not advocate military methods in their struggle against the regime.

Moreover, the leftist groups splintered into numerous subgroups, a process which weakened their capacity to resist the regime. The fact that these illegal organizations were so fragmented, and lost members as the repression increased, is evidence that they were less of a threat to national security than the authorities claimed. Nonetheless, the existence of the armed guerrilla groups was a pretext for the military to carry out full-scale repression against both suspected leftists and the population at large.

The clandestine groups were mainly Marxist in orientation. They were formed largely as offshoots of the Brazilian Communist Party (PCB), which was founded in 1922. Until the late 1950s, the PCB included virtually all Brazilian Marxists, but this unity collapsed in the 1960s, as new organizations emerged. These groups differed in their visions of how Brazilian society should be restructured, the strategies they advocated for taking power and effecting those changes, and their plans for more immediate political action. Although the organizations generally agreed on the common goal of a socialist society to be run by the workers, they differed significantly as to how to achieve the transformation.

One important point of divergence was whether there were to be intermediate stages between the present social order and the envisioned socialist goal. While some groups insisted upon measures that would lead directly to socialism, others defended a slower transformation that would pass through "bourgeois-democratic" or "nationalist-democratic" stages. Still others advocated intermediate views between these two positions. Another point of divergence was whether violence was a legitimate means for obtaining political power. The groups disagreed as well about questions of political alliances, whether to participate in elections called by the government, and what were the most effective propaganda methods.

Almost all groups did adopt Marxist arguments that sanctioned the revolutionary violence of the oppressed in their struggle against governments supported by force and responsible for maintaining socioeconomic systems based on the exploitation of labor, itself a form of institutionalized violence. In specifically adapting this struggle to the post-1964 Brazilian situation, however, many of these groups did *not* advocate the immediate use of military methods. On the contrary, as the relevant proceedings make clear, at least one of the main organizations targeted by the repression, the Brazilian Communist Party, proposed the peaceful transition to socialism.

For purposes of clarity, the dozens of organizations cited in the court proceedings have been divided into seven major groups on the basis of their origins and political characteristics.

THE BRAZILIAN COMMUNIST PARTY (PCB)

Sixty-six of the legal proceedings examined by the BNM project, involving 783 defendants, referred to the Brazilian Communist Party. The PCB was founded in March 1922 during a workers' congress in the city of Niterói, in the state of Rio de Janeiro, as a response to the 1917 Russian Revolution. Its appearance coincided with the decline of anarchist influences on the Brazilian labor movement. The PCB was a legal party for three brief periods only: twice during the 1920s and once at the end of World War II, after the fall of the Vargas dictatorship. The same enforced clandestinity to which the PCB was subject would later be imposed on all the leftist organizations that appeared during and after the 1960s.

In 1962, the PCB suffered its first significant split. Two party lines emerged at that time, and they are still recognizable in Brazil. One retained the PCB name. The majority of the party members supported Khrushchev's ideas as they were presented during the 1956 Soviet Communist Party Congress: namely, a criticism of Stalin; the defense of peaceful competition between the socialist and capitalist camps; and a belief in the peaceful transition to socialism.

A group of important PCB leaders, however, disagreed with these positions and formed a dissident movement. In 1962, they formalized their opposition and formed a party that would be known by its acronym, the PC do B: Partido Comunista do Brasil (Communist Party of Brazil). The origin of the two acronyms, PCB and PC do B, is curious. The PCB was originally known as the "Communist Party *of* Brazil"—PC do B. In fact, the government had banned the party in 1947 on the grounds that it was an international organization connected with a foreign power, a mere Brazilian section of the worldwide Communist Party. In 1961 the traditional party leadership changed the name of the party to PCB in order to make clear the Brazilian nature of their organization. When the dissident group formed a new party, it reassumed the orginal name, the PC do B, to indicate its Stalinist orientation.

The PCB characteristically defended the implementation of social transformations that would lead to the development of national capitalism, which was seen as a precondition for the development of socialism. To this end, it was necessary to construct an alliance among workers, peasants, and the national bourgeoisie. This united force would then challenge the agents of "imperialism" and their allies, the major landowners. In the 1960s, the PCB stuck to this strategy of a peaceful transition to socialism. This was the principal reason why so many militants split from the party and formed other clandestine parties.

The PCB was taken by surprise by the April 1964 coup. Despite its "peaceful road" philosophy, it was hard hit by repression. The party apparatus in the labor unions—two decades in the making—

was practically dismantled. Intellectuals linked with the party were persecuted and prosecuted throughout the country. In addition, "Military Police Inquests" (Inquéritos Policial Militares—IPMs) were organized against the PCB in every Brazilian state. These inquests charged the PCB with responsibility for promoting virtually all the support that existed for the deposed government, whether among loyalist troops in the armed forces or among progressive state governors. The PCB was thought to be behind the "Groups of Eleven Comrades," nationalist commando groups which had in fact been proposed in 1963 by then-federal congressman Leonel Brizola in order to implement a series of pronationalist reforms. The PCB was also accused of instigating student demonstrations led by the Catholic-linked Popular Action group, and provoking the activities of the Nationalist Parliamentary Front, a group of pronationalist congressmen. As if that were not enough, the PCB was also thought to be behind the formation of the Peasant Leagues, rural organizations led by the popular organizer Francisco Julião.

In 1966, the PCB was shattered by an internal struggle over the "mistakes and causes of the 1964 defeat." The question of armed struggle in Latin America was also hotly debated at the time, especially since guerrilla movements inspired by the 1959 Cuban Revolution were in fact already in action. The death of guerrilla leader Che Guevara in Bolivia in October 1967 added more fuel to the fire. The orthodox wing of the PCB, united around the old-time party leader Luís Carlos Prestes, rejected the armed struggle and allied itself with the officially permitted opposition party, the Brazilian Democratic Movement (MDB), in order to participate legally in the Congress. As a result, this PCB faction was relatively protected from the repression unleashed after 1968, which was directed primarily against organizations that adopted guerrilla tactics.

Curiously, a general attack against the PCB was launched only after 1974, when Geisel's program of gradual liberalization had already begun and security forces claimed to have controlled the activities of armed organizations and radical Marxist groups. Between 1974 and 1976, the PCB was subjected to successive waves of detentions in which hundreds of members and important party leaders were imprisoned, tortured, and killed throughout the country.

The deaths of two detainees allegedly associated with the PCB, journalist Wladimir Herzog in October 1975 and the worker Manoel

Fiel Filho in January 1976, had a particularly strong political impact. Both died under torture in the DOI-CODI of the Second Army, on Tutóia Street in São Paulo. These episodes forced then-President Geisel to rein in the security forces by sacking the Second Army commander, General Ednardo D'Ávila Mello. In retrospect, it is clear that these murders in particular, and the public demonstrations which repudiated them, represented the awakening of a national conscience against repression.

THE ARMED DISSIDENTS

As indicated, the internal struggle in the PCB generated numerous splinter organizations. Some had a national following, while others were confined to a single region of the country. All these groups, however, aimed to join the armed guerrilla struggle inspired by Che Guevara that was growing throughout Latin America.

The most significant guerrilla organization, and the group with the largest membership of all those that joined in the Brazilian armed struggle between 1968 and 1973, was the National Action for Liberation (ALN). The history of the ALN, organized in 1967 as a splinter group of the PCB, is inextricably linked with the name of former PCB leader Carlos Marighella.

At the end of 1966, Marighella broke with the Executive Committee of the PCB and traveled to Havana. There he participated in the meeting of the Latin American Organization for Solidarity, which sought to develop a continental plan for revolution. Marighella rejected the idea of creating a formal political party in Brazil, and he began to draw away from other dissident sectors of the PCB. His own organization was created without a formal structure. Its motto was "action makes the vanguard."

Marighella's group broke with the orthodox theses of the PCB, which considered the bourgeoisie an ally of workers and peasants in the Brazilian revolutionary process. It proposed the immediate launching of armed operations in the large Brazilian cities, which would in turn provide resources for rural guerrilla warfare. According to Marighella, the armed struggle in rural areas would produce a national army of liberation, which would defeat the military regime and implement "antiimperialism" in Brazil.

In September 1969, the ALN, acting with another group known as the 8th of October Revolutionary Movement (MR-8), gained both national and international attention by kidnapping Charles Elbrick, the American ambassador to Brazil. Elbrick was later released in good condition, but the militants negotiated the release of fifteen political prisoners and the publication of a manifesto in exchange for the ambassador's safe return.

Following the kidnapping, there was a notable escalation of repression against leftist groups. Just months later, in November 1969, Marighella himself was killed in São Paulo. The murder was engineered by civilian police chief Sérgio Paranhos Fleury, a notorious torturer, in a highly controversial maneuver that drew on alleged connections between the Dominican order and the ALN. In October of the following year, Marighella's successor, Joaquim Câmara Ferreira, was abducted in São Paulo and killed under torture by the same police chief Fleury on a secluded farm that operated as a clandestine repression center. Between 1969 and 1971, security agents detained hundreds of ALN members in various Brazilian states.

The ALN, for its part, attempted to avoid the repression by redirecting its activity to "work with the masses." The objective was to break the vicious cycle of armed actions conducted simply to support the group's members. This strategy ultimately proved unsuccessful. In the first half of 1974, a final sequence of arrests and disappearances of ALN members in Rio de Janeiro and São Paulo resulted in the final dismantling of the organization.

In the BNM research, 76 of the legal proceedings studied covered activities of the ALN. More than 1,000 persons were named in the proceedings; 722 were called before military courts.

Three other small groups are referred to in the documents as splinters of the ALN. The Movement of Popular Liberation was the object of seven of the legal proceedings researched. It disbanded after the summary execution or death under torture of the majority of its members. Another, called "Marx, Mao, Marighella, and Guevara" (M3G), operated in Porto Alegre, the capital of Rio Grande do Sul, in 1969 and 1970. The group's founder, Edmur Péricles de Camargo, had been a companion of Marighella's. The M3G, however, was of dubious legitimacy as a revolutionary political group, since the proceeds from its armed assaults were divided among the individual group members rather than serving to finance the organization. The story was made additionally murky by doubts about Camargo's whereabouts. Detained in April 1970, and among those political prisoners released in exchange for the liberation of the abducted Swiss ambassador, Camargo went to Chile. Some militants affirmed that he was killed during the Chilean military coup in September 1973. Others, however, raised the possibility that Camargo was in fact a double agent. The other splinter group of the ALN was known as the Front for the Liberation of the Northeast. It was being organized at the beginning of 1972 in the northeastern states of Ceará and Pernambuco by militants who had formerly belonged to the ALN and another armed group known as the Armed Revolutionary Vanguard when its members were detained by security agents.

The Revolutionary Brazilian Communist Party (PCBR) had a trajectory similar to that of the ALN. Its origins go back to the immediate aftermath of 1964, when its principal leader, Mário Alves, a prestigious journalist and intellectual and member of the Executive Committee of the PCB, began to take exception to the positions of party leader Luís Carlos Prestes. Alves formed a "Revolutionary Current" with support in Rio de Janeiro and in the northeast of Brazil. The PCBR was only formally constituted as a party, however, in April 1968, in Rio.

The general objective of the PCBR was to reformulate the traditional position of the PCB, which posited the necessity of an alliance with the Brazilian bourgeoisie. Nonetheless, the PCBR did not adhere to the notion of an immediate "socialist revolution." In fact, the strategy of the PCBR for taking power was similar to that of the ALN, especially in choosing rural areas as the most important staging ground for the struggle toward a "popular revolutionary government."

After April 1969 the PCBR dedicated itself to armed activities in urban centers, primarily for the purpose of promoting revolutionary propaganda. The intensification of the repression during the second half of that year drove the party deeper underground and made its operations even riskier. After their first attack on a bank, in Rio de Janeiro, half of the group's Central Committee was imprisoned. Mário Alves was brutally murdered with a series of tortures that included the scraping of his skin with a steel brush and the medieval torment of impalement. To this day, the military regime has not assumed responsibility for his death, which occurred in the barracks of Rio's army police, on Barão de Mesquita Street, in January 1979.

Between 1970 and 1972, the PCBR engaged in activities similar to those of other groups that practiced urban guerrilla warfare. Since the party had to be financed by illicit means, successive operations to obtain funds were carried out. These operations absorbed the full attention of the group's members. At the beginning of 1973, members of the last designated Central Committee of that phase of the organization were killed in Rio when the DOI-CODI of the First Army set fire to a car in which some of the militants were present. To this day, it is not known whether the militants were already dead when the car was ignited.

In the BNM project, 31 of the legal proceedings investigated were about the PCBR. Close to 400 individuals were named as defendants or accused in preliminary inquests.

The 8th of October Revolutionary Movement (MR-8) was consolidated in the 1970s. The group was named in honor of Che Guevara, who was killed in Bolivia on 8 October 1967. After the MR-8 abducted American Ambassador Elbrick in September 1969, it suffered its first wave of violent reprisals. Nonetheless, the group continued to carry out armed operations in Rio throughout 1970. Although some group members were captured, many of the operations were successful. In 1971, as a result of the break-up of the Popular Revolutionary Vanguard (VPR), a group of former VPR militants, including leader Captain Carlos Lamarca, requested admission into the MR-8. After Marighella, Lamarca was perhaps the best known of the guerrilla leaders. It was as a member of the MR-8 that he was killed in an ambush in the remote interior of the northeastern state of Bahia. His death, which occurred only after a prolonged nationwide search by the authorities, was a serious blow to the armed struggle. The MR-8 was dismantled in 1972, when virtually all its surviving members fled to Chile. In subsequent years, however, the organization was rebuilt. It resurfaced in other Brazilian states, after members had repudiated armed struggle and adopted political positions that differed substantially from their former views.

In the BNM project, 33 of the legal proceedings analyzed were concerned with MR-8 activities. Almost 500 persons were named as defendants in the military courts or were charged in preliminary inquests.

In the same internal struggle within the PCB in which the ALN, the PCBR, and MR-8 orginated, other groups of more limited importance appeared. Among the series of arrests that led to the break-up of one of these groups, the Armed Forces for National Liberation, was the nationally known case of Mother Maurina Borges da Silveira. Mother Maurina was barbarously violated by her torturers in an episode that led the Catholic Church to excommunicate two Ribeirão Preto DOPS officers, Miguel Lamano and Renato Soares Guimarães. Despite the innumerable actions of the Catholic Church on behalf of political prisoners and torture victims, the excommunication of known torturers was unusual.

COMMUNIST PARTY OF BRAZIL (PC DO B)

A "Special National Conference," organized in São Paulo in February 1962 by the followers of PCB dissidents João Amazonas, Maurício Grabois, and Pedro Pomar, is generally cited as the occasion when the PC do B was founded. Despite its relatively recent origin, the PC do B has always competed with the PCB over which group was in fact the true historical continuation of the Communist Party created in Brazil in 1922.

From its inception, the PC do B directed strong criticism against the "peaceful line" of the PCB. Gradually, it began to evolve its own policy about the proper course for the revolutionary struggle in Brazil, heavily influenced by Mao Tse-tung's thought and the Chinese Revolution of the 1927–1949 period. For the PC do B, the most important stage of the revolutionary struggle would take place in rural areas. The struggle would be waged by means of a war supported from its inception by strong popular participation, particularly among peasants. Like the PCB, the PC do B envisioned a "bourgeois democratic, antiimperialistic, and antifeudal" stage as a preliminary step to future struggles that would implement a socialist order.

Tactically, the PC do B differed from the PCB in that it defended more radical forms of social mobilization. In particular, the PC do B condemned the urban guerrilla actions initiated by other groups in 1968, condemning them as "petit-bourgeois" *foquismo*, a reference to the Frenchman Régis Debray's theory of guerrilla warfare, which propounded the creation of foci of armed resistance from which the general revolution would then spread. For the PC do B, the actions of the Brazilian armed groups gave too little importance to the participation of the "masses" in the revolutionary struggle.

There was disagreement within the PC do B that culminated in the formation of two dissident groups: the Red Flank in São Paulo and in the center-south of the country; and the Revolutionary Communist Party in the northeast. Both groups were formed in 1966–

1967 by militants who distrusted the PC do B leadership and the adequacy of their preparation for the armed struggle. They assumed a political position similar to the other urban guerrilla groups already described.

From the end of 1966 on, the PC do B devoted itself to relocating party members to the Araguaia River region in the state of Pará, in the north of the country. This region was chosen as the most likely site for the rise of a future "popular army." The transfer was accelerated after the declaration of AI-5 in order to avoid the repression unleashed by the regime.

In April 1972 security organs detected the presence of the PC do B in the Araguaia region. Large numbers of army troops engaged in successive siege operations against the militants, which continued until 1974. When the battles began, the party constituted itself as the "Araguaia Guerrilla Forces." Although their number was small, they did win some military victories. They also wrote communiques in an effort to make their political goals known. In the end, however, government troops won a clear military victory. In the process of eliminating the rebels, moreover, the government resorted to a virtual reign of terror against the local population.

In spite of this defeat, the PC do B was reconstituted in subsequent years. This was possible in large measure because of the incorporation (described below) of the majority of militants from another resistance group, the Popular Action.

In the BNM project, 29 of the legal proceedings studied covered PC do B activities, scattered over ten states. More than 300 individuals were accused of connections with the party. The Red Flank was the object of 10 of the legal proceedings studied, in which approximately 150 persons were named as defendants or accused during preliminary hearings.

Two splinter groups of the Red Flank appeared in São Paulo in the 1969–1970 period. They were known as the Tiradentes Revolutionary Movement (Movimento Revolucionário Tiradentes—MRT), and the Marxist Revolutionary Movement (Movimento Revolucionário Marxista—MRM).

POPULAR ACTION (AP)

Popular Action (Ação Popular—AP) was founded in 1962. It was composed of progressive Christians connected with Catholic activist groups such as Catholic Action and, in particular, the group known as Catholic University Youth. Originally, the AP defined itself as a "political movement" rather than a "party." It was inspired by the humanist ideas of Jacques Maritain, Teilhard de Chardin, Emanuel Mounier, and Father Lebret. In its "basic document," written in 1963, the AP proposed to struggle for a just society. Significantly, the group condemned both capitalism and existing socialist countries.

The AP was most influential among students, controlling successive directorates of the National Student Union (União Nacional dos Estudantes—UNE). It also penetrated worker and peasant circles, especially in the northeast, where it was active in the Grassroots Education Movement promoted by the Brazilian National Bishops Conference (Conferência Nacional dos Bispos do Brasil—CNBB). During the early 1960s the AP was deeply committed to the basic reforms proposed by the Goulart government. In this regard, it was to the left of the PCB, since it sought immediate social transformation.

After the April 1964 coup, the AP suffered the full impact of repression. Many members were arrested or forced into exile. Subsequently, the group gradually reorganized and began to redefine its political and philosophical principles. From its inception, the AP had points of contact with Marxist thought. From 1965 to 1967, the organization engaged in an extended and polemical debate, but leaned toward adopting Marxism as a theoretical guide for its activities.

There was some dispute, however, over how the transition to Marxism would occur. Eventually, the faction proposing a "painless transition"—in large measure because it was apprehensive about creating conflicts between the Christian faith of the militants and the new official philosophical position—lost out to another faction that supported the ideas of Mao Tse-tung and the Chinese Cultural Revolution, which was then being debated among Marxists worldwide.

From this period onward, the AP evolved until it became a typical Maoist organization. Its political position was very similar to that of the PC do B. In practice, however, the AP was never involved in guerrilla actions. The spirit of the Cultural Revolution, moreover, inspired a "proletarianization campaign" among the markedly middle-class AP members, most of whom were university students.

Hundreds of them went to work in factories or rural areas in an effort to transform the social composition of the organization. The results of the campaign were contradictory. On the one hand, the severe discipline required of militants (which reached the point of compulsory atheism, through a "self-criticism of God") caused some members to leave the organization. On the other hand, some militants did settle successfully in working-class and rural areas, including the large industrial zone around São Paulo known as the ABC Paulista, the sugar-producing area of Pernambuco, the cocoa-growing region of Bahia, and the Pariconha and Água Branca areas of Alagoas, where a bean-producing cooperative was located. AP militants also secured a foothold among rice-growing peasants in the Vale do Pindaré in the northern state of Maranhão, where peasant leader Manoel da Conceição was based.

In 1968, when the AP began to publish its official paper, *Libertação* (*Liberation*), an internal struggle took place that resulted in the formation of a new dissident group. The group took the name Workers' Revolutionary Party (Partido Revolucionário dos Trabalhadores—PRT). The founders of the PRT did not agree with the orthodox Maoism propounded by the AP leadership, which proposed an antifeudal struggle, the siege of cities by peasants, and other features of the Chinese experience. The PRT was small but claimed as members two former UNE presidents, a controversial priest associated with the Peasant Leagues, Father Alípio Cristiano de Freitas, and José Porfírio de Souza, a peasant leader from the central state of Goiás who had exercised a legendary role in rural land conflicts in his region back in 1955. The PRT executed some armed actions in Rio de Janeiro and in São Paulo, but broke up in 1971 after being attacked by the repressive organs.

In 1971, when the AP had already drawn quite close to the PC do B through alliances within the student movement, the AP modified its bylaws and became the Marxist-Leninist Popular Action of Brazil (APML). From that point on, the influence of those members who defended the fusion of the AP with the PC do B grew even stronger. The fusion between the organizations was completed in the 1972–1973 period, after a heated internal struggle that divided the highest leadership of the AP. A significant portion of the organization membership chose to follow those leaders who opted to incorporate into the PC do B. A sector led by Jair Ferreira de Sá and Paulo Stuart Wright, however, maintained the AP as an independent organization.

From 1973 on, the group that had rejected the incorporation of the AP into the PC do B became better known as the "Socialist AP." It joined with the POLOP (see below) and the MR-8 to edit a magazine called *Brasil Socialista*. The publication affirmed the "socialist character of the Brazilian revolution," in contrast to the "bourgeois-democratic" proposal defended by the PCB and the PC do B.

In 1973 and 1974, the Socialist AP suffered harsh repression by the security organs. Important leaders like Paulo Stuart Wright, a former state legislator in the southern state of Santa Catarina, and Honestino Guimarães, who had been the highest-ranking leader of the National Student Union, were detained and killed by the DOI-CODI. To this day, they are listed as "disappeared."

Of the legal proceedings studied by the BNM project, 49 scattered over 13 states covered activities of the AP. More than 500 persons were named as defendants. Approximately 250 others were involved only in preliminary inquests. In a number of these cases, Church activities were also investigated, since the AP and its members came from a Christian background.

The PRT was featured in five legal proceedings, two of which investigated the events in Trombas-Formoso in which the peasant leader José Porfírio played such an important role. Porfírio "disappeared" in 1971, shortly after his release from a military installation in Brasília.

POLOP AND ITS OFFSHOOTS

The Marxist Revolutionary Organization–Workers' Politics (Organização Marxista–Política Operária—POLOP) was created in February 1961, bringing together students from the "Working Youth" of Minas Gerais, the "Socialist League" of São Paulo (sympathizers of Rosa Luxemburg), a few Trotskyites, and dissidents from the PCB in Rio, São Paulo, and Minas Gerais. From its inception, POLOP gave more importance to the theoretical and doctrinal debate within the Marxist left than to the task of building a political alternative to the PCB. It consequently did not become a national organization, although it did achieve some prestige in university circles in the states of Rio de Janeiro, São Paulo, and Minas Gerais. Even prior to 1964, POLOP also counted among its sympathizers military personnel connected to nationalistic activities within the armed forces.

POLOP was critical of positions defended by the PCB, especially in regard to the need for an alliance between the left and the "national bourgeoisie" in order to win the struggle against "imperialism" and "feudalism." POLOP proposed instead a sociaiist program for Brazil which affirmed that the level of capitalism already attained in the country not only allowed for but required immediate socialist transformation, and could dispense with any "national-democratic" stage of development.

After the overthrow of Goulart, POLOP tried to design a guerrilla strategy to confront the new regime. In alliance with military personnel identified with a philosophy of "revolutionary nationalism," the organization elaborated two plans for an armed resistance movement. Both were aborted. The first was a thwarted effort in 1964 in Rio de Janeiro, which was given the ironic name of "Copacabana Guerrilla." The second, which occurred in 1967, was an unsuccessful effort led by military personnel connected to an embryonic organization called the National Revolutionary Movement. This movement became known as the "Caparaó Guerrilla."

In 1967, POLOP, like the PCB, was affected by the spreading guerrilla warfare in Latin America, inspired by the Cuban Revolution and the revolutionary fervor of Che Guevara. Two important splinter groups were formed in response to this trend. In Minas Gerais, the majority of POLOP militants left to create the National Liberation Command (Comando de Libertação Nacional—COLINA). In São Paulo, a "left flank" of POLOP joined military personnel from the disbanded National Revolutionary Movement to form the Popular Revolutionary Vanguard (Vanguarda Popular Revolucionária—VPR).

The COLINA was very short-lived. It was limited almost entirely to the state of Minas Gerais, with some impact in Rio. It adopted the ideas defended by the Latin American Solidarity Organization— namely, the development of a continental plan for revolution in Latin America. From 1968 on, COLINA engaged in armed actions designed to obtain funds that would be used to create a "strategic area"—a revolutionary staging ground—in a rural region of Brazil. At the beginning of 1969, however, COLINA was hit by a series of arrests. From then on, both because of political affinity and in order to survive, COLINA merged with the VPR. The result of the merger was a new organization called the Armed Revolutionary Vanguard– Palmares (VAR–Palmares), named in honor of a historic rebel slave settlement.

The VPR was better known than COLINA, since it was connected from its inception with Brazilian army captain Carlos Lamarca. Lamarca earned his revolutionary credentials shortly after the imposition of AI-5, when he left his unit, leading several soldiers and taking with him a large stock of armaments for the purpose of resisting the regime. The VPR's political line, as formulated by Lamarca, was somewhere between the theses of Guevara in the Latin American Solidarity Organization and the POLOP position, especially in regard to the thorny question of whether the revolutionary struggle was to be immediately socialist in character or whether it was primarily "antiimperialist."

The VPR joined with the COLINA group in July 1969, forming the VAR–Palmares. Yet in September of that same year, the new organization split once more. One dissenting faction withdrew and reconstituted the VPR, with Lamarca once again its central figure.

Despite successive waves of imprisonments of militants, the VPR kept up a strong rhythm of armed actions from 1968 to 1971, mainly in São Paulo and in Rio. Some actions received ample media coverage. In 1970, for example, the organization assumed responsibility for the widely publicized abduction of three foreign diplomats, who were exchanged, unharmed, for political prisoners. Beginning in 1971, however, the VPR rapidly disintegrated. The death blow occurred in 1973, when police infiltrator "Cabo Anselmo" supervised the slaughter of the remaining militants, who were trying to restructure the organization in the Recife region.

In mid-1969 a former army soldier named Eduardo Leite, known as "Bacuri," withdrew from the VPR. He formed a small dissident group called Democratic Resistance or Nationalist Democratic and Popular Resistance, which existed for only one year. It perpetrated armed actions in São Paulo, collaborating with the ALN, the VPR, and the MRT in a combined "Front." Bacuri himself was captured in August 1970, in Rio de Janeiro, by São Paulo policeman Fleury and by agents of Rio's Navy Information Center. By that time, Bacuri was a member of the ALN. He was subjected to prolonged tortures until December of that year, when he appeared on the list of prisoners to be freed in exchange for the safe return of the kidnapped Swiss ambassador. Instead of releasing Bacuri, security agents executed him. After the murder, they released a public version of the events, claiming that he had been killed during a shootout.

Before the September 1969 split that led to the reconstitution of the VPR, the VAR–Palmares, for its part, executed the most successful of all urban guerrilla assaults designed to obtain funds for the clandestine groups. Acting on inside information, the group robbed a safe containing $2.5 million. According to the VAR–Palmares, the money had come from the corrupt activities of Adhemar de Barros, the former governor of São Paulo.

In 1970, the VAR–Palmares was faced with strong internal dissent over how to confront the growing repression. In Rio de Janeiro, one faction withdrew from the parent organization and formed the VAR–Palmares Dissidence, later renamed Unified Group. Among those militants who remained with VAR–Palmares were some who called for the end of armed actions. They turned instead to organizing urban workers in "Workers Unions." Others insisted upon preparing for armed struggle in rural areas.

As of 1971, both the VAR–Palmares and the VPR began to disintegrate. Efforts to reverse the process were rendered useless when important leaders like Carlos Alberto Soares de Freitas, one of the founders of the COLINA, and Mariano Joaquim da Silva ("Loyola"), a veteran of the Peasant Leagues, were imprisoned and murdered by the repression. Both disappeared in the clandestine prisons of the DOI-CODI in Rio de Janeiro.

It should be emphasized that the internal splits within the parent organization POLOP that led to the formation of the VPR and the COLINA left POLOP clearly debilitated. In order to shore up its dwindling strength, POLOP approached a local subgroup of the PCB called the Leninist Dissidence of Rio Grande do Sul, as well as several other small militant groups, to form the Communist Workers' Party (Partido Operário Comunista—POC). The POC attained a certain status in the 1968 student movement, where it was known as the "Critical University Movement." Its program was a clear continuation of the POLOP positions. The POC also tried to establish a presence among workers in Brazilian state capitals.

In April 1970 a group of militants left the POC to reconstruct POLOP. Those who remained in the POC soon developed profound internal differences, because some members defended joint actions with urban guerrilla organizations and even became involved in armed operations. Between 1970 and 1971, the POC was hit by the repression several times. Hundreds of militants, mainly in the cities of São Paulo and Porto Alegre, were imprisoned. The arrests brought their activities virtually to an end, although some sectors remained organized in exile.

In 1970, a small group of militants left the POC and created the Communist Revolutionary Movement (Movimento Comunista Revolucionário—MCR). The group executed a few joint armed actions with the VPR. Those who reorganized themselves in 1970 under the POLOP acronym, however, condemned armed actions and concentrated their few cadres in worker organization efforts. They also renamed their group the Marxist-Leninist Combat Organization-Workers' Politics. In exile, this group cooperated with the socialist AP and the MR-8 to publish a magazine called *Socialist Brazil*.

After less than a year, a splinter group called the Bolshevik Fraction of the POLOP was created from within the POLOP ranks, in Rio de Janeiro. In 1976, this name was changed to Movement for the Emancipation of the Proletariat (Movimento pela Emancipação do Proletariado—MEP).

Project BNM studied 5 legal proceedings covering the POLOP, which cited approximately 100 defendants. The POC was the object of 8 legal proceedings in São Paulo, Minas Gerais, Paraná, and Rio Grande do Sul. More than 200 individuals were named as defendants or included in the preliminary hearing phase. The MEP was detected by the repression in 1977, resulting in detentions and the initiation of legal proceedings in Rio de Janeiro and São Paulo.

The VPR was the object of 30 legal proceedings. Almost 500 persons were involved either as defendants or named in the preliminary hearing phase. The COLINA was investigated in 6 legal proceedings, all held in 1969. Four legal proceedings initiated in São Paulo in 1969 and 1970 investigated the VPR splinter group headed by Bacuri, while 35 trials referred to the activities of VAR–Palmares. More than 300 defendants and 110 additional persons called to testify in preliminary hearings were named in these trials.

TROTSKYITE GROUPS

Since 1929, Trotskyite groups have existed in Brazil. The most important of these was the Trotskyite Revolutionary Workers' Party (PORT), founded in 1953 under the influence of a curious figure named Homero Cristali, an Argentine known by the pseudonym J. Posadas. For many years Posadas wrote articles for the periodical *Workers' Front (Frente Operária)*, addressing subjects from the arrival of flying saucers on Earth to the sexual life of the revolutionaries. Posadas was also in charge of the Latin American Bureau of the IV International, founded by Trotsky in Mexico in 1938.

At the beginning of the 1960s, PORT began to acquire some prestige, especially because it had adopted a political position to the left of the PCB. It had a small membership confined mainly to the states of São Paulo, Rio Grande do Sul, and Pernambuco. The organization gained notoriety during the Goulart administration, however, when its members were subjected to detentions and political persecutions because of their involvement in the controversial Peasant Leagues.

With the 1964 coup, PORT was struck in earnest by political repression. Nonetheless, it stayed alive in the ensuing years, especially in student circles. Some of the group's members went to work in industry. This was the case of Olavo Hansen, who was killed under torture in the São Paulo DOPS in 1970, after distributing pamphlets at a peaceful May Day demonstration. Between 1970 and 1972, PORT was hit by repeated waves of detentions.

Aside from the eccentricities of the texts written by Posadas, the political line of PORT in the 1960s and early 1970s was characterized by the energetic condemnation of armed struggle as carried out by other leftists groups; a certain defense of the role of the Soviet Union in the international context (in clear disagreement with the opinions of other Trotskyite groups around the world); and propaganda in favor of a "Peruvian" solution for the Brazilian political process, that is, the expectation that a group of military nationalists would create a regime in Brazil similar to that of Peru's General Alvarado.

The Trotskyite Bolshevik Fraction (FBT) was organized in 1968 inside PORT itself, mainly in Rio Grande do Sul, while another dissident group called the First of May was formed in São Paulo. Many years later, in 1976, those two organizations, which had broken away altogether from the ideas of Posadas, would unify under the name Internationalist Socialist Organization. This would become better known for its student branch called Liberty and Struggle. The internal splits within PORT developed less as a result of the internal programmatic, strategic, and tactical differences that led to splits in other organizations and more as a reflection of conflicting positions on questions debated by Trotskyites worldwide.

Twelve of the legal proceedings studied in the BNM project referred to PORT. Four other sets of proceedings covered the Trotskyite Bolshevik Fraction, and one referred to the Workers' League, an offshoot of an FBT group. Indirect references to other Trotskyite groups were found in testimonies and in documents appended to the legal proceedings.

"REVOLUTIONARY NATIONALISM"

Finally, there was a group of small organizations dedicated to "revolutionary nationalism." Although these groups shared the nationalist ideals of the leftist groups, they were not Marxist in orientation.

Most of these groups were formed during the early 1960s by activists who supported Goulart's basic reforms. The groups also found supporters among the lower-ranking military. Above all, they were connected to the activities of Leonel Brizola, a former governor of the state of Rio Grande do Sul who was at that time a federal congressman.

Even before the overthrow of Goulart in November 1963, Brizola had broadcast an appeal over a Rio de Janeiro radio station, asking supporters throughout the country to band together in "nationalist commandos" to be known as the "Groups of Eleven Comrades" (Grupos de Onze). These groups would have three goals: the defense of the democratic conquests of the Brazilian people; immediate social reforms; and national liberation. Brizola's appeal spread throughout Brazil, and although the BNM project studied only twelve sets of legal proceedings dealing specifically with the activities of the Groups of Eleven, references to them appeared in practically all the inquests and legal proceedings initiated during the first several years of the military regime. Several hundreds of these groups were no doubt already in existence when the coup occurred in April 1964.

It was said that the armed resistance promised by the "revolutionary nationalist" sectors should there be any threat to depose the constitutional president was in fact planned in Uruguay *after* the coup. This was an ironic reference to the fact that Goulart, Brizola, and members of the left wing of the Brazilian Labor Party, as well as military personnel opposed to the regime, had all gone into exile in that neighboring country. Virtually all of these resisters had had their electoral mandates canceled and their political rights revoked in Brazil. The "revolutionary nationalist" efforts enumerated below were all initiated in Uruguay, inspired by this circle of exiles.

The National Revolutionary Movement ended up as one more embryonic political effort rather than an effectively consolidated structure. Inspired in what might be called the "Brizolista" philosophy, its fundamental constituency was a group of military personnel who lost their posts under the new regime. This group was known as the "Caparaó Guerrilla," although its activities mounted to no more than a sequence of military training exercises carried out in the vicinity of a mountain called the Pico das Bandeiras, in Minas Gerais. All the members of the group were detained for interrogation in March 1967, and one of them, Milton Soares de Castro, was killed. When militants involved in the "Caparaó Guerrilla" began to be released from prison, during the second half of 1969, they initiated a new organization. It was first known as the Independence or Death Movement and later became known as National Armed Resistance.

A similar group also connected with the exiles in Uruguay was founded in Rio Grande do Sul. Colonel Jefferson Cardim Osório, the group's main leader, led a guerrilla column that tried in March 1965 to unleash an armed movement in the Três Passos and Tenente Portela regions of the state. The movement was defeated in a few days, and those militants who had not been captured organized the 26th of March Revolutionary Movement (MR-26) in honor of those who had fought with Osório and who remained in prison after suffering barbarous tortures. The MR-26 was also involved in a few armed actions in the city of Porto Alegre. In 1969, after several of its members were captured, the group disbanded.

The National Liberation Front (FLN) was born in 1969, incorporating some survivors of the MR-26. It lasted one year only, executing some urban guerrilla operations in Rio Grande do Sul and Rio de Janeiro in conjunction with other groups. Its leader, Joaquim Pires Cerveira, was imprisoned in April 1970. In June 1970, when the German ambassador was abducted, Cerveira was among those prisoners for whom the ambassador was exchanged. He was banished from Brazil upon his release from prison. Three years later he was arrested by security agents when he and other exiles tried to reenter the country. To this day he remains on the list of "disappeared political prisoners."

The 21st of April Revolutionary Movement (MR-21) was the name adopted by a group of militants connected with the journalist Flávio Tavares, who worked for the Rio newspaper *Última Hora* (The Final Hour). The paper was identified with leftist currents associated with the political tradition of former president Getúlio Vargas. Between July and August of 1967, in the midst of plans for initiating military training with the objective of launching a guerrilla movement in the interior of Minas Gerais, the group was discovered by the repression and forced to disband.

Flávio Tavares was also involved in efforts to create another organization in 1969. The Movement of Revolutionary Action represented military personnel who were held in the Lemos Brito Penitentiary in Rio de Janeiro. These individuals had been prosecuted and condemned in military courts for their involvement in the Association of Navy and Marine Personnel of Brazil and in the "Sergeants Uprising" in 1963. In brief, they represented those forces within the military that had been loyal to the Goulart government. In May 1969 this group made a spectacular escape from the penitentiary, eluding authorities who pursued them for several days in the mountains around Angra dos Reis on the Rio coast. The group carried out several armed actions in the city of Rio, but almost all members were captured in August of that year. Those who escaped became members of other urban guerrilla organizations.

The BNM project analyzed one set of legal proceedings referring to the National Revolutionary Movement, two related to the National Armed Resistance, three covering armed actions of the Movement of Revolutionary Action, one related to the MR-21, three about the MR-26, and three covering the National Liberation Front.

ELEVEN

AGAINST TARGETED SOCIAL GROUPS

THE BNM project collected 263 sets of legal proceedings that did not focus upon clandestine political organizations. In 179 of them it was possible to classify defendants as members of six clearly identified social groups: the military, union leaders, students, politicians, journalists, and religious workers. These groups were singled out by the military regime as special targets for repression largely because they represented broad areas of resistance to the authoritarian government.

One of the BNM project's most significant conclusions was that the military itself was one of the social sectors most affected by the repression. From the first hours after April 1964, the military regime engaged in a systematic effort to purge military units of all persons identified with the deposed government and its pronationalist stance. The purges affected all military ranks, from infantry to the highest officers. No fewer than thirty-eight of the legal proceedings researched involved navy, army, and air force personnel. In one case, the accused were members of the Military Brigade of Rio Grande do Sul. Many of these proceedings were voluminous and involved many defendants.

The second largest social sector targeted in the early period of the regime was organized labor. Worker-organized activities such as the invasion of large properties by landless peasants and the formation of the Peasant Leagues to seek redress of grievances among the rural population also sparked repression and are included in this category. Thirty-six sets of legal proceedings investigated these activities.

Student groups were the object of fifty-three of the legal proceedings studied. The major concentration of trials investigating this sector was in 1968 and 1969, when the traditionally militant student movement took on a vanguard role in the opposition.

Twenty-two of the legal proceedings were brought against political figures, including congressmen, administrators, and candidates for office. In the first years of the military regime, the major party targeted was the Brazilian Labor Party to which the deposed president belonged. In subsequent years, the most frequently targeted party was the Brazilian Democratic Movement, created in 1966 by the government as the official opposition party.

Fifteen of the legal proceedings studied concerned journalists. In an additional fifteen cases, the target was the Catholic Church.

What follows is a synthesis of the proceedings directed against these six important social groups.

MILITARY PERSONNEL

Spokesmen for the military regime customarily affirmed that the final decision to break with the constitutional order and overthrow President João Goulart was made when mobilization in defense of Goulart's proposed "basic reforms" spread to sectors of the armed forces. As early as September 1963, when the Supreme Federal Court prohibited a military man from registering as a candidate for public office, there was a strong protest movement among military. The uprising began in Brasília on 12 September 1963 and became known as the Revolt of the Brasília Sergeants. Fifty-four defendants were investigated, almost all of them air force sergeants. The accused were singled out for acts of insubordination, including the imprisonment of officers and other authorities, the closing down of the Brasília airport, the sabotage of airplanes and machine-gunning of tires, and the incitement of fellow soldiers in the army and the navy. Three other sets of legal proceedings were also initiated in 1963 as a result of the same episode.

Overall, the legal proceedings initiated in 1964 aimed principally to punish military personnel who remained faithful to Goulart. The most curious trial was initiated in May 1964. The defendants were petty officers, sergeants, corporals, and soldiers. In a seemingly absurd proceeding, they were prosecuted for meeting in the casino of the Fortaleza Air Base on the day of the coup and marching in formation to the unit commander in order to request clarification about the ongoing political events. Their request was met with imprisonments, punishments, and judicial sanctions.

Another example of the typical charges brought against military personnel was a suit against twelve sergeants and a sublieutenant of the army's First Battalion of Combat Engineering. The only concrete charge in the proceeding was the accusation that on 1 April 1964 these military personnel moved in formation toward the city of Areal in the state of Rio in order to support loyalist troops and combat rebellious units. Although the battalion commander decided at that moment to join the anti-Goulart movement, his troops refused to obey his orders to throw their support to the rebels. They stuck to the nation's laws and constitution, but when the coup was victorious, the price of their loyalty was a military inquest.

Many of the military police inquests were initiated in this fashion. The BNM project collected thirty-eight sets of legal proceedings specifically directed against "subversion" within the armed forces. In these actions, a total of 747 persons were tried in military courts, while 1,692 were named in the preliminary hearing stage only. As a general rule, moreover, implicated military personnel were dismissed from active service, sometimes expelled even before the military court rendered a verdict.

One trial, initiated in Rio de Janeiro in April 1964, deserves special mention. The proceedings began with the April 4th suicide, registered in the military court records, of 3rd Sergeant Ivan Pereira Cardoso. Cardoso killed himself immediately after he was interrogated by a secret service captain named Luís Carlos Zamith. Because only one defendant—one of Sergeant Cardoso's military buddies accused of subversion—was named in this proceeding, the trial outcome is less important than the fact that the trial record is one of the earliest documents to refer to interrogation followed by suicide, a pattern that would become commonplace in political investigations. Although the incident occurred during the first days of the new military regime, higher authorities never questioned what happened.

Although the navy was a much smaller force than the army, it suffered the largest number of punitive legal proceedings, This reflects the fact that navy personnel had achieved a more advanced level of political organization, especially after the founding of the Association of Navy and Marine Personnel of Brazil (AMFNB) in 1962. The influence of a few high-ranking officers strongly identified with the political positions of João Goulart, among them Admiral Cândido Aragão, commander of the Marine Corps, was also important.

The most voluminous of all proceedings against military personnel resulted from a military police inquest ordered by the new minister of the navy, Admiral Augusto Rademaker Grunewald, on 3 April 1964. The purpose of this inquest was to investigate events that finally catalyzed the insurrection against Goulart.

On 25 March 1964 the Association of Navy and Marine Personnel of Brazil met in the Metalworkers' Union headquarters in Rio de Janeiro to celebrate its second anniversary. The expectation that the AMFNB president, José Anselmo dos Santos (known as "Cabo Anselmo"), was about to be arrested marked the celebration. Agitated speeches were made, and, on the morning of March 25th, the ranking officers put all navy and marine troops on alert. A detachment of marines was sent to repress the "mutiny." The situation was made more tense when a marine commander widely known to sympathize with AMFNB chose to fraternize with the navy personnel. By March 28th, the ranking officers were provoked into open rebellion against the pro-Goulart faction represented by the AMFNB. Using the pretext that discipline had broken down among the troops, they were able to move against the constitutional government. Preliminary hearings accused 1,123 individuals; the trial ended in July 1966 when close to 250 of the defendants were condemned to sentences of more than five years each.

Another four sets of legal proceedings against the crews of four navy vessels deal with the events of 25–27 March 1964. The documents describe how unarmed navy personnel advanced in the direction of the Metalworkers' Union, singing the national anthem and waving the Brazilian flag, until they were stopped and wounded by gunfire from officers who—in the days that followed—would overthrow Goulart.

The AMFNB also appeared in several other legal proceedings. "Cabo Anselmo," who in 1973 would be named as a police infiltrator of the armed left, was a central figure in these cases. In retrospect, it is possible that his leadership in the AMFNB and in the events of 1963 and 1964 was spurious.

In other proceedings, high-ranking officers were named. On 3 April 1964, for example, a military police inquest was initiated with the interrogation of the former minister of the navy, Admiral Paulo Mário da Cunha Rodrigues, who had been deposed just two days earlier. The admiral whom Rodrigues himself had replaced just a week earlier, Sylvio Borges de Souza Motta, was also called to testify at the hearing. Another former minister of the navy, Admiral Pedro

Paulo de Araújo Suzano, was charged as well. The central personality in the investigations, however, was Admiral Cândido Aragão, known as the "admiral of the people" within the nationalist ranks but dubbed the "Red Admiral" by the rightist press. Aragão escaped into exile but was sentenced in absentia to almost ten years in prison.

Significantly, of the thirty-eight proceedings against military personnel, only four were initiated after 1964. Most of the trials were in fact begun during the year of the coup. This suggests that the military acted swiftly and decisively to eliminate all sources of opposition within its own ranks.

UNION LEADERS

The distribution of legal proceedings aimed at labor unions during this period is similar to the pattern of investigations of military personnel. Trials were concentrated in 1964, with only sporadic investigations of the labor sector in following years.

There are two complementary interpretations for this pattern. First, the high frequency of legal proceedings initiated against these sectors in 1964 indicates the threat they represented to the new regime. Thus the generals who led the 1964 coup most feared the spread of a pronationalist stance among sectors of their own troops, and resistance from the labor unions to their economic programs, which were based on tightening salaries and denationalizing the economy. Second, the low incidence of punitive action against these sectors in later years indicates that the immediate repression of these groups successfully forestalled further resistance on their part. As will be seen later in this chapter, the opposite pattern would develop in student circles and among Church activists.

The results of the BNM project, moreover, are in full agreement with other historical and journalistic accounts of the pre-1964 years. It is clear that the agitation unleashed by the more conservative sectors of society, ostensibly to defend a political rupture that would implant a "strong government," in fact used pretexts to justify the overthrow of the constitutionally elected president by force of arms. One pretext was the supposed breakdown of military discipline; another, the specter of communism that was presumably infiltrating the federal, state, and city governments. The imminent victory of a "unionistic republic" was also one of the "dangers" most frequently invoked by the insurrectionary forces.

The Goulart years were characterized by a highly inflationary economic situation as well as growing freedom for popular organizing and participation; the growth of labor unions was inevitable. The centerpiece of the worker's movement at that time was an organization known as the General Workers' Command (Comando Geral dos Trabalhadores—CGT). Invariably mentioned in the military legal proceedings affecting the labor sector, the CGT was an effort to create a central coordinating body of labor unions. The labor legislation then in effect in Brazil, which was a holdover from Vargas' "New State" copied directly from Mussolini's labor code, specifically prohibited the formation of an organization that represented workers from different trades and professions. Given the political freedom of the Goulart period, however, workers and labor organizers attempted to circumvent the authoritarian legislation and to build a truly representative central organization.

Some further background regarding the CGT is useful in understanding why the repressive forces so feared its activities. The CGT was founded in August 1961 as an outgrowth of the General Strike Command (Comando Geral de Greve—CGG), which had led a successful campaign for the equivalent of an extra month's wages (the "13th salary") to be added to a worker's wages. The General Strike Command was composed of representatives from official labor union entities on a state and national level, such as federations and confederations. These union organizations were largely controlled by leaders connected with the Brazilian Communist Party and the Brazilian Labor Party, who therefore became influential in the newly created CGT. The actual political influence of these left-wing parties in the labor organization permitted the pro-coup forces to charge that the repeated strikes of 1963 and 1964 were communist-inspired. The fact that the communists in the CGT leadership at that time advocated a peaceful, legal stance based on permanent dialogue with the authorities and gradual social change achieved through "basic reforms" was of little importance to those who saw the labor movement as the very incarnation of pernicious communist influence.

In the countryside, the Peasant Leagues had a role equivalent to the CGT. First founded in the 1950s, the Leagues were established largely in the northeast of the country under the leadership of Catholic lawyer Francisco Julião. They represented an effort to create a more flexible and less bureaucratized union structure than had previously existed for peasants. The Leagues were founded for the expression of absolutely elementary demands, such as the right to individual coffins. As macabre as that sounds, it was of great importance to peasants, who previously were dumped into their graves from a government-owned coffin with a false bottom.

The Peasant Leagues grew rapidly; on the eve of Goulart's overthrow, there were approximately 2,181 Leagues scattered over twenty states and the federal district that included Brasília. The Leagues had also undergone considerable political evolution. After winning the right to unionize in rural areas at the beginning of the 1960s, they were repudiated by the communists who had inspired them on the grounds that they had become "ultra-left." The propagandists of the coup, however, ignored these ideological nuances. The Peasant Leagues of Francisco Julião, whatever their political position, became the bête noire of northeastern landowners. The strength of the Leagues was evident in the onset of land takeovers made in accordance with the peasants' campaign for "agrarian reform by law or by force," as the slogan of the day went.

In view of these active labor and popular groups, classified here under the generic name of "unionist movements," it is understandable that the authorities who took over in 1964 were especially careful to "clean out" this sector. Of the thirty-six sets of legal proceedings targeting labor union activities, eleven investigated rural episodes. The police phase of three of these proceedings was initiated even before April 1964. The first, for example, was begun in November 1962 in Magé, in the state of Rio de Janeiro, although the actual trial did not take place until 1970. The defendants were accused of mobilizing union members and of occupying an area of land belonging to a textile company, Companhia América Fabril, in order to carry out agrarian reform.

Two other rural proceedings investigated the Peasant Leagues in three counties in the Brazilian northeast, and the activities there of almost legendary rural leaders: Júlio Santana, "Leather Hat," and Joca. In one of these cases, the immediate cause of the events in question was the October 1963 imprisonment of Júlio Santana in response to pressures exerted by rural landowners. The peasants reacted strongly, and on the night of 11 October they abducted the local police chief, who was also a lieutenant in the state militia. The incident led to an exchange of gunfire between the police and the peasants, who were entrenched in the Rural Workers' Union headquarters.

Numerous similar activities were investigated in penal actions that have been classified elsewhere in this book. In addition, an incalculable number of investigations of the Peasant Leagues never reached the trial stage but were shelved during legal discussions regarding whether civil or military courts had jurisdiction. These discussions were frequent prior to the decree of Institutional Act No. 2 in October 1965, which expanded the jurisdiction of military courts over all civilians charged with political crimes.

In another of these proceedings, dated 1964, the activities of the federal office in São Paulo charged with coordinating the agrarian reform were investigated. Those responsible were charged with inciting citizens to class struggle through union organizing, promoting occupation of land areas, and publishing a bulletin that carried propaganda in favor of agrarian reform. The proceedings clearly demonstrate that individuals were punished for the simple fact that they had been associated with the deposed government.

A set of legal proceedings initiated in 1964 in the town of Governador Valadares demonstrates the kinds of event that could occur in Brazil at that time. The suit charged three farmers who allegedly killed two farm workers connected with union struggles. This case is the only one among all the proceedings studied in which defendants were not accused because they supported the deposed government. In their testimony, the three farmers declared that on 1 April 1964 they had been summoned by the police to help detain union leaders active in the region. The farmers discharged several shots when they found one of the leaders, Wilson Soares Cunha, injuring Cunha and killing his father and brother. In August 1966 the military coup absolved the defendants. In January of the following year, however, the Supreme Military Court modified the verdict, condemning the defendants to seventeen years and six months in prison.

The legal proceedings initiated in São Paulo after the death of a farmer named José da Conceição Gonçalves, "Zé Dico," demonstrates another kind of event—the beginning of armed struggles against the military regime. "Zé Dico," known for his repeated disregard for the law, was killed on his farm in an ambush set up by nineteen farm workers with whom he had been feuding. The workers were led by Edmur Péricles de Camargo, a companion of Carlos Marighella and a member of the PCB dissident group, the M3G.

In the legal proceedings against urban unions, dock workers, railroad employees, and employees of state-run corporations were the defendants most frequently charged. This suggests that these groups had the most active union movements at that time, in contrast to subsequent years when metalworkers would become the labor vanguard in Brazil. Throughout the proceedings initiated in 1964 the CGT appears as an omnipresent demon to be exorcised in penal actions directed at many diverse workers' sectors. Defendants included unionist workers in Rio de Janeiro commercial enterprises, bank workers, workers at the giant Verolme shipyard in Angra dos Reis, textile workers in the state of São Paulo; and even food industry workers in very small places like Santa Rosa do Viterbo, also in the state of São Paulo. What united these groups, at least in the eyes of the new authorities, was their political participation in forming the CGT, and, more generally, in the social struggles of the pre-1964 period.

In all the legal proceedings, phrases such as "crypto-communist," "Maoist-Castroist propaganda," "orders from Moscow," "unionist republic," "unionist subversion," "agitation in favor of basic reforms," "illegal strikes," "illegal entities," etc., monotonously reappear. Vast numbers of activities were included in these categories, considered criminal for the simple reason that they were inspired by a political philosophy opposed by the authorities.

Of the six sets of legal proceedings that covered urban union activities after 1964, three merit more detailed discussion.

The first resulted from a public protest meeting held on 1 May 1968, in the center of São Paulo. Union leaders subservient to the regime and São Paulo's Governor Roberto de Abreu Sodré had called for a commemorative May Day celebration, but rebellious workers' leaders and the recently formed Union Opposition organization, an umbrella group which included representatives of several trade categories, united to transform the proposed celebration into a public demonstration against the exploitation of workers. At that time workers were suffering from four years of real wage cuts imposed by the new regime. When Governor Sodré tried to begin his speech, he was roundly booed, and the speaker's platform was taken over by the rebellious union leaders. The governor was hit on the forehead by a stone and forced to take refuge inside a nearby cathedral. Unable to identify those responsible for the disturbance, police authorities opened an investigation charging a small number of citizens with inciting the events. Among those charged were journalists and passersby who had little to do with what had happened.

Two months later, metalworkers inspired by this demonstration carried out the most important strike attempted since the beginning of the military regime. Military police and army troops intervened under orders from the minister of labor, Jarbas Passarinho. The repression was brutal, with beatings of strikers, imprisonment of the strike leaders, and government intervention in the local Metalworkers' Union activities. The legal proceedings investigating these events were directed primarily at José Campos Barreto, who worked for the Cobrasma Metalworks Company. Barreto had been a seminarian in Bahia. He died there in September 1971 at the side of Carlos Lamarca, murdered by the repression in the final clandestine struggle of the VPR. Barreto is one of many individuals who embraced radical opposition activities after living through experiences which demonstrated that all possibility for democratic political participation had been extinguished by the military regime.

The third noteworthy legal proceeding against the unions after 1964 was initiated in the barracks of a military unit called the "Cannon Group 90." The defendants' principal offense was that they had met for the 5th National Meeting of Petroleum Union Leaders and had sent several protest telegrams to government authorities and a paper to the International Labor Organization of the United Nations denouncing the repression of labor unions in Brazil. The case against them was evidence of the extent of the government's intolerance at a time when frequent public demonstrations marked widespread discontent with the regime.

Overall, the BNM project determined that 472 individuals were named as defendants and another 114 were named in the preliminary inquiry stage of 36 legal proceedings directed against labor union movements as broadly defined here. A more complete account of the political repression directed at the labor movement would have to examine government intervention in the labor unions, the unilateral cancellation of mandates of elected union officials, the laying off of workers in various industries, and the hardships caused by forced unemployment. This task is beyond the scope of the BNM project. Nonetheless, such an inventory would be an indispensable part of a broad effort to document the repressive period in Brazil.

STUDENTS

As they have throughout the world, students in Brazil have played a very important role in crystallizing political and social struggles. They actively participated in all the great political changes in Brazil, for example, in the sharpening of nationalist sentiment in the face of colonial domination, and in the struggles for the abolition of slavery and the creation of the republic.

In 1937, the National Student Union (UNE) was founded. From its inception, UNE was a powerful symbol as well as an organizational base for student involvement in national-level politics, not only in the area of education, but also in general causes such as the defense of democracy, solidarity with workers, the protection of human rights, and opposition to dictatorships. As early as August 1961 UNE threw its weight behind the constitutional forces that defended Goulart's succession to the presidency after the sudden resignation of President Jânio Quadros. In the period immediately preceding the April 1964 coup, UNE played an important and highly visible role in the growth of nationalist sentiment and in the campaigns for Goulart's basic reforms. When the military ministers in the cabinet tried to prevent Goulart's inauguration, UNE transferred its national headquarters in Rio de Janeiro to the Goulart stronghold of Porto Alegre, where it participated in pro-Goulart mobilization led by Governor Leonel Brizola.

Also during this period, UNE launched its famous Popular Center for Culture, roving cultural activities which used Brazilian music, theater pieces, poetry, and other artistic forms to disseminate messages promoting nationalism and social justice. The CPCs, as they were known, became the primary vehicle through which Brazilian artists and intellectuals sought to transcend class boundaries and integrate the reformist political ideals of the period into artistic forms that would reach the working classes.

In view of these activities, it is hardly surprising that the country's conservative elite, agitating against the Goulart government, denounced UNE as one of the "seven heads of the communist dragon" in Brazil. The fact that the headquarters of UNE on Flamengo Beach in Rio de Janeiro was occupied, plundered, and burned down by a paramilitary organization called the Command for the Detection of Communists on the very day of the coup, 1 April 1964, is evidence of how important the pro-coup forces felt the student organization to be.

Nonetheless, repression of the student movement was not an immediate priority of the regime. The leaders of the coup had considerable support among the middle class, from which UNE activists and other student leaders were largely drawn, and military authorities believed that, at least in the short term, they might win over university students through the promotion of an anticommunist ideology that was supposedly based on the ideals of the "free world."

While some legal proceedings were initiated in 1964 to investigate student activities in support of the deposed government, they were relatively few in comparison to the number of military and trade union investigations. In one typical case, a set of legal proceedings was initiated in the Second Naval Military Court in Rio de Janeiro against dozens of students connected with UNE, but the case was dropped before reaching the trial stage.

Of the fifty-two sets of legal proceedings studied that referred to student activities, only five were initiated prior to 1968. In contrast, forty-four cases were initiated between 1968 and 1970. Only three proceedings were initiated during the later years covered by the BNM project.

This distribution faithfully mirrors political events in Brazil and the evolution of the student movement during the years of military rule. While the repression unleashed in April 1964 was less severe in the student sector than in other areas, it was sufficient—at least at first—to paralyze the student movement. After the initial impact of the coup faded, however, the student movement embarked on three years of a slow but impressive renewal of its activities. By 1968, riding the explosion of sentiment produced by student mobilizations that erupted from Paris to Prague, the Brazilian student movement took the lead in organizing protests against the military regime.

The events of 1966 were a major dress rehearsal for the street marches and confrontations with military forces that characterized the 1968 political scene. For the first time since the military had come to power, students went into the streets of Rio, São Paulo, Belo Horizonte, Porto Alegre, Brasília, and other state capitals. Their protest marches culminated on 22 September 1966 with a National Day of Protest. Known as the "setembrada," the demonstration made public student demands, including the defense of UNE, free tuition, university autonomy, and the rupture of university ties with American organizations. The students also expressed their general political position with slogans like "Down with the Dictatorship!"

Student protests continued. On 28 March 1968 secondary school student Edson Luís Lima Souto was killed by police during a peaceful student demonstration protesting the imminent close of a popular restaurant. Like a fuse on a powder keg, the murder provoked street demonstrations throughout the country. Confrontations with the police and general repression intensified in every Brazilian state. On June 25th events reached a climax in Rio with a street march that came to be known as "The March of the 100,000." Spurred by the brutal murder of the young student Edson Luís, demonstrators also protested the economic policies and the numerous restrictions on civil liberties which had been imposed since 1964.

In this way, the student movement was the spearhead of and the main spokesman for the general dissatisfaction with the military regime. At the same time, and in some measure because the student-led demonstrations had little effect except to intensify the repression, the arguments of those who thought that all possibilities for achieving democracy through peaceful means had been exhausted were also gaining currency. By the end of 1968, the regime cracked down in earnest with the decree of AI-5. To the opposition, AI-5 formalized the imposition of an unmasked dictatorship. After 1969, student demonstrations decreased, while clandestine armed operations against the regime increased.

Student political activities, therefore, declined during the Médici period from 1969 to 1974. Student organizations disintegrated and their leaders were persecuted and driven into the clandestine opposition. The simplest expression of demands in universities was swiftly repressed. Several proceedings were initiated against student activitists after 1969 but were suspended before reaching the trial stage, often because the principal defendants were charged with more serious crimes—e.g., armed actions and militancy in revolutionary organizations—or because they had left the country, sometimes as voluntary exiles, sometimes banished by presidential decree. Only after 1974 did the student movement reemerge. The first demonstrations to take to the streets occurred in 1976, and they revived student participation in the reconstruction of UNE.

Many student leaders were shot or tortured to death by the security organs during the repressive period, both in the capital cities and in remote rural area like the region around the Araguaia River, in the Amazon region. Among the dead was Honestino Monteiro Guimarães, the last president of UNE before the organization was dismantled in 1964. Guimarães was detained in 1973, but no further news regarding his whereabouts was ever made available.

The only set of legal proceedings examined by the BNM project dating from the first year of the military regime was initiated on 1 July 1964 in the Reserve Officer Training Center in Curitiba, the capital of the state of Paraná in southern Brazil. The investigation covers the "student agitation" of the period prior to the military regime, focusing especially on UNE's Popular Center for Culture

(CPC). The authorities charged with carrying out the investigation were so inventive that they saw evidence that UNE was a front for the Communist Party in the similarity of the acronyms "CPC" and "PC."

In 1966, legal proceedings again focused upon student protest activities in Brasília. Among those specified were street marches, the distribution of fliers, public rallies, and, in particular, the stoning of the Thomas Jefferson House, a cultural center connected with the American embassy.

Of the proceedings dated 1967, one was begun to investigate slogan-painting on the walls of a well-known center for conservative students. A second set of proceedings investigated charges including the publication of opposition newspapers.

In contrast to this scarce number of proceedings in the early period of the military regime, twenty-three sets of proceedings covering student activities were initiated in 1968 alone. They are small in scope, with few defendants named. In addition, they focus upon local episodes, for example, the distribution of a bulletin called *O Acadêmico* (The University Student) during an event dubbed "University Week" in the small city of Taquaritinga, in the state of São Paulo. Another typical proceeding was one initiated by the military court of the 10th military Judiciary District against a student and a professor who were detained in Fortaleza, Ceará, after participating in a march protesting the death of student Edson Luís. The two were carrying a Vietnamese flag.

There are voluminous proceedings which indicate that hundreds of students thoughout the country were subject to police persecution and detainment. In the days preceding the declaration of AI-5, for example, the dormitories of the Universtity of São Paulo were surrounded by military forces. Hundreds of students were detained, and allegedly subversive material was confiscated. Those military officers who sought to justify further crackdowns by the regime organized a public exposition in the foyer of a major newspaper organization of the material confiscated from the dormitories. A few small boxes of birth control pills were prominently displayed.

A prime example of these proceedings was one initiated after 693 students were detained on 12 October 1968 for trying to hold UNE's 30th conference at a rural site in the town of Ibiúna. This proceeding was later divided into subparts, and only a few groups of defendants were finally tried in military court. Nonetheless, because of their involvement, hundreds of students were forced to choose a clandestine life, especially in the repressive situation that worsened after AI-5 was decreed.

This episode also had an aftermath. According to the records, another penal procedure was initiated to investigate students who protested in Brasília against the detainment of the Ibiúna group. The Brasília students were themselves imprisoned after invading a bazaar organized by the wives of military personnel and using the loudspeaker there to denounce what had happened to their fellow students in Ibiúna. Another small incident followed. On 17 December 1968, four days after the declaration of AI-5, students again tried to hold the 30th UNE conference. This gathering, held in a place called "the German's Farm," in Curitiba, Paraná, was also interrupted by the police, and another penal action resulted.

Following the death of the student Edson Luís at the end of March 1968, in fact, at least one set of legal proceedings against students was initiated in each of the country's main capital cities. These focused on marches, rallies, protests, and students' union activities. In most cases, moreover, the formal beginning of the legal proceedings was after the decree of AI-5 on 13 December 1968, as if to signify that AI-5 was a signal to step up the repression.

University students were not the only targets of these investigations. Secondary school students were also named in numerous inquiries and judicial proceedings. On 7 September 1968, for example, the secretary of the Brazilian Union of Secondary School Students was detained in the city of Goiânia and prosecuted by the military court in Juiz de Fora, Minas Gerais. On 10 May 1968, two leaders of the Gaúcha Union of Secondary School Students, from Rio Grande do Sul, were detained while trying to reopen the student association of the Júlio de Castilhos School in Porto Alegre. From that time on, one of these students, Luís Eurico Tejera Lisboa, was systematically persecuted by the police. Lisboa felt compelled to enter into clandestine resistance activities. He died in São Paulo in 1972 at the hands of the repression. Secondary school students were also charged in a legal proceeding initiated in October 1969, resulting from the detainment of several students who were meeting with a few Catholic priests in an effort to organize the 21st conference of the Brazilian Union of Secondary School Students.

Finally, at least one of the legal proceedings initiated in the especially repressive period after 1968 deserves special mention for what it indicates about the anticultural bias of the authorities. In this proceeding, students and faculty of the History and Geography

Department of the University of São Paulo were accused of participating in groups known as "parity committees for educational reform," which had been set up by students in 1968. During this
period, historian and university faculty member Emília Viotti da
Costa suffered special persecution. In a military police inquest initiated in the general headquarters of the Second Army in São Paulo,
da Costa was accused of spreading subversive propaganda in her
university classes.

Many members of the university and the intellectual community
were also targeted by the repression. Another set of legal proceedings, for example, charged the students in the School of Philosophy
at the University of São Paulo who protested the sacking of some
of their most distinguished professors following the decree of AI-5.
Complicating this situation was the fact that the minister of justice
at the time, Luiz Antonio da Gama e Silva, was also a professor at
the University of São Paulo. He utilized the immense arbitrary
power of his position to settle old political disputes with his colleagues—by summarily removing them from the university.

POLITICAL FIGURES

The BNM project studied twenty-two sets of legal proceedings initiated against citizens for speeches made during the exercise of
their office or during political campaigns. These trials bring to light
some of the most petty aspects of the political repression that existed
in Brazil during the fifteen years covered by this study.

There were clearly two distinct periods in the repression of political figures. The first affected those individuals who were called
before military courts because they supported the deposed Goulart
government. These politicians belonged either to Goulart's party,
the Brazilian Labor Party, or to the Brazilian Socialist Party. The
second period of repressive action included cases initiated and tried
after the October 1965 decree of Institutional Act No. 2 (AI-2), which
abolished all existing political parties and created the National
Alliance for Renewal (ARENA), the official government party, and
the Brazilian Democratic Movement (MDB), the government-
sanctioned opposition party. In almost all cases, the political figures
tried belonged to the MDB.

Unlike other dictatorships, the Brazilian military regime never
banned political parties altogether. Nonetheless, as the military court
proceedings summarized in this section demonstrate, this electoral

"democracy" was a mere façade. It was in fact the military regime that established the allowable limits for criticism by opposition politicians. These were adjusted by the authorities in accordance with the internal necessities of the regime. For those critics who passed the official limits for dissent, punishment was rapid. Hundreds of electoral mandates were canceled, and political figures brought to military court for trial.

The twenty-two sets of legal proceedings investigated by the BNM project, moreover, were not the only juridical actions taken against popular political figures. In 1964, for example, the "IPMs [military police inquests] of subversion" were initiated throughout the country, leading to trials in which hundreds of city councilmen, mayors, state and federal legislators, and even state governors were subjected to official investigation, incriminations, accusations, and even legal sentences. It was decided by the BNM project, however, to separate the legal proceedings exclusively directed against politicians from those resulting from the "IPMs of subversion." The latter explored the connections of politicians with the Communist Party, trade union activities, the Peasant Leagues, Brizola's "Groups of Eleven," and Goulart and his basic reforms—among other "miscellaneous" subversive activities.

Of the proceedings exclusively against politicians, six date from 1964. In Minas Gerais, for example, a penal action was initiated against three state legislators. Although the three were also leaders of the General Workers' Command, the authorities in this particular proceeding emphasized their activities as elected officers. Elected in 1962, their mandates were canceled in April 1964 as part of the general purge against Goulart supporters by the new authorities. The anticommunist hatred underlying the legal proceedings was manifested in the absurd charges levied against the defendants. In falsehoods reminiscent of those fabricated by the Nazis, the legislators were accused of planning to poison the Belo Horizonte water supply. They would allegedly have begun with the water used by the 12th Infantry Regiment, which was stationed where the hearing took place.

Another example is provided by the penal action against Armindo Marcílio Doutel de Andrade, a federal congressman. The episodes investigated in the hearing went back to the pre-coup period, when Andrade participated in various pro-Goulart organizations. At that time, he allegedly delivered "subversive" speeches in support of UNE and the CGT. Furthermore, Andrade was associated with Leonel Brizola and Goulart himself. While the IPM involving Andrade began in 1964, the actual penal action against him was initiated only in 1969. For five years, Andrade was hostage to the decisions of the military officers in charge of the investigation.

Several legal proceedings from the years after 1964 should also be mentioned. They faithfully illustrate the way in which the military courts pressured the regime's opponents to drop their dissenting views.

On 2 September 1969, for example, at the Brasília general headquarters of the 6th Air Zone, an IPM was initiated against Senator João Abrahão Sobrinho. The senator was from the state of Goiás, and had been elected in 1962 by the Social Democratic Party. He was accused of having made several speeches from the Senate rostrum in April, August, and November, 1968, in which he attacked the military regime, the federal authorities, and even the president of the republic. Among these speeches was a denunciation of the violence by police that had invaded schools and killed students. In a democratic regime, such pronouncements might have been refuted by a senator's colleagues, and the matter would have died then and there. In Brazil in 1969, however, the senator who made the denunciations was put on trial, charged with having threatened national security.

City councilmen from counties in the interior of Rio Grande do Sul were targeted specially in these legal proceedings, against politicians. In April 1969, for example, city councilman Irany Guilherme Muller was investigated because of a speech he had made in a city council meeting, criticizing the commander of an artillery unit for having called the opposition sectors "communist."

In May an IPM was begun against two city councilmen from the town of Santo Ângelo who were critical of the repressive policy of the military regime. In 1970, in the same military unit, another proceeding was initiated against city councilman João Batista Santos da Silva of the MDB. Silva was investigated because of a speech he made denouncing tortures applied to political prisoners in Santo Ângelo's army barracks.

Legal proceedings that drew national attention were those initiated against federal congressmen Hélio Navarro, Hermano Alves, and Márcio Moreira Alves, all elected officials of the MDB party and outspoken government critics. Navarro, for example, was detained on the day AI-5 was decreed. The charge against Navarro was that in a television program aired during the campaign for municipal elections that took place on 15 November 1968, he called

President Costa e Silva a "dictator." Navarro was sentenced by the Second Military Court in São Paulo to twenty-one months in prison.

On 6 October 1969, Hermano Alves, a well-known journalist for the Rio newspaper *Correio da Manhã* (Morning Post) as well as a federal congressman, was condemned to two years and four months in prison by the navy's First Military Court in Rio. The proceedings against Alves were initiated at the request of no less than the general secretary of the National Security Council, General Jaime Portella, who had been criticized in one of Alves' newspaper articles. In the brief he presented to Justice Minister Gama e Silva for initiating the proceeding, Portella also appended transcripts of several of Alves' congressional speeches.

Márcio Moreira Alves was also prosecuted for several congressional speeches in which he denounced police violence against the student movement as well as other dictatorial actions of the military regime. Like Hermano Alves, Márcio Moreira Alves was both a federal congressman and a well-known journalist.

On 12 December 1968 the Congress denied the government's request for permission to prosecute Márcio Moreira Alves. This was a gesture in defense of legislative autonomy. The session in which this position was taken was so emotional that it closed with the congressmen singing the national anthem. On the following day, the government decreed AI-5. The Congress was closed, and a number of congressmen, including Márcio Alves, were stripped of their mandates. The penal proceedings against Márcio Alves, however, were only initiated later, on 20 May 1970. Not only his congressional speeches, but also his newspaper articles, his connection with the 1968 student demonstrations, and the publication of a book entitled *Tortura e Torturados* (Tortures and the Tortured), describing tortures imposed on political prisoners during the first administration of the military regime, led to Márcio Alves' prosecution.

Finally, two other sets of legal proceedings must be mentioned. They clearly demonstrate the abusive spirit with which the National Security Law was invoked by the provincial authorities in rural Brazil.

In 1970, in the city of Barra in the state of Bahia, four city councilmen of the government's ARENA party as well as another councilman from the opposition MDB were prosecuted under the National Security Law for continuing to participate in council meetings, even though their mandates had been revoked by other councilmen loyal to the local mayor. In brief, the exercise of the elementary right of opposition to a mayor in a remote area of Bahia led to the prosecution of five legally elected councilmen for crimes against national security.

On 26 May 1969, in Poços de Caldas, Minas Gerais, city councilman Dgeney Diniz de Melo was prosecuted under the National Security Law for having protested in a council meeting against the way in which he was treated by soldiers of the military police in a traffic incident that had occurred the month before. The logic was apparently simple. If in its most important decisions, the government confused national security with the security of a military regime imposed by force, who was to distinguish national security from traffic safety in the tiny town of Poços de Caldas?

JOURNALISTS

Fifteen of the military court proceedings studied by the BNM project referred to journalists, who were criminally prosecuted for performing legitimate professional activities, that is, publishing articles in legally sanctioned publications. Invariably, these defendants were accused of criticizing government authorities in a way that allegedly stimulated "hatred between classes" and "animosity against the armed forces." The military regime promulgated a specific Press Law in February 1967 in order to limit the freedom of information, but press professionals were often charged instead under the National Security Law, which permitted more severe penal actions.

The following summary demonstrates that in the majority of cases involving journalists there was no actual violation of national security. In reality, the threat of prosecution under the National Security Law served as a powerful form of intimidation, which curbed individual rights to inform, criticize, and disagree with the official version of events. The fact that criticism—whether of high federal officials or lowly municipal bosses—was punishable as a criminal offense also made the authorities virtually unassailable.

The distribution of these fifteen legal proceedings indicates that repression against the press, which reached the point of installing government censors in the newsrooms of the country's major newspapers, escalated after the declaration of AI-5 on 13 December 1968. Only one of the trials is dated prior to that time.

In February 1968 the owner of a newspaper from Passo Fundo was prosecuted at the request of several regional mayors, in retaliation for criticisms and attacks made against them in the paper in

1967. In the proceeding, references were also made to "offensive" words written against Tarso Dutra, then the minister of education.

On 7 January 1969, Niomar Muniz Sodré Bitencourt, the director-president of Rio de Janeiro's prestigious daily, the *Correio da Manhã* (Morning Post), was detained and subjected to a humiliating investigation. In one of the penal actions brought against her, "Dona Niomar" was accused of publishing an offensive editorial the day after AI-5 was declared. A few weeks later, on 31 January 1969, the *Correio da Manhã* was again targeted by the repression. This time, a penal action was brought against psychoanalyst Hélio Pllegrino for articles he published toward the end of 1967 and 1968 in which he not only criticized the Brazilian regime but "exalted" the figure of Che Guevara.

Dickson Fragoso Veras, owner and editor of a newspaper called the *Gazeta Popular*, was subjected to an investigation begun by the Federal Police in Curitiba on 30 September 1969. The reason for the investigation was the publication of a news item referring to a request for habeas corpus that had been filed on behalf of former army major and political prisoner Joaquim Pires Cerveira. The immediate cause of the penal action was the title of the news item, which quoted a sentence from the habeas corpus plea: "The police invaded and plundered my home."

In January 1970, journalist Hélio de Azevedo of Guarapuava, Paraná, was prosecuted for articles he had published in 1969 and 1970 that criticized the local mayor. Also in 1970, Paulo da Costa Ramos was taken to military court for an article he published in 1968 that allegedly criticized the minister of education. The two-year delay between the publication of the article and the beginning of the penal action is evidence of the purely political motivations that inspired this type of legal procedure, since no real threat to national security would have gone unpunished for so long a period.

On 12 April 1971 journalist Sebastião Nery published some comments about the prime minister of Portugal, Marcelo Caetano, which proved prophetic. Nery wrote that Caetano's statement to the effect that "Portugal would never abandon control over its African provinces" had the same lack of validity as Mussolini's assertions about Ethiopia, Hitler's about Yugoslavia, and Nixon's about Vietnam. Brazilian authorities considered Nery's statement to be "injurious and offensive," and ordered that a penal action be initiated against him. The Brechtian adage, however, proved to be true: "Truth is a child of time, not of authority."

There are more examples of journalists' "crimes" in the proceedings. On 10 February 1971, a correspondent for the newspaper *O Estado do Paraná* (The State of Paraná) submitted a news item to the paper about the lynching of a prisoner. That was reason enough to accuse him of a crime against national security. In August of that year journalist Carlos Augusto Vinhaes was accused of a crime against national security for commenting in a Rio newspaper called *Luta Democrática* (Democratic Struggle) about a traffic accident in which a child was injured.

In Porto Alegre, two journalists and a police chief from Camaquã were accused of crimes against national security for publishing articles about a prisoner who had been in the Camaquã public prison for eighteen years for having slapped his wife.

Finally, there is the case of a journalist who was prosecuted under the National Security Law despite the fact that he was a notorious propagandist for the military regime. In his regular column for a Brasília newspaper, José de Arimatéia Gomes Cunha, known as "Ari Cunha," denounced the tortures suffered by a pregnant political prisoner, Hecilda Mary Veiga Fonteles de Lima, in the Brasília Squad for Criminal Investigations. This was a unique case: a proponent of the Doctrine of National Security himself suffered from the onus of the National Security Law. His offense, ironically enough, was that he published an account of an episode that represented, even to him, excessive repression. Thus even the apologist for the military believed that it was unnecessary to go to such lengths to guarantee the stability of the regime.

RELIGIOUS WORKERS

The political transformation that occurred in Brazil in the beginning of the 1960s coincided with changes in the Catholic Church. After the Vatican's Second Ecumenical Council, from 1962 to 1965, the Church sought greater identification with marginalized sectors of society and their hopes for justice. Although they were in the minority, some bishops, priests, nuns, and laity supported the struggles for Goulart's proposed basic reforms. Bishops like Recife's Dom Hélder Câmara were already becoming identified with pressures for the change of unjust social structures, in accordance with the decisions reached by the Second Vatican Council. Lay movements like the Catholic University Students and Young Catholic Workers became deeply involved in struggles of the oppressed. In the same way in which people referred, with some exaggeration, to the existence of "generals of the people" and "admirals of the people"—those who were in sympathy with pronationalist sectors of the army and the navy—they also referred to the existence of "priests of the people," like Fathers Alípio, Lage, Josafá, and many others.

The overthrow of João Goulart, however, took place at a time when those Church sectors sympathetic to popular mobilization were still limited in size and influence. The Church hierarchy was engaged in the anticommunist crusade backed by the conservative elite. They joined together against agrarian reform, strike movements, the demands of pronationalists in the armed forces, and the alliance between Christians and Marxists that was formed in trade unions and student organizations. The consensus among historians, in fact, is that the Church hierarchy played a fundamental role in the creation of a favorable ideological climate for military intervention.

After the military regime took power in Brazil, however, and especially after the 1968 crackdown, the Church experienced a constant evolution of its social preoccupations. As a result, government authorities became increasingly estranged from the Church. They were puzzled by its criticisms of government measures and its forthright defense of human rights. Confrontation with the Church became inevitable.

For several reasons 1968 marked a shift in the Church's attitudes. First, it was a time of numerous protest demonstrations and consequent police repression that was condemned by Christians. Second, it was the year in which AI-5 was decreed. Third, many of the first experiments with "ecclesial base communities" were begun in 1968. These neighborhood organizations would eventually become the foundation of a whole new movement for social reform. Finally, the decennial conference of Latin American bishops was held that year in Medellín, Colombia. The worsening social injustices present in all countries represented at the meeting led the bishops to affirm, in their final resolutions: "It is not enough to reflect upon, to obtain greater clarity, and to speak. It is necessary to act. This has not ceased to be the hour of the Word; it has become, with dramatic urgency, the hour of action."

It should be noted that many of the legal proceedings mentioned earlier affected members of the Church. A summary of the fifteen proceedings *exclusively* concerned with the Church, however, will help to clarify the nature of the political repression that existed in Brazil from 1964 to 1979.

Two procedures initiated prior to 1964 were directed against Father Alípio Cristiano de Freitas, a Portuguese priest who had become well known at the beginning of the 1960s as one of the most daring and controversial "priests of the people." One of the IPMs against him was begun *before* the coup, in no less a place than the office of the minister of war. It accused Father Alípio of maintaining an "intense agitation campaign, systematically attacking the powers of the republic and the armed forces" in numerous speeches delivered in several states. The other IPM against Father Alípio accused him of having delivered an impassioned speech at a rally held at the local law school. The occasion was the first anniversary of the assassination of João Paulo Teixeira, leader of the Peasant Leagues of Sapé, in Paraíba. In his speech, the priest allegedly incited the people to violence and to the struggle between social classes.

Another set of military court proceedings that originated during the first days of the new regime investigated Father Francisco Lage Pessoa's activities from 1948 until 1964 and charged him with subversion. His work with slum dwellers, his support of strike movements, and his defense of Goulart's basic reforms are mentioned.

On 17 July 1968, Father José Eduardo Augusti of Botucatu, São Paulo, was detained in that city for helping to organize local medical school students who sought better teaching conditions. Augusti was also accused of offering his seminary to house the protesters after the police occupied and broke up their camp, and of promoting subversive propaganda in a bulletin called *Manifesto* and on Church radio programs. In another proceeding, Father Augusti was accused of collaborating with students preparing for the 21st conference of the Brazilian Union of Secondary School Students. He remained in the São Paulo Tiradentes penitentiary for almost a year.

In 1968, a voluminous set of military court proceedings was initiated in Belo Horizonte against thirty-four religious personnel, including priests, former priests, and professors of theology. Their crime: writing, signing, printing, and distributing a "Declaration of Priests" to protest the death of the student Edson Luís. The manifesto was dated 29 March 1968 but the inquest did not begin until December; this interval between the alleged subversive act and the ensuing reprisal once again reveals the purely political motive that inspired authorities to initiate such military court procedures. In this case, military officers evidently sought to fabricate the "subversion" that would justify the escalation of repression; indeed, AI-5 was decreed just three days after the inquest began. In June 1973 the military court in Juiz de Fora, Minas Gerais, found for the defendants. The court admitted that the activities cited did not constitute crimes. The case documents do, however, make recommendations as to what the role of the Church should and should not be. The reasoning is repeated time and again in penal actions against religious personnel:

> It is being verified that they are evangelizing in the light of Marxism or teaching socialism in the light of the Gospel, instead of teaching love toward the Nation, respect toward laws and authorities as it behooves the Church as a recognized, immaculate and eternal institution.

In May 1969, the Porto Alegre DOPS initiated an inquiry against religious and lay personnel of the St. Paul Parish, in Canoas, Rio Grande do Sul. They were accused of staging a play called "The Boss and the Worker," which allegedly was an incitement to class struggle. Sister Leonilde Boscaine and the parish priest, Father Oscar Albino Fuhr, were included among the defendants. Other religious personnel were also detained during the interrogation phase of this case. Among them was Affonso Ritter, of the Workers' Pastoral Commission, and laywoman Alceri Maria Gomes da Silva, who entered the clandestine opposition at the time the inquest began. In May 1971 da Silva was killed in São Paulo by DOI-CODI agents.

In November 1969 numerous Dominicans were detained in São Paulo, accused of association with rebel leader Carlos Marighella. One of the seminarians detained, Francisco Carlos Velez Gonzales, was also prosecuted individually for having written and mimeographed an adaptation of Pope John XXIII's encyclical under the title "Populorum Progressio and Brazil—The Drama of the Brazilian People."

Sacramentine Father Hélio Soares do Amaral was sentenced to one year and eight months in prison, which he served at the Tiradentes penitentiary in São Paulo, for having preached an allegedly subversive sermon during Sunday Mass. In that sermon, Father Amaral allegedly affirmed that Brazil had never been independent because it had emerged from Portuguese domination only to fall under American domination, and that the Brazilian government was responsible for the poverty that prevailed in the country.

In January 1970 two priests from Rio Grande do Sul, Roberto Egídio Pezzi and Mariano Callegari, were prosecuted by the Porto

Alegre military court. Pezzi was accused of committing a crime against national security because, in a sermon he preached on 30 November 1969, he denied the official account of the Dominican order's involvement in Carlos Marighella's death. Callegari was prosecuted for his role in the local rural labor union movement.

These legal proceedings were usually written in a style replete with adjectives and almost hysterical anticommunism. The military prosecutor thus referred to Father Callegari as follows, offering no proof whatsoever to substantiate his charges:

> The second person being denounced has a clear Marxist orientation; he has traveled to Russia and Cuba under sponsorship of the Caxias do Sul Diocese; he carries out great activity in his parish, a place called Estância da Roça; he proclaims the need to implant the Cuban regime in Brazil for the solution of national problems; and uses his priestly status to spread his subversive propaganda.

Apparently the military court was not convinced. Both Pezzi and Callegari were acquitted in June 1971.

In December 1972, Father Carlos Gilberto Machado Moraes was sentenced to one year in prison for a "crime" against national security: criticizing the government, the military leaders, and the rich in sermons, talks, and radio programs. Singled out was the sermon he preached on 26 July 1970, in which he criticized the popular slogan of the Médici period: "Brazil: love it or leave it." The legal document also condemned the priest's custom of wearing a red shirt in lieu of his cassock, describing him in very nonjudicial language: "He is given to parables, intelligent, slick, slippery. Deep down [he is] red and subversive."

In January 1971 a penal action of great importance—because it marked a courageous stance on the part of the church in São Paulo in the defense of human rights and of political prisoners in general—began in São Paulo with the detention of Father Giulio Vicini and of laywoman Yara Spadini. Their crimes against national security were spelled out as follows: Father Vicini carried a stencil for printing a pamphlet titled "Mass Imprisonment of Workers in Mauá and Santo André" that denounced the death under torture of worker Raimundo Eduardo da Silva; Yara Spadini had a copy of a newsletter called *Metalworkers' Struggle*.

A few days after these detentions, the recently installed archbishop of São Paulo, Paulo Evaristo Arns, was able to visit Vicini and Spadini, and he verified that they had been victims of "ignominious tortures." Cardinal Arns stated this fact in the sermon that was either read or posted in churches throughout the archdiocese on the following Sunday. With this action the São Paulo Church began to take an ever more courageous position on behalf of political prisoners and in defense of human rights in general.

Finally, this section should conclude by mentioning one of the most odious persecutions carried out against the Church in Brazil. This is the case of the court proceedings initiated in the state of Mato Grosso following numerous military operations against farm workers and religious personnel in the São Félix do Araguaia Prelacy, an area of land struggles as well as a fledgling guerrilla outpost.

The inquest was carried out by the Mato Grosso state militia. It began on 4 March 1972, one day after conflicts had taken place between homesteaders of Santa Teresinha and militiamen and hired thugs of a farm called Codeara. Before this armed conflict took place, Codeara tractors had already destroyed a medical post that was being built by homesteaders with the help of the Church.

The formal judicial procedure accused only two persons: Father François Jacques Jentel, who had lived in that area since 1955, engaging in pastoral work among Indians and homesteaders; and a Codeara manager. In May 1973 the military court sentenced the priest to ten years in prison. The case of the Codeara manager was classified as falling outside of the jurisdiction of the National Security Law. In practical terms, this decision was equivalent to an acquittal.

In May 1975, Father Jentel's defense attorneys were also able to prove that the LSN did not apply to his case. He was freed from prison and soon afterward traveled voluntarily to France to visit his relatives. When he returned to Brazil in December he was detained by the Federal Police in Fortaleza despite the fact that his passport was in order. The operation, in fact, had all the characteristics of an abduction. Father Jentel was immediately transferred to Rio, where he remained in prison at a navy unit. He was accused of having violated an "informal decree" of expulsion from Brazil.

On 15 December 1975, President Ernesto Geisel signed a decree formally expelling the priest. Soon afterward, Father François Jacques Jentel died in Europe.

TWELVE

AGAINST "SUBVERSION"

Of the legal proceedings collected by the BNM project, a final group of eighty-four cases merited the creation of a separate category from those that referred to leftist clandestine organizations or targeted social sectors. In these penal actions, the defendants were not accused because they were members of a specific clandestine political party, though they were often described as communists or as members of a somewhat vague and imaginary Communist Party. Nor were the defendants members of a single social or professional group; instead, they were drawn from many walks of life. In some of the proceedings, for example, intellectuals, peasants, students, trade union leaders, and political figures were included.

The crimes attributed to these individuals fell into three groups: activities in support of or participation in the Goulart government; the spread of "subversive propaganda"; and criticism of the authorities. A synthesis of the penal actions directed against civilians who engaged in these three targeted activities will reveal a great deal about the extent and characteristics of the repression practiced by the regime through its military courts between 1964 and 1979. Although this group is comprised of significantly fewer legal proceedings than those involving leftist parties and targeted social groups, these episodes were no less important to the overall pattern of repression.

CONNECTIONS WITH THE
DEPOSED CONSTITUTIONAL GOVERNMENT

Most of the thirty-four penal actions included in this category stemmed from the controversial "IPMs of subversion" initiated throughout Brazil after João Goulart was overthrown. These preliminary inquests allowed judicial action to be brought against the thousands of individuals who were detained in the period immediately following the coup on 1 April 1964. Since the National Security Law, which institutionalized many of the arbitrary powers claimed by the regime, was not passed until 1967, in virtually all cases the defendants were charged under a 1953 law that established criminal liability for acts against the state and the political and social order.

Overall, this punitive effort by the military government bordered on vengeance. The right of Brazilian citizens to hold opinions contrary to those of the victorious insurgents was completely abrogated. Indeed, dissent became a criminal act.

In particular, those who just weeks or months before had held important posts in the Goulart government were singled out as criminals. The proceedings charged governors, mayors, heads of public offices and government agencies, diplomatic representatives, special assistants to deposed leaders, and political figures in sympathy with Goulart's philosophy and his campaign for basic social reforms. Their "crimes" were all the activities in which they had participated in earlier years, which included promoting social change, defending the nationalization of the Brazilian economy, strengthening popular organizations, and expressing socialist ideas.

An "IPM of subversion" in the northern zone of Paraná and another investigating the government of Miguel Arraes, the militant governor of Pernambuco in the Goulart period, are typical of the investigations that led to these penal actions. Both investigated a grab bag of allegedly subversive activities: the "Groups of Eleven"; the Peasant Leagues; strikes; the distribution of nationalist or "communist" papers; the occupation of land areas; participation in trade unions; UNE-inspired student movements; and the political records of a suspect governor, state secretary, mayor, congressman, or city councilman—to name just some of those cited.

In these investigations, the defendants' political and ideological convictions were of little importance. Rather, those accused were routinely referred to as "communists," "crypto-communists," and "communist sympathizers or allies." In fact, all suspect political activities were allegedly planned by the Communist Party, which became hundreds of times more powerful in the minds of the military authorities than was in fact the case.

An IPM of subversion initiated in May 1964 typifies these investigations. Initiated in Curitiba, Paraná, the investigation expanded in the following months to include numerous neighboring cities. All individuals who had participated in political activities sympathetic to the deposed government were required to testify. Declarations were made in police departments, army units, and government offices. Six of the legal proceedings that resulted—each investigating subversion in a particular Paraná city—were directed specifically against Goulart sympathizers and activists in the deposed government. In one set alone an assortment of allegedly subversive activities were investigated: the organization of strikes; the formation of trade unions; pro-Cuba meetings and trips to that country; the constitution of the "Groups of Eleven" and connections with Leonel Brizola; invitations to the Peasant League leader Francisco Julião; propaganda in favor of agrarian reform, etc.

Investigations similar to the one focusing on the "Northern Zone of Paraná" were carried out in various counties of the states of Rio Grande do Sul and Santa Catarina. In the state of Rio de Janeiro, inquests were initiated to investigate "communizing [sic] subversive agitation" in the cities of Cachoeiras de Macacu, Campos, Santo Aleixo, Magé, Macaé, Três Rios, and Teresópolis. In addition, an extensive inquiry was initiated to investigate activities in support of Goulart and his basic reforms at the city of Rio de Janeiro Post Office and Telegraph Department.

Other inclusive inquests were initiated in the state capital cities Teresina, Belém, Florianópolis, and Curitiba. In addition, investigations were conducted in the Bahia branch of the national petroleum corporation, Petrobrás. In Natal, the capital of Rio Grande do Norte, an investigation began with the mayor and implicated municipal officials, city councilmen, and trade union leaders. In this case, the mayor was Djalma Maranhão, whom the military considered to be a communist. Djalma Maranhão was also the brother of Luiz Inácio Maranhão Filho, a known communist leader who "disappeared" in the agencies of the repression in 1974. The mayors of five other cities were also targeted in official investigations.

In view of its scope, mention should be made again of an IPM conducted in Pernambuco. State governor Miguel Arraes, who was detained immediately after the coup, was the principal defendant. In one way or another, all social conflicts that had taken place in Pernambuco during the three previous years were investigated in these proceedings, and 984 persons were forced to testify. The subversive agitation attributed to the "Communist Party that had embedded itself in the government" rendered suspect even the notable popular education campaign developed by world-renowned educator Paulo Freire. Like numerous other Brazilians forced into exile by the new regime, Freire left to avoid further persecution by the military authorities.

Finally, special mention should be made of a most vindictive and perhaps the most absurd inquest initiated during the period. The principal defendants were nine mainland Chinese who happened to be in Brazil when the coup occurred. These Chinese included a group of journalists who had been working as foreign correspondents in Brazil since December 1961; a delegation that arrived in June 1963 to organize an exposition; and a commercial mission that had been traveling in Brazil since January 1964. The defendants were accused of meeting with Brazilian communists in order to plan subversive activities, of spreading communist propaganda, and of distributing material praising the Chinese regime. The imprisonment of these Chinese, who had diplomatic credentials for their activities, provoked one of the first human rights scandals of the new regime. The violent treatment they received at the hands of the authorities made international headlines.

SUBVERSIVE PROPAGANDA

In thirty-two sets of legal proceedings, the common accusation against the defendants was that they spread "subversive propaganda." Legally, the crimes with which they were charged fell under different provisions of the National Security Law, but a philosophical constant in all the proceedings was the arbitrary and broad definition of "subversion" utilized by the authorities. That definition followed a primitive logic: "to subvert" is to seek the transformation of the existing order, and since the existing order—the military regime—represented the "will of the Nation," any effort to change that order constituted a criminal act and had to be punished.

This generic concept of subversion is referred to in some proceedings as "communist indoctrination." It appears in others as "incitement toward the class struggle," the "preaching of inter-class hatred," and "acts of adverse psychological warfare." Almost always, the accusations refer to the instigation of "animosity against the armed forces and constituted authorities." The range of activities included as subversive was wide: classroom lectures, art, the publication of certain books and magazines, the distribution of fliers, and painting slogans on walls. Significantly, only seven of these thirty-two penal actions were initiated prior to the decree of AI-5 in December 1968.

The single military court action in this group dated 1964 had as its only defendant a janitor who worked for the Institute for Retirement and Pensions of Industry Workers; he was charged with criticizing the region's plantation owners over a loudspeaker and inciting protests against them in speeches praising Fidel Castro. The following year six individuals were accused of starting a Puppet Theater that represented stories similar to those developed by the UNE Popular Center for Culture; the defendants were also accused of corresponding with their counterparts in socialist countries about their theater and other forms of cultural expression.

In October 1967 an inquest, followed by a military court trial, was begun in São Paulo against the well-known historian, publisher, and university professor Caio Prado Júnior. Two students from the school of philosophy of the University of São Paulo were named as co-defendants. In this case, the "subversive propaganda" was a student-sponsored magazine called *Revisão* (Revision), which was dedicated to theoretical debates. For simply having given an interview that appeared in the magazine, Caio Prado Júnior was sentenced by the Second Military Court in São Paulo to four years and six months in prison.

In 1968 in Rio de Janeiro, two sets of legal proceedings referred to "acts of subversive propaganda" in support of North Vietnam. Notably, the charges did not involve either the student movement or leftist organizations. In one case the three defendants were accused of painting slogans on walls reading "Long Live the Vietcong" and "The Vietcong Show Us the Way." In the other, two young men were detained for distributing pamphlets denouncing the plan of the Costa e Silva government to send Brazilian soldiers to fight with the Americans against the Vietcong.

After AI-5 was decreed at the end of 1968, this kind of repression intensified. On 19 December 1968 Professor Roberto Jorge Haddock Lobo Neto, 69, a philosophy professor at the university in São José dos Campos, was prosecuted for lectures he had given in education history. Lobo was accused of promoting Marxist-Leninist indoctrination and of attacking the Brazilian regime. On 2 January 1969 university professor and economist Jairo Simões was charged with pursuing "high power communizing action," through lectures, speeches, and activities carried out in executive and legislative positions in Bahia during 1968. Curiously, despite the charges, Simões' accusers praised his professional activities. That same year two students were charged with teaching a course in "subversive literacy training."

In July 1969 the Department for Political and Social Order in Rio de Janeiro initiated three inquests against publishers that led to military court actions. In the first inquest and trial, four individuals were accused of promoting subversive propaganda for publishing a book called *Fundamentals of Philosophy*, by the Russian author Victor Grigorievitch Afanassiev. Two of those charged were accused of having published the first translation of the book in 1963, six years earlier; the third defendant was the well-known publisher Ênio Silveira, head of the prestigious publishing house Civilização Brasileira, which had republished Afanassiev's volume in 1968; the final defendant in the case was responsible for the actual printing of the book. The second inquest and trial accused those responsible for the publication of Che Guevara's book *Textos* at the Editora Saga in Rio de Janeiro. One of the defendants was Saga's director-president, José Aparecido de Oliveira, formerly the private secretary of President Jânio Quadros, Goulart's predecessor. In the third inquest and subsequent trial, Ênio Silveira was again the defendant. Accused with him was Maia Netto, the former director of radio station Mayrink Veiga. Both were charged for publishing a book that defended pro-nationalist positions.

Also in 1969, military court proceedings initiated in Minas Gerais indicated that national security was "threatened" in the forgotten Minas town of Inhapim when a resident painted slogans all over the walls of the town, condemning the military and the local Lions Club alike by scrawling "Down with oppression" and "Down with the filthy [Lions] Society!"

By orders of the air force minister himself, an inquest was initiated on 19 November 1969 against film producer Olney Alberto São

Paulo. São Paulo was accused of violating the National Security Law with his film *Manhã Cinzenta* (Grey Morning), which showed the violent street battles between police and students in Brazil in 1968. In 1969 student Humberto Rocha Cunha, in his second year at the Amazônia agronomy school, was prosecuted for having written a paper praising mechanization and rural development in socialist countries in a course on "Practical Agricultural Activities." He was also accused of having widely distributed an open letter to school officials responsible for the course, who had not permitted him to present his paper in the classroom. Cunha was sentenced to one year in prison and forbidden to continue his studies.

Similar accusations of subversive propaganda were made in a military court proceeding that charged four individuals from Joaçaba, Santa Catarina, for criticizing the military regime of 1969 through various forms of verbal expression. In January 1970 an IPM was initiated in the Fifth Combat Engineering Battalion in Porto União, Santa Catarina. One of the defendants was charged with giving lectures on subversive topics and including in exams such questions as "Name five socialist countries" and "Who was Che Guevara?"

In May 1971 a Portuguese teacher was accused of violating the National Security Law for discussing the themes of "the proletarian woman" and "sugar production" in her classes. According to the Federal Police inquest, she was also accused of admiring Fidel Castro and Che Guevara and of lending books about socialism to her students. In April 1972 she was acquitted by a military court in Brasília. In September 1972 she was sentenced to one year in prison by the Supreme Military Court for the crime of "carrying out subversive propaganda and seeking to convince persons in workplaces and educational locales."

This kind of cultural persecution was also evident in proceedings initiated in January 1974 in São Paulo, in which educator Maria Nilde Mascellani and two collaborators were accused of publicizing a study that analyzed how the teaching of "moral and civic education"—a kind of militarized civics course—had been imposed by the military regime upon all Brazilian school curricula. The accusations demonstrated that the authorities were particularly irritated because this text had been sent to the Geneva headquarters of the World Council of Churches and to Italy.

Two other military court proceedings in this category proved conclusively that police censorship of correspondence distributed by the Brazilian postal system in fact occurred, despite the authorities' repeated assertion to the contrary. In one of the penal actions, the defendant, a social work student, was detained while mailing several letters denouncing human rights violations. In the second set of legal proceedings, both the individual who had written the suspect letter and the individual who mailed it were charged with violating the National Security Law.

This description of crimes of "subversive propaganda" will conclude with two penal actions initiated against individuals who were already in prison for political crimes. In one of these proceedings, a group of political prisoners from the Juiz de Fora penitentiary were charged with organizing "a veritable communist cell" in prison, with the help of their relatives. Through this group, the accused had allegedly practiced subversive indoctrination among the other prisoners. They were also charged with jointly writing denunciations of tortures suffered by prisoners during interrogations. The second case was initiated in August 1971, when the guards of the Tiradentes penitentiary in São Paulo confiscated books and manuscripts belonging to political prisoners. These materials were considered to be instruments of subversive indoctrination among the political prisoners themselves.

CRITICISM OF AUTHORITIES

Eighteen sets of legal proceedings were included in this group. Defendants were charged with violating national security by speaking out or holding attitudes that criticized, insulted, or attacked the constituted authorities. All of these proceedings were initiated after AI-5 was decreed. While a summary of the most representative cases will indicate that some of the alleged offenses could in fact be interpreted as insulting to an official's honor, it is nonetheless astonishing that such insults were criminally prosecuted under the National Security Law. In retrospect, it may even appear that the "insults" were praiseworthy. Be that as it may, the following summary demonstrates still another aspect of the political repression that was directed against the opponents of the Brazilian military regime. All those who opposed the status quo were considered "internal enemies." The National Security Law, which originally was intended to forestall threats against the state, became a plaything that was used by petty provincial officials to persecute their adversaries. Under the elastic concept of authority permitted by the National Security Law, even a petty bureaucrat like an employee of the highway department could claim official status and charge that he had suffered an insult. This led to the application of the law in episodes so futile and picturesque as to constitute a "folklore" of the repression.

In January 1969, for example, a farmer in Uberlândia, Minas Gerais, stopped his pickup truck at the entrance to the 36th Infantry Battalion barracks. He invited a few soldiers to go with him to his farm to eat mangos. Three months later he was accused of insulting the garrison officers during that ride to his farm and charged with defamation of the armed forces and the incitement of animosity against the superior officers of those soldiers who had accompanied him.

In June 1969 a chief inspector of the Rio state finance department complained at a monthly inspectors' meeting that a general had tried to have him sacked. The general was the president of the Rio General Committee for Investigations, charged with conducting political investigations. According to the inspector, the general sought revenge against him for having fined another military officer in the interior of the state. This same general opened an official inquest against the inspector through his investigating committee. In this case, the National Security Law and military court action were used to resolve petty conflicts, as well as to conceal the official patronage of corrupt persons.

In São Sebastião, on the São Paulo coast, a municipal civil servant denounced the mayor, who had fired him, as a thief, a swindler, and a corrupt person. Following these denunciations an inquest was initiated at the São Paulo DOPS in June 1970. The man who had been fired was accused of violating national security.

A similar "folkloric" episode took place in the state of Amazonas. This case reveals that clientelism, the traditional political patronage system in Brazil, still predominates in certain areas of the country. In August 1970, an inquest was initiated against a state legislator from the town of Manicoré. The legislator's wife, who was the town mayor, and several other members of the ARENA party were also named as defendants. All were accused of inciting demonstrations against the local judge in violation of the National Security Law. The judge, for his part, had denied a request to facilitate the registration of new voters for the upcoming elections. The demonstrations took place during the first three days of August. The judge was morally insulted and even physically attacked. In the end, he was forcibly put on a boat called "Comandante Careca" (The Bald Commander) and chased out of the town, which is so small it has no roads. This case was tried in Belém's military court.

In 1970, in the police department of Uraí, Paraná, a defendant was taken to the Paraná military court for having affirmed that an employee of the highway department had put a bus stop sign right in front of a fruit store in return for a suckling pig the proprietress offered him.

In two cases, the defendants were already political prisoners. In the course of their trial, the defendants refused to stand when the military judges entered the courtroom. When forced to do so, one of the defendants stated that he was complying only out of respect for the others present and for the Brazilian people, since he did not recognize the right of those judges to be carrying out the trial. Another penal action for contempt of authority resulted, and the defendants were sentenced to two years and six months in prison for that offense alone. In another such episode, Antonio Sérgio Melo Martins de Souza was being held in the Tiradentes penitentiary, accused of participation in the Popular Action group. During his testimony in the military court, Souza declared that the Brazilian regime was an antipopular dictatorship, subservient to capitalists and imperialists. The military judge ordered his immediate arrest—even though the defendant was already in prison—and initiated a new penal action in which the defendant was accused of "insulting the government leadership of the country and especially the president of the Republic."

PART IV

DISTORTION OF THE LAW

THIRTEEN

THE NATURE OF JUDICIAL PROCEEDINGS

IN THE course of the BNM project, it was possible to reconstruct what actually took place in the punitive legal proceedings and to compare these practices with the laws and codes of military justice that regulated inquests and the judicial process in Brazil during the repressive period. This examination indicated that both the military justice system implemented by the regime itself as well as universally accepted judicial norms were systematically violated by the Brazilian military authorities.

During the course of the military regime, the legislation regulating the conduct of police and military police inquests (IPMs), the course of judicial proceedings, and the structures of legal jurisdiction, which separated the functions of civil and military justice with respect to political crimes, was changed numerous times. For example, between April 1964 and October 1965, individuals charged with subversion could still appeal to civil courts—in most cases, directly to the Supreme Federal Court (STF). In this period, moreover, the STF courageously handed down decisions in accord with the 1946 federal constitution that was still in effect at that time. These decisions precluded the completion of hundreds of IPMs, which were dropped either before legal proceedings were formalized or before actually reaching the courtroom. Habeas corpus petitions filed by those accused of political crimes also often halted these investigations, because the authorities were incapable of sustaining any formal charges against detainees. These petitions, often filed directly with the STF, were in fact the suspects' most frequent recourse until AI-5 suspended habeas corpus for political crimes.

On 27 October 1965, AI-2 was decreed, transferring jurisdiction over all crimes against national security to the military justice system. Henceforth, civilians accused of political crimes could be prosecuted and tried by military courts. All the proceedings collected by the BNM project, therefore, were processed by the federal system of military justice as it developed under the authoritarian regime. In a few cases, short periods of civil court activity were recorded.

THE PURVIEW OF MILITARY JUSTICE

The administration of military justice was governed by the Code of Military Justice, dating from 2 December 1938. After AI-2 was decreed, this code regulated the investigations of "national security" crimes. In 1969, the governing military junta decreed a legislative package that modified the regulation of the military court system. It also decreed three all-inclusive codes: the Military Penal Code, the Military Penal Procedure Code, and the Law for Military Judiciary Organization to regulate all proceedings brought to military courts, including those generated by infringements of the National Security Law. These codes permitted relentless repression against opponents of the military regime.

The Law for Military Judiciary Organization, for example, established that a given legal proceeding would be assigned to a particular military court in accordance with the order in which it was filed, but that in cases dealing with crimes against the National Security Law, cases could be assigned to particular courts without reference to the order of receipt. This additional provision allowed courts to "specialize" in proceedings against a given political group. In this way, the system of military justice worked hand-in-glove with the repressive apparatus.

There are other examples of this collaboration. Although the illegality of double jeopardy is a universally recognized judicial norm, the Brazilian military justice system provided a mechanism whereby individuals could in effect be tried and convicted twice—and often many times—for essentially the same crime. Thus charges were divided into subaccusations, and the defendant could be penalized and sentenced for each of the infractions. For example, a person accused of belonging to an allegedly subversive group, who used a false identity, and who was detained with the organization's propaganda material in his possession, could be found guilty on three charges: membership in a clandestine party, the use of false documents, and the possession of subversive material. This subdivision of charges, common particularly in Rio de Janeiro and in Recife, violated the legal norm in Brazil that requires the "unity of proceedings based on the connection of deeds." Obviously, this subdivision allowed the military courts to mete out harsher sentences to those charged with political crimes, and defendants invariably were subject to the interpretation of the law that had the most unfavorable consequences for them.

THE POLICE PHASE:
THE MILITARY POLICE INQUEST

The objective of an inquest is to investigate crimes and those responsible for them without delay. The right of an accused person to contest charges by presenting evidence to the contrary, known in Brazilian law as the principle of "contraditório" (contradiction), is not permissible in an inquest. Strictly speaking, therefore, no defense is possible during the police stage of investigations. In the cases of political prisoners, no defense was possible for another reason as well, namely, that detainees were subjected to long periods of incommunicability, in which they were separated from all outsiders, including relatives and lawyers.

From 1969 on, police inquests of political prisoners were divided into two stages: the phase conducted in the intelligence centers known as the DOI-CODIs or in security organizations of the armed forces; and the "notary phase," when prisoners were turned over to the DOPS (Department for Political and Social Order) or the Federal Police, who then "formalized" the inquests.

In the first phase, the so-called preliminary interrogations were characterized by incommunicability and physical and mental mistreatment. In the majority of cases, not even the military courts were advised of the detentions made by security organs. In the few cases when the courts were advised, the dates of the detainments were reported incorrectly. When lawyers forced the military courts to request information from the DOI-CODIs about a certain imprisonment, a negative response was almost always given.

Forged depositions

When they were taken to military courts, many defendants denounced the fact that they were forced to sign forged depositions during the police inquest phase. This happened to teacher Luiz Andréa Fávero, 26, who testified:

> that, in said room, the interrogated was again subjected to tortures, in which Captain Júlio Mendes and Lieutenant Expedito participated; that, after those tortures, they brought a paper, rather several papers for him to sign; that, in view of the already described facts, he signed, not knowing, however, the content of said papers . . .

Quite often the defendant was not given the right to read the papers that he was asked to sign. This was the case of social worker Luiza Gilka Oliveira Rabelo, 29, who testified in Fortaleza's military court, in 1973:

> that, at the end of the interviews, Inspector Xavier presented her with a typed document for her to sign; that she was unable to read properly the content of the typed documents, because they did not allow her to do so; that she verified, however, at a first look, that the document contained horrible things not only about herself, but about other persons as well, and that those references, it seems, were about the formation of groups and activities contrary to the regime; that she signed said document in order to free herself from the vexation she was going through . . .

Journalist Nelson Luiz de Morais Costa, 22, told the council of military court judges how he was forced to sign depositions while almost out of control:

> . . . that the depositions included in the court proceedings were made under physical and moral coercion, at which time he was forced to sign several typed white papers, and that he did not know their content; that, at no time, rather, for a period of 43 days, he had no access to any lawyer, for he was in prison and incommunicado; that, at the time he signed the papers, he was incapacitated, speaking disconnected words, in an indiscriminate monologue, and that, because of this condition,

he was taken to the Souza Aguiar Hospital, where he was medicated.

The panic and fear provoked by torture led some defendants to sign whatever papers were presented to them:

> He was forced to sign pages 62 to 74 because of what some men of the Army Police said, that if he did not sign, he would have to return to the first barracks in which he had been, where he suffered ill-treatments . . .
> [João Luiz San Tiago Dantas Barbosa Quentel, 21, student, Rio, 1973.]

> He wants to add that, in reality, he made no declaration whatsoever, having limited himself to sign depositions that were presented to him . . .
> [João Henrique dos Santos Coutinho, 25, teacher, Salvador, 1972.]

Mechanical engineer Ivan Valente, 31, declared to the military court in 1977 that the parts of the proceedings presented as his deposition at the police department were in fact nothing more than a dictation made by a police officer to the notary:

> The declarations given by him in the DPPS were dictated by the police officer to the notary, in spite of his protests, at which time he received new threats to be sent back to the barracks of the Army Police; that, in spite of the way in which his declarations were taken down, he signed [the statement] because of two basic motives . . . (1) fear of being tortured again; (2) that the type of evidence obtained by the police would have no juridical value whatsoever; that, in spite of not being an expert on the subject, he was right in thinking that declarations taken under physical and moral tortures had no value in court; that, up to the 20th day after being tortured, his body showed signs of electric shocks on his hands, feet, and genital organs; . . . that he signed the declaration that was presented to him in the DPPS because he was afraid of being tortured again in the barracks of the Army Police . . .

In short, the DOI-CODIs and similar organs acted with impunity, in accordance with their own laws. They did not respect the national laws, not even the time limits established by the national security legislation for certain procedures. Persons were interrogated with hoods over their heads, while the interrogators used code names or nicknames and did not identify themselves to the prisoners. Virtually no prisoner who passed through their hands escaped torture.

When the security organs had terminated the "preliminary interrogations," the prisoner was transferred to the DOPS or to the Federal Police. At this stage, detainments were usually communicated to the military courts. After this transfer, furthermore, depositions were recorded by "notaries" who tried to maintain the essence of the confessions obtained by force at the DOI-CODI. The voluminous testimonies extracted in the "preliminary interrogations" rarely appeared in the records of inquests forwarded to the military courts. At times, torture was also carried out in the DOPS. In addition, the prisoner could be returned to the DOI-CODI for further interrogations. Often, too, further interrogation or the threat of it dissuaded the prisoner from making changes in the testimony he had given in the preliminary interrogation when presenting it again at the "notary office."

False confessions

During their testimony in military courts, many defendants who had "confessed" to crimes revealed that their depositions had been obtained under torture and were false. Their confessions were always made in order to end the violence against them.

Testifying in São Paulo in 1972, journalist Renato Leone Mohor, 30, told the military court:

> that, a certain night, he heard screams of a woman and the crying of a child mixed with intervals of music and they told him that his wife and daughter were being tortured; that, therefore, he asked that they let his wife and daughter go and that he would answer questions in the way they wanted him to, and that he invented a number of things that were included in his statements . . .

In Recife, in 1972, mechanic Leonardo Mário Aguiar Barreto, 38, testified:

that he wanted to state that his declarations on page 114 of the proceedings were false, that they were only signed by him because of the beatings and tortures to which he had been submitted ever since his detainment on 22 January of the current year; that those tortures were applied to him, in the beginning, at the DOPS, and later, at the DOI of the Second Army. Asked if he would like to be submitted to a *corpus delicti* exam, the answer was affirmative, because he suffered the fracture of two ribs which, although already fused, should reveal the bone callosity through an X-ray . . .

In a 1975 letter appended to the proceedings of his trial, 2nd sergeant of the São Paulo military police, João Buonome, described how depositions taken under torture were made to look like real manuscripts, written without coercion:

On 14 July 1975, several policemen who were detained there were taken with me to an auditorium where they were each handed a folder containing typed declarations that had been obtained in interrogations under pressures and tortures. We were instructed to copy them in our own handwriting and, later, to sign them. This was the sine qua non condition for bringing to a close that period of suffering and for being sent back to our military police unit.

An extreme case of complete abuse of authority was reported by Inês Etienne Romeu, 29, kept in a private prison in Petrópolis, in 1971:

In this phase, they increased my food, gave me clean clothes, including someone else's glasses, for I am quite nearsighted and had gone three months without wearing them. At that time I was forced to sign blank papers and to write declarations dictated by them regarding my situation, from the moment of my detainment. They also forced me to sign a "work contract" in which I promised to collaborate with security organs, in exchange for my freedom and money. There was a clause in that contract in accordance with which, if I did not carry out my part, my sister, Lúcia Etienne Romeu, would be detained because I myself, her own sister, was accusing her of being connected with subversive groups. Even that was done by my jailers; I was overcome, sick, reduced to a worm and obeyed like a puppet. Taking advantage of this, they made me accuse my sister, who never became involved in political activities, as the security organs know very well. They also made me record a tape in which I declared myself to be a paid agent of the government, and they made a movie of me counting ten cruzeiro notes after reading my "work contract." I declared in that tape that I had been well treated by my jailers. They took scenes of me dressed only with a bra and panties to show that the marks on my body resulted from a traffic accident. I don't remember everything I said, but I affirm that [the statements] were all lies and falsehoods. The answers that they forced me to give and the affirmations and gestures that they obliged me to make were previously rehearsed.[1]

It is important to emphasize that investigations carried out by the security organs were not only clandestine but illegal insofar as they violated the requirements of the military penal code. According to this code, it is the duty of the person in charge of the inquest to go to the scene of the crime, confiscate the instruments and all objects related to the events, arrest the suspect, and collect all evidence that might serve to elucidate the facts and circumstances of the crime. The only individual empowered to make arrests is the agent in charge of the inquest. However, since all these duties were carried out by the military security organs and merely formalized later by the police, the inquests initiated in this fashion had no legal validity.

Another important illegality has to do with the time limit for inquests. Military law states that inquests are to be concluded within twenty days if the indicted person is already in prison. If the person is at liberty, that period can be extended to forty days. Only in the latter case can the period of the inquest be further extended. Such an extension requires judicial authorization, and it must be made at the request of the person in charge of the inquest and before the expiration of the original inquest period. In practice, the inquests based on national security legislation were systematically extended beyond these limits. There was in fact no time limit whatsoever for the conclusion of inquests. Individuals who were abducted and detained for questioning remained in prison indefinitely.

After 1968, it was no longer possible to file a writ of habeas corpus, which would have ensured that the person held was lawfully detained, because AI-5 extinguished the right of habeas corpus "in cases of political crimes against national security, the economic and social order, and the popular economy." Without the right of habeas corpus, without the power to communicate his detainment, and without a fixed time limit for the conclusion of the inquest, the political prisoner, once inside the security organs, was absolutely defenseless, from the day he was abducted to the moment he appeared in military court. The prisoner—subjected as well to long torture sessions—had little choice but to confess everything his interrogators wished. Only after these confessions were obtained, moreover, were the inquests "legalized" and the detainments communicated to military courts.

There were other infractions of the Military Penal Procedure Code as well. For example, the law stipulates that interrogation sessions can last no more than four consecutive hours, with an obligatory rest interval of one-half hour, and that no testimonies are to be recorded after 6:00 P.M. Obviously these legal stipulations were disregarded in political investigations. Prisoners were interrogated for endless hours and deprived of rest and food. The proceedings analyzed by the BNM project mention interrogations that lasted for days without interruption.

In addition, the norms for taking a prisoner's deposition are also established by law. Two witnesses are supposed to be present throughout the interrogation. In the proceedings studied by the BNM project, the "witnesses" in the majority of cases were police agents of the investigating agency. When this practice was denounced in the military courts, the agencies which had to "legitimize" the inquests brought passersby in from the street to sign the depositions of political prisoners, without their having either witnessed the investigation or read the deposition.

It is clear, therefore, that the police inquests were characterized by many irregularities. Nonetheless, the investigations would proceed to their next phase in military courts.

THE JUDICIAL PHASE: PENAL ACTION

The indictment

Penal actions are the judicial procedures that stem from indictments and are carried out before judicial authorities. It was the judge's duty to guarantee the regularity of these proceedings, the execution of the law, and the maintenance of order. In theory, the judge had his own legitimacy and did not depend on outside authorities to carry out his functions. Furthermore, the judge was excluded from presiding over any case in which his neutrality was suspect, whether because of friendship or kinship with the defendant or because of having given an opinion or advice to the defendant or the plaintiff.

In the proceedings, the parties were to be represented by the prosecutor and by the defense attorney, on an equal basis. The prosecutor also had to maintain neutrality, since he represented the "people's case." Because "the people" did not wish to punish innocent persons, the prosecutor was entitled at his discretion to request the acquittal of the defendant. The accused had the right to be defended by a qualified lawyer. When the defendant had no lawyer of his own, the judge was to name one. The lawyers, finally, were supposed to act in accordance with their rights and obligations as contained in the statutes of the Brazilian Bar Association. In addition, they were to be independent and faithful to their profession's code of ethics.

Once an indictment was received by a military court, the accused was submitted to an interrogation before a group known as the Council of Justice, composed of four military officers and one civilian. The presiding judge was the highest-ranking officer. Military judges themselves were chosen by lot from among qualified officers, from lists submitted by the personnel departments of the three branches of the armed forces. Officers served as judges for three months, before others also chosen by lot replaced them. The civilian judge in the Council of Justice was not subject to the quarterly rotation.

What was verified during the BNM project, however, was that certain officers served on successive councils of justice with a highly improbable statistical frequency, indicating that they could not possibly have been chosen by lot. Even more incriminating was the fact that the military judges were almost always either directly or indirectly connected with the security organs.

On occasion, defendants were tried in military courts by military judges who had served as their interrogators during the investigation at the security agencies. For example, army captains Maurício Lopes Lima and Roberto Pontuschka Filho, accused of torturing political prisoners in the DOI-CODI of the Second Army in São Paulo, also served as judges during political trials in the São Paulo military courts. (Captain Pontuschka, a member of Gideons International, was known for distributing biblical texts to his victims in the DOI-CODI, during intervals between torture sessions.) It was also clear that military judges were subject to superior orders, for example, in cases in which defendants were convicted despite substantial evidence of their innocence.

Proof that the authorities took no chances of losing cases is provided by Article 73 of the National Security Law: "The prosecutor is obliged to appeal to the Supreme Military Court if 1) a judge rejects, entirely or in part, an indictment; and 2) a sentence absolving the defendant is handed down." This meant that although the prosecutor could argue for acquittal of the accused, if it were conceded, the same prosecutor was obliged to appeal the decision! Moreover, lawyers who defended political prisoners were subject to constant coercion. Some were detained, while others were prosecuted and found guilty. In other words, the traditional qualities attributed to the judiciary—impartiality, independence, and autonomy—were demonstrably absent from military courts in political proceedings. The system of military justice was designed to function as a simple extension of the repressive apparatus.

Prerequisites for indictment

The starting point for a judicial procedure was a legally valid indictment. According to Brazilian military law, an indictment was to contain specification of the judge to whom it was addressed; the name, age, profession, and residence of the accused, or an explanation why this information could not be provided; the time and place of the crime; information about the person offended and the name of the injured juridical person or institution; narration of the criminal act with a complete description of the circumstance in which it occurred; the reasons for the firm belief or the presumption of guilt; the classification of the crime; and a list of witnesses. The law further required that the indictment fully describe the way in which the accused carried out the crime, in accordance with the constitutional rule of ample defense: only when the crime and all its circumstances are clearly identified can an adequate defense be mounted.

In violation of this principle, the indictments in military courts for crimes against national security were as a rule vague and imprecise. It was said that the accused was "subversive" or had practiced "acts of subversion," but such acts were not clearly described. The witnesses listed at the end of the indictment by the prosecutor frequently declared that they did not know the facts narrated, or, at best, that they intended to testify about "what they had heard."

In brief, the indictments for crimes against national security generally did not comply with the legal requirements. In addition, they often narrated actions that were construed as crimes under national security legislation, but that were in fact the exercise of freedom of thought and opinion or the expression of legitimate social demands. Finally, the legal time limits for the preparation of an indictment— five days if the defendant were already detained and fifteen days if he were at liberty—were almost never respected by military justice. The accused were usually imprisoned and remained incarcerated for months before the indictments were formally presented.

Preventive imprisonment

The Military Penal Procedure Code permitted the individual in charge of the inquest to detain those accused of crimes against national security and to keep them incommunicado for ten days. While this arbitrary period in itself compromised an individual's right to due process, even this limit was systematically ignored in the investigations of political crimes. The detainee remained incommunicado for months, with no notification of his imprisonment sent to the appropriate judges.

Also according to the Military Penal Procedure Code, the civilian judge of the military court was responsible for ending detainments that were not communicated to him by the authority in charge of the police investigations—if he determined them to be illegal. Very rarely, however, did the judges analyze the legality of imprisonments.

Furthermore, when the official in charge of an inquest considered that it would be "inconvenient" to free a defendant, he would request that the judge decree his preventive imprisonment. According to the Military Penal Procedure Code, preventive imprisonment is to be ordered only when there is evidence of a criminal act, sufficient clues as to who committed said act, and, furthermore, a necessity to guarantee public order. The criminal potential of the accused and the certainty of the applicability of military law are also supposed to be demonstrable. In addition, the dispatch ordering or denying preventive imprisonment must always be well substantiated. Contrary to the code, however, the dispatches ordering preventive imprisonment of those accused under the National Security Law were emitted simply at the request of the police authorities.

The prisoner, for his part, according to statutes of the Brazilian Bar Association, has the right to be visited by his defender, even while held incommunicado in a police, civil, or military unit. In political cases, however, lawyers were prevented from giving professional assistance to detained clients. The rights of both the prisoner and his lawyer were thus violated, in most cases arbitrarily, demonstrating the disregard of the authorities for the constitutional principle of ample defense.

Evidence

The Military Penal Procedure Code establishes that "the judge shall form his own conviction through the free appreciation of the body of evidence collected in court. In the consideration of each piece of evidence, the judge shall compare it to all others, to verify whether there is compatibility among the various pieces of evidence presented."

The defendant's rights are guaranteed by the requirements regarding the obtaining of evidence and the principle of contradiction referred to earlier, which gives the accused the right to deny the charges against him. From a juridical point of view, evidence is the way in which the responsibility for a crime is demonstrated. All means for gathering evidence are acceptable to the justice system, as long as they do not threaten the morals, health, and security of the individual. Nonetheless, the BNM project's analysis of legal proceedings indicated that virtually all the convictions of political prisoners were based upon testimony elicited during police inquests, with all their irregularities and coercion. Evidence collected during the judicial phase of the proceedings was largely ignored in sentencing.

Furthermore, in the majority of cases involving guilty verdicts and punitive sentences, instead of the prosecution proving its allegations, the defendant had to prove his innocence. In crimes against national security, the accused was always assumed to be guilty, and never given the benefit of the doubt. When the court was in doubt, the defendants were found guilty. This practice ran counter to the fundamental legal principle that places the burden of proof on the accuser, explicitly stated in Article 296 of the Military Penal Procedure Code.

A final observation about the use of evidence in these proceedings can be made. The code classifies as inadmissible evidence produced by spouses, descendants or forebears, or siblings. Such evidence is considered immoral and useless for juridical purposes. The legal proceedings studied, however, include numerous inquests in which spouses and relatives accused one another and many in which implicated individuals accused each other. This kind of evidence was obviously collected under torture, in interrogations which produced all manner of reckless charges. Yet the military courts did not declare this evidence invalid. On the contrary, individuals were sentenced on the basis of just this "evidence."

Confession

The Military Penal Procedure Code stipulates that the court can consider as evidence only that which was produced or repeated in court. Even for the military justice system, therefore, the interrogation of the accused in court is an essential element of the proceeding. The accused is not obliged to answer any questions formulated by a judge, although his silence might count unfavorably. The law establishes, furthermore, that the accused shall be asked only about facts included in the indictment.

In the military courts, however, those accused for political reasons were subjected to extensive interrogations that were not limited to matters contained in the indictments. Interrogations examined the items included in the police inquests and even probed into the philosophical, religious, and ethical concepts of judges and defendants. At times, a climate of coercion was established in the military court itself. There were moments, for example, when the judges, dissatisfied with answers given by the defendant, would qualify them as false before any verdict had been reached.

In addition, when military justice had to choose between defendants' answers obtained by the police and those given in court, priority was given to the information provided by the police, despite the fact that the confessions the police or security agents extracted from defendants had no legal validity. To be considered as evidence a confession must be made before competent authorities, it must be freely and spontaneously given, it must deal with the principal facts of the case, and it must be credible and compatible with all other evidence in the proceedings. Confessions obtained in the security agencies obviously did not meet these conditions. The police agents could not be legitimately considered competent authorities, because their names did not appear in inquests, they did not identify themselves to their prisoners, and they almost always used false names. Defendants' testimony was clearly not free or spontaneous. Furthermore, confessions were often not credible, since many times prisoners were forced to agree with prior information the authorities had collected about them. Finally—and this is a crucial point—confessions gathered by the police were not compatible with all other judicial evidence. In court, in the presence of his lawyer, it was possible, although difficult, for the defendant to deny or retract his extrajudicial confession and recount how it had been obtained.

Nonetheless, such retractions were considered by the judges as one more sign that the accused was guilty. For the military courts, the defendant's retraction of confessions given to the police and also the revelation of the methods by which such confessions were obtained were simply part of the defense strategy that attempted to malign the security organizations and the military regime through denunciations of torture.

Evidence by experts

The Military Penal Procedure Code regulates the use of evidence by experts. Article 330 makes mandatory a *corpus delicti* examination to prove the existence of a crime against a person. The examination can also exhume a corpse or identify the victim through other means. In the event of the victim's death, an autopsy is mandatory.

However, examination by experts carried out for penal actions against political prisoners served other purposes. The results of the examinations were manipulated to incriminate the accused, but never to favor the defense. For example, whenever examinations of defendants for bodily lesions were requested to prove that they had been tortured, the results were negative: either the doctors appointed by the court to conduct the examinations were in the service of the repressive apparatus or the marks of torture had disappeared by the time the examination was conducted. Autopsies of persecuted political figures were prepared so that they agreed with the official versions of the deaths released by the authorities.

The code also stipulates that "the judge shall not be bound by the medical report, and he may reject it entirely or in part." This releases the judge to form his own opinion about the proceedings in light of all the evidence. Nonetheless, military justice accepted without question the negative conclusions of medical examiners about the existence of bodily lesions on defendants, as well as autopsy reports that confirmed the official versions of how political prisoners had died. These conclusions were considered incontrovertible evidence that took precedence over all other testimony, especially over the denunciations made by defendants while on trial.

Evidence by witnesses

The Military Penal Procedure Code regulates the production of evidence by witnesses. Persons who give false depositions are to be charged for giving false testimony. However, this regulation was often violated, since witnesses for the prosecution were as a rule agents of the security organs or persons called in to sign depositions who had not witnessed the police interrogation of those accused. The code also stipulates that witnesses who claim to know nothing about the facts narrated in the indictment shall not have their declarations taken into account by the judges. Moreover, a witness is forbidden from expressing his personal opinion, unless it is inseparable from the narration of facts. Nonetheless, the BNM research verified that witnesses for the prosecution were allowed to give their opinions, but that witnesses for the defense were not.

The BNM project also examined the question of the identification of persons. According to the penal code, the witness should describe the person he is identifying, and the person to be identified should be placed side by side with others who have similar physical traits, whereupon the person making the identification must point him out. The code also recommends that in order to avoid intimidation or any other influence, the person making the identification should not be seen by those in the line-up.

In the legal proceedings studied, however, there was a total disregard for these legal formalities regulating the identification of persons. As a rule, the person to be identified was placed alone in a room, and the individual who was supposed to identify him was pressured by the authorities into making the identification. Although these identifications were revealed as worthless when questioned in court, the judges nonetheless used them in finding the defendants guilty and in determining their sentences.

Confiscations

According to the military legislation, those in charge of inquests are allowed to seize only those goods that were acquired with illegally obtained funds or that are important in continuing investigations. The rules regulating such confiscations are clearly established.

Persons detained by the security forces, however, routinely had their property seized and distributed among those who had abducted them. The homes of abducted persons were invaded and sacked. Clothing, household appliances, cash, and personal objects were taken. When persons were freed after being interrogated, they did not recover their property.

Documentary evidence

The Military Penal Procedure Code stipulates that any public or private written or printed matter relevant to the facts being investigated is admissible as documentary evidence.

In the legal proceedings studied by the BNM project, documents were frequently attached to the records as if they had been confiscated from the accused and proved their culpability. When the defendants were interrogated, however, it became clear that many of these documents did not in fact belong to them. Apparently security agents had placed them in the court records to influence the judges. Those documents that the defendants did claim as their own, moreover, were not admissible evidence. Eventually it was established through litigation that the simple possession of allegedly subversive material is not a crime, nor does it constitute proof of guilt.

THE JUDICIAL PHASE: SENTENCING AND APPEALS

When members of the councils of justice were sworn in, they took the following oath of office: "I promise to evaluate impartially the facts that are submitted to me and judge them in accordance with the law and the evidence of the court proceedings." Nonetheless, it is evident that the councils did not comply with this oath. Inquests marked by coercion; confessions obtained through torture; vague, general, and imprecise indictments; and councils of justice working hand-in-glove with the repressive forces—all led to sentences clearly marked by injustice, illegality, and sometimes absurdity.

After 1969, military councils were empowered to lend to the judged fact "a juridical definition different from the one contained in the indictment, even though that might mean the application of a stiffer penalty." This provision allowed military courts to hand down sentences, without supporting evidence, that were colored by a strong ideological position presuming the guilt of the defendants. Many of the sentences meted out were in fact based exclusively on the inquest, and ignored evidence presented in court that undermined the case against the accused.

Finally, the penal code requires that aggravating or attenuating circumstances should be taken into account in calculating the length of the sentence. These factors include the gravity of the crime, the personality of the defendant, the intensity of the malice involved, the circumstances of time and place, the background of the defendant, and his behavior during the proceedings. Study of the military court proceedings, however, revealed that sentences were arbitrarily determined. In general, ameliorating factors were ignored while aggravating factors were emphasized.

Both the defense and the prosecution could appeal decisions made by the councils of justice in the lower military courts to the Supreme Military Court (STM). A comparison of the sentences of the lower military courts and the appeals decisions showed that, as a general rule, the STM sustained convictions. The only modification seemed to be a superficial reduction of penalties applied by the lower courts.

As noted above, the legislation of the military regime required prosecutors to appeal to the Supreme Military Court each time a defendant was acquitted, in spite of the fact that both the councils of justice and the prosecutors were so linked to the security organs that they were not likely to set any defendants free. In any case, the STM was charged with preventing any liberal gestures that might—at least in the eyes of the regime—have compromised national security.

There were some episodes, however, in which the STM adopted a posture that was more independent and liberal than that of the lower military courts. On occasion, some STM ministers did contest their colleagues, writing minority opinions which defended legality and even contained courageous condemnations of torture.

More frequently, however, the STM covered up the irregularities practiced by the military justice system in political cases. The prosecution was favored, while decisions detrimental to the defense were routine. For example, the defense was required to present its "reason for appeal" before the prosecution presented its case. The defense was also barred from secret sessions attended by the prosecutor and the STM ministers in which the court decisions were reached.

Finally, the Supreme Military Court decision could be appealed to the Supreme Federal Court, which is the country's highest court of justice, and a civil court as well. Among the proceedings collected by the BNM project, there were relatively few that reached the Supreme Federal Court. The decisions in the cases were mixed. More liberal and juridically defensible positions were found, along with those that implicitly defended the irregularities described here. Overall, it could be concluded that the decisions of the Supreme Federal Court varied in accordance with the political situation of the regime. During the first years after the military coup, for example, the Supreme Federal Court repeatedly disagreed with the decision of the military courts. It disavowed the attitudes of the military officers in charge of the IPMs, and it sought to protect the constitutional rights of citizens and avoid the arbitrary exercise of power.

In important cases of political persecution, such as those involving deposed Pernambuco governor Miguel Arraes, former president Juscelino Kubitschek, deposed governor Mauro Borges of Goiás, Peasant League leader and former federal congressman Francisco Julião, journalist Carlos Heitor Cony, and Father Tomás Domingo Rodrigues, as well as trade unionists, students, and many others, the Supreme Federal Court issued memorable decisions that defended citizens' rights. Particularly significant during this period was the Court's receptivity to writs of habeas corpus filed on behalf of the persons implicated in IPMs or on behalf of defendants in court proceedings that had already begun. These writs allowed some who were detained to be freed, transferred some charges to civil courts, guaranteed the right of special jurisdiction in some cases, and stopped penal actions when no crime could be established.

Castello Branco, the first military president, empowered by the early institutional acts, forced several members of the Court into premature retirement in order to appoint others more in sympathy with the military regime. As this chapter makes clear, the military justice system was further strengthened when, with the exception of final appeals that could be made to the Supreme Federal Court, military courts were given exclusive jurisdiction over crimes against national security.

FOURTEEN

SIX SAMPLE CASES

THE purpose of this chapter is to present selected cases that demonstrate the behavior of the Brazilian judiciary and the judicial system in the 1964–79 period. In particular the cases illustrate judicial attitudes regarding both traditional legal norms and the system of exceptional national security legislation imposed after 1964.

NINE YEARS IN THE SOVIET UNION: PROOF OF INTENTION TO COMMIT AN OFFENSE

In 1972, Thomás Antônio da Silva Meirelles Netto was sentenced to three years and six months in prison for "constituting, becoming a member of, or maintaining an organization of a military type, for purposes of combat."

The evidence against the accused consisted of his deposition, given in the course of a police inquest, and documents confiscated from his residence. Although the deposition had been interpreted as a confession by police authorities, it was retracted in court by the defendant, who stated that he had been forced to sign it under coercion and violence. That left the confiscated documents as the only solid evidence in the case. Yet the court records showed that the confiscation was witnessed only by the police officers themselves, in violation of the legal requirement that two persons who were not involved in the incident act as witnesses to the confiscation and sign a document to that effect.

In view of the weak evidence presented, the guilty verdict and sentence lent great importance to the fact that the defendant had "spent nine years in Russia." The military prosecutor also stressed that fact in his opinion, adding that "Russia is the cradle of international communism." When the case was appealed to the Supreme Military Court, the crime was reclassified as coming under a law prohibiting "affiliation with or maintenance of an organization with foreign help." The basic argument of the higher court stated:

> The retraction [of the defendant's deposition] does not have the force of evidence, especially because in his residence a copious amount of subversive material was confiscated, including maps and armaments. It should also be added that the defendant lived in Russia for nine years, where he surely . . . received instruction for the practice referred to in the court records.

Even though the STM reduced the defendant's sentence, it also justified his conviction on the basis of the nine-year residence in the Soviet Union.

SILENCE OF THE COURT IN THE FACE OF AN INVALID PROCEEDING

On 13 August 1971, the São Paulo Second Army Court notified the lawyer representing Dominican friars accused of connections with the clandestine organization National Action for Liberation that a court session was scheduled for August 19th, and that the defense was invited to present witnesses. Since the accused Dominicans were in the Tiradentes penitentiary, however, it was difficult for the lawyer to contact his clients in order to find out whom they wished to call before the court. The lawyer therefore requested an extension of the time period before the court session was convened. Although the prosecutor agreed to the defense attorney's request, the military court rejected it unanimously.

In addition, the defense also requested a meeting between two of the defendants because, according to the opinion of the military court, the declaration of one of the priests was an "astounding piece of evidence" against the other. This request was also denied.

In short, the defendants lost their right of defense, even though it was guaranteed under military law. The upshot of the proceedings was the conviction of the Dominican friars in the lower military court. The defense appealed to the Supreme Military Court with a preliminary request that the case be nullified in view of the flagrant violation of the constitutional right to ample defense. The STM, however, upheld the decision of the lower court and did not even mention the illegality in the proceedings. An appeal was made subsequently to the highest court in Brazil, the Supreme Federal Court, which also upheld the conviction in a unanimous vote and did not mention the constitutional issue.

In accordance with the legislation then in effect, both the military and the civilian high courts should have declared the proceedings null and void from the moment when the right of defense was denied. In addition to being prevented from presenting witnesses, the defense was impeded from clarifying conflicting points in the prosecution's evidence.

DECISION BASED ON A MILITARY POLICE INQUEST

João Henrique Ferreira de Carvalho, accused of belonging to a clandestine organization, was convicted in 1974 and sentenced to one year in prison. The prosecutor, however, did not present any evidence in court for the indictment. The defendant appealed to the Supreme Military Court, arguing that his conviction was illegal because it was based entirely upon the proceedings of a Military Police Inquest (IPM). According to the Military Penal Procedure Code, the sole purpose of the IPM is to furnish material on which the military prosecutor can base his proposal for a penal action.

Nonetheless, the STM ministers unanimously ignored the argument for the defense and upheld the lower court's decision. The defendant then appealed to the Supreme Federal Court, reiterating the argument that the prosecution had presented no evidence for the indictment. The attorney general for the republic admitted that "in fact, only in the police inquest is there evidence against the defendant, but in accordance with the repeated decisions of the Court, it is meritorious evidence." The ministers' unanimous opinion read:

> In accordance with the principle of free conviction, based upon the examination of the body of evidence, that conviction based on police recommendation and not revoked by evidence col-

lected in the judicial proceedings is legitimate, because the judge's conviction is based on the reality of facts impartially collected, and not on the place where the collection of evidence takes place.

The law, however, clearly states that "the judge shall sentence defendants by the free appreciation of the body of evidence *collected in court.*" This condition guarantees the right of an indicted person to contest in court accusations made in the police inquest, where he is totally at the mercy of interrogators. In a public court session the defendant is not threatened by prison guards, and his lawyer is present as well. The Supreme Federal Court decision in this case demonstrated that the legal proceedings—that is, the judicial phase of the penal action—were in fact a mere accessory to the inquest. The decision therefore established that the military courts were simply instruments to confirm police findings.

"IN DUBIO PRO CONDEMNATIO"

Professor Guilherme Simões Gomes, of Ribeirão Preto in the state of São Paulo, was accused in 1969 of crimes including the practice of acts for the provocation of a revolutionary war, connection with a military-type organization or reorganization of a prohibited political party, the spreading of subversive propaganda, and possession of armaments to be used exclusively by the armed forces.

In finding the defendant guilty, São Paulo's Second Military Court nonetheless admitted that there was no certainty regarding the case:

> Although the participation of the defendant in the facts [of the case] is very strange, if his claims in court are to be considered true, the Council finds itself, with reference to this defendant, in a situation of definite doubt, which should weigh in his favor.

The decision recognized, also, that the "confession given to the police, in circumstances unclear to the court," was the only element favoring conviction in the case. Despite that admission, the court went on to challenge the defendant's courtroom declarations, asserting what are clearly its own opinions about a publication with which the accused was associated:

No one in Ribeirão Preto, especially in student circles, could
be totally unaware of the bizarre, cynical, slimy, and provoc-
ative content of *O Berro* (The Shout).

Furthermore, the court convicted the professor on the basis of the
testimony of another defendant in the same case:

The defendant's affirmation is, however, unacceptable [in view
of] the declaration made by A. . . . in court, which clarifies
that the professor "FURNISHED 50 CRUZEIROS PER MONTH TO
HELP THE PAPER *O BERRO*, DOING THIS FOR EIGHT
MONTHS." . . . The crime stipulated in Article 45, Item I, of
Decree-law 898/69 has been proved, with relationship to this
accused person—subversive propaganda. It is the decision most
favorable to him, in the context of the facts that have been
reported here.

Thus the professor was sentenced to one year in prison, despite the
fact that doubt regarding his guilt was admitted in the court's opinion. Worse yet, the military court also recognized the claims of a
co-defendant, violating the traditional consensus among jurists and
the considerable body of legal precedents which establish that the
declaration of a co-defendant cannot be taken in good faith and is
insufficient grounds for a conviction. In this case, the council of
military court judges not only disregarded its own doubts but also
utilized evidence that it recognized as invalid. This decision inverted
the legal principle accepted by all civilized nations: *In Dubio Pro
Reo*.

CONTINUOUS PERSECUTION
TO INCRIMINATE DEFENDANT

In November 1974, the Supreme Federal Court nullified the trial
in which Olderico Campos Barreto was convicted for violating an
article of the law different from the article on which his indictment
was based.

The indictment charged the defendant under Articles 25 and 33
of Decree-law 898/69 with "acts to provoke revolutionary war and
with the use of violence for reasons of socio-political non-conform-
ity." The conviction imposed by the military court in Salvador,

Bahia, considered that Barreto's crime was really one described in a different article of the same law: "to reorganize, in another form, a party prohibited by law." Barreto was thus convicted of a crime of which he had not been accused in the indictment, and in regard to which, therefore, he could not defend himself.

The Supreme Military Court had examined the same proceedings, confirmed the sentence, and rejected the arguments of the defense in favor of voiding the conviction. Then the case was brought before the Supreme Federal Court, which did nullify the trial. This led the military court to try the defendant again, this time examining only those crimes that had been mentioned in the original indictment. In May 1975 Barreto was acquitted. The Bahia state military prosecutor subsequently appealed the acquittal to the Supreme Military Court, which sentenced the defendant to five years in prison.

Once again an appeal was made to the Supreme Federal Court, which reestablished the acquittal of the defendant. Not to be thwarted, the military prosecutor presented yet another indictment to the military court. On this occasion, Barreto was accused of membership in the clandestine 8th of October Revolutionary Movement.

On 14 March 1979, on the eve of the inauguration of João Baptista de Figueiredo as president of Brazil, and with the liberalization in full swing, the Supreme Military Court rejected a habeas corpus petition filed by the defendant. Barreto escaped a third round of trials based on the same set of circumstances only because the Amnesty Law was passed in August 1979. Under the amnesty, he was no longer legally responsible for political crimes.

In this case, the military court system managed to keep the defendant *sub judice* for eight years. He was imprisoned during most of that time. For eight years, the military justice system searched for a way to incriminate the defendant. This persecution in itself constituted punishment.

SUBVERSION OF JUDGMENT

Santana de Jaguaiba is a small town in the state of Rio de Janeiro, inhabited by impoverished peasants. There is virtually no public assistance. In 1968, Father Gerson da Conceição served as the local parish priest. Within two years, with the help of the people, he had built six churches and a school in the town. This work drew the attention of authorities, and the priest and several peasants were soon charged with subversion.

In the 3rd Army Court, in Rio de Janeiro, the military prosecutor declared that the priest indoctrinated peasants because he taught that:

> there are two classes in our Country, that is dominant classes and dominated classes; that agrarian reform should be on socialist terms, and not the one promoted by the Brazilian Institute for Agrarian Reform; that they should use force to overthrow the Government; that they should follow Cuba's example, whose people live in freedom, and that this struggle was not only here but in all the world.

The prosecutor added that in 1968 the priest had participated in guerrilla exercises carried out in the region called "Mata do Marino," for the purpose of preparing participants for armed warfare. According to the prosecutor, the priest

> became a member of the subversive organization VAR-Palmares, whose objective is the overthrow of the constituted government, through violent methods, in order to open the way for the socialization of Brazil . . .

For these activities, the priest and other defendants were charged under laws that criminalized membership in a subversive movement and that made it an offense to entice others into subversive activity. In the course of the proceeding it was proved that the "training of guerrillas" was nothing more than a hunting session, common in that region. Father Gerson's lawyer revealed in court the tortures suffered by the defendants while they were detained in an army unit. All defendants denied the accusations in military court. Father Gerson added, in his deposition, that he belonged to the "idealist" line of the Church, which was committed to social work among the poor. Even so, the priest was sentenced to one year in prison, because "the activities of the defendants are in reference to an organization which, with foreign help, upholds the subversion of the political and social order, by violent means."

An appeal was made to the Supreme Military Court, which affirmed that the priest, in the deposition he made to the person in charge of the inquest, had confessed "the criminal occurrence in detail." The ministers also affirmed that, in those same declarations, the priest "finally confessed that his deposition was given in a spontaneous way and without any coercion."

The court's decision transcribed sections of the opinion of the attorney general for military justice. After criticizing Father Gerson's behavior as a priest, the attorney general accused him of being "mixed up with a bunch of subversives and communists." He also stated that the priest "divorced himself from Holy Scriptures and the commandments of the Lord," especially the commandment to "love one another as I have loved you."

The Supreme Military Court decided to acquit the peasants, because

> it is evident that they are simple-minded men, with little knowledge, easily enticed by Father Gerson. It might be said that the defendant contradicted himself before the Council but, in truth, he testified that he belongs to another flank of the Church, that is, to the IDEALIST, which really makes one wonder. . . . In truth, Gerson da Conceição does not carry, within his bosom, the celebrated Alter Ego and, of Christianity, little or no profession of faith does he nourish, in view of the fact that he has withdrawn from the supporting column of the philosophy of Christ: *Whatever you wish that men would do to you, do so to them.* Or does not Father Gerson da Conceição belong to the true Church of Peter, the only one, indivisible and universal? If he did, would it not be more noble that his "apostleship" be another one, rather than this one which is so different from mystical meaning of the term sacrifice? Or, even, between the sanctifying devotion of his priesthood and the ignominious stigma of *homo sacer,* would he have preferred, sacrilegiously, to repudiate the former and remain with the latter? Without any doubt, finally, the behavior of Father Gerson da Conceição, affiliated with the doctrinal system of a subversive organization, at the service of the Communist Party, is of such an order that it would cause to tremble the flaming sword in the right hand of the statue of Doctor Evangelicus at his grave . . .

If the Supreme Military Court had adhered strictly to the law, its decision could not have included speculation about doctrinal matters of the Church. The court's judgment was more against the role of the Church than against the individual priest's behavior. Yet an individual's choice of beliefs and teachings has no place in a court of law. Whether or not one is a communist is equally irrelevant. The law cannot punish ideas, for it is only empowered to deal with actions or omissions that may constitute a crime. In this case, what should have been considered were the facts. Neither the indictment nor the sentence describes what actions were practiced by the defendants and how they may have justified the priest's conviction. In the final analysis, the priest was convicted for the way in which, guided by his conscience, he had decided to exercise his ministry.

PART V

"THIS IS WHERE WHERE HELL IS . . . "

FIFTEEN

THE HOUSES OF HORROR

IN THE special language of political militants, houses, farms, or apartments designated as hiding places were known as "aparelhos," from the Portuguese word for "apparatus" or "device."

The repressive system also made use of "aparelhos," private prisons where political detainees were held following their abductions. These torture centers, where many prisoners were killed, allowed the security agencies to conduct their work beyond the reach of the law. Those who did survive their passage through the "aparelhos" found it very difficult to identify them later, since hoods were placed over their heads during their stay. Only a few individuals were permitted to see the torture chambers, and fewer still were able to commit to memory details such as access roads or time elapsed between geographical points en route that would have allowed them to identify precisely the *aparelhos* of the repressive system.

Bank worker Gil Fernandes de Sá, 29, detained in Fortaleza, Ceará, testified to the military court in 1973:

> that from the barracks . . . he was taken in a red station wagon, lying down on the floor, to a place distant from the city, about an hour's trip; . . . that the police told him that they were taking him to a house called "the house of horrors"; that when he got there he realized that it was a serious thing because he heard screams and groans . . .

The existence of that particular clandestine prison was confirmed the same year through the testimony of businessman Geraldo Magela Lins Guedes, 24:

> After arriving here in Fortaleza, the station wagon was driven for about an hour until it finally arrived at a place unknown to the defendant; that at this place he was taken to the upper floor of the building where the flooring was made of wood; . . . that on this top floor he saw and heard persons being tortured; . . . that during the time in which he remained in that unknown place he saw all kinds of torture, and heard screams and noises resulting from the application of beatings and other ill treatments; that during the night he would go down to the ground floor to lie down in a long room that gave the impression that this was a house in the country, because on this ground floor there were old tires, ears of corn, straw mats, fuel cans . . .

Given the fact that prisoners were taken blindfolded to this mysterious place, the location was difficult to identify precisely even though they were allowed to see the prison once inside. This is confirmed by the testimony of pharmacist José Elpídio Cavalcante, in 1974:

> that from those barracks he was taken by the police, with a hood over his head, to a place outside the city; that he noticed a change in climate when he left the city limits; that this house is surrounded by a high wall; that when he arrived there the defendant was taken to the upper floor of the building; . . . that he heard from another policeman the explanation that "THIS IS NOT THE ARMY, [THE] NAVY OR THE AIR FORCE; THIS IS WHERE HELL IS" . . .

Student Ottoni Guimarães Fernandes Júnior, 24, described to the 1st Court of the Air Force, in 1974, what happened to him after he was detained in Rio de Janeiro by a security team commanded by police officer and notorious torturer Sérgio Paranhos Fleury:

> that he was taken to a private house located in São Conrado [an outlying district of Rio]; that the defendant was taken from the vehicle handcuffed, with his eyes blindfolded and his feet also tied; that the defendant was carried and noticed that they

were descending a steep staircase with about forty steps; that
the house in question had two floors; that on the upper floor
there was a porch and that the rear part of the house was backed
up to a stone mountain; that the bathroom was located on the
lower floor with the stone mountain serving as one of its
walls; . . . that it was a high class residence in colonial style
that was uninhabited at the time because neither the electricity
nor the water were connected; and that he could see the National Hotel from the porch . . .

Testifying before Rio's military court system in 1972, bank worker
Inês Etienne Romeu, 29, reported the existence of another such
house:

She was [held] one hundred days in a private prison where she
was submitted to coercions and tortures of a physical, psychological, and moral order . . .

Ten years later, Romeu distributed to the press a detailed account
of her detention. It included a description of the place in Petrópolis,
a city in the mountains near Rio, where she had been held:

Arriving at the place, a fine-looking house, I was placed on an
army cot that was marked with the initials CIE, where the
interrogation continued. . . . They would put me on the humid
cement floor completely naked, early in the morning before
dawn when the temperature was quite low. [1]

She was later able to ascertain that the house was owned by Mario
Lodders and located at No. 120 Arthur Barbosa Street.
    Hairdresser Jussara Lins Martins, 24, also referred to a house in
Petrópolis when, in 1972, she testified in the Minas Gerais military
court:

that she was sent to Guanabara where she was submitted to
torture again, this time in a house that she believes to be located
on the way to Petrópolis, and that she remained there for a
period of four days . . .

The magistrate of the military court in Juiz de Fora, in the state
of Minas Gerais, ordered into court records the following testimony

of photographer-reporter José do Carmo Rocha, 39, interrogated in 1976:

> that he was detained in his residence in the morning by several armed men, approximately six, and taken to an unknown place; that he remained nine days in that place after which he was interrogated at the Federal Police department; that when he was detained in that unknown place, he was beaten; . . . that after testifying at the Federal Police department he was taken back to the place from which he had come before, where he remained two more days . . .

Several sets of military court proceedings registered that the military school in Belo Horizonte, an educational institution for minors, was utilized for torture. José Antônio Gonçalves Duarte, 24, a teacher, testified in military court in 1970:

> that after this episode he was taken to the Military School where he was submitted to tortures on the "parrot's perch," where he also saw defendant Neuza being tortured in the same way . . .

His testimony is confirmed in the deposition of sociologist Neuza Maria Marcondes Viana de Assis, 33, given in 1970:

> The defendant, when taken inside the wooded area of the Military School to be placed on the parrot's perch, saw that José Antônio Gonçalves Duarte was tied there and being beaten with a whip on his back . . .

The 1970 testimony of Lamartine Sacramento Filho, 28, a professor, also supports the charge that the educational institution was used for repressive activities:

> that after that period he was taken to the Military School where he was interrogated without any of the authorities making official note of his declarations, during which he was threatened with torture; that after this he was transferred to Neves where he spent approximately 40 days, during which time he was brought back to the Military School once in a while to be interrogated; that during the last times in which he was at the Military School he signed several depositions . . .

The most significant depositions about the private prisons of the "clandestine arm of repression" in São Paulo were made in 1975.

Journalist and salesman Renato Oliveira da Motta, 59, wrote in a letter included in court records:

> The building had several rooms but I was able to observe the existence of only three: a room approximately 4 x 4 square meters, with a closet where torture instruments and clothes were kept. It had a window that gave the impression that the house was located on a large tract of land, although [it was] not very far from the road. There was a smaller room that was used as an office; next to it there was a bedroom which could be reached through the kitchen. It had a sealed window and two large rectangular cement blocks on the floor. One of the blocks had a metal ring attached to its side; on the other, there were two rings for holding the feet of prisoners. In the small room there was a radio and a record player being tuned alternately to their highest volume. . . . The unfinished house had no electricity. Sometimes there was no water. For illumination they used gas lamps that were placed upon pedestals two meters high. The food was prepared by the same individuals who tortured. . . . On 17 May I was finally transferred to another place. They blindfolded me with wide adhesive tape and dark glasses. They drove for hours on end in unending circles until we came to a residence. In order to reach the main part of the house there was a staircase. The house had electricity and a complete bathroom and a radio transmitter, as in the other place. In the room that served as my prison cell there was a table and a bed. There was also a block of cement similar to those already described. There was a small opening near the ceiling for air to enter.

Store clerk Ednaldo Alves Silva, 31, refers to a similar location, according to a letter of his that was included in the military court proceedings. After being detained on 30 September 1975 by a group of men who abducted him in downtown São Paulo, he was forced to enter a Volkswagen and was taken to a place where his black hood was changed for dark glasses. Then the trip continued:

> We drove a lot. At a certain point I perceived that we were on a highway and that there was a problem of tolls. That was when they warned me to remain quiet and not move or else

they would shoot me. . . . I now perceived that those who were
transporting me were not the same ones who had abducted me
from the street. . . . After a trip of an hour and a half or two
hours, I felt by the absence of traffic and because we were on
an unpaved road that we had left the main highway. The car
stopped soon afterwards. They made me get out and I was
taken to a house that I judge to be located far from an inhabited
place. . . . They immediately took me down a staircase and
when we arrived at a room with coarse cement flooring they
began to beat me savagely. . . . After that they guided me up
the stairs and through a corridor [until] we came to a small
room. They placed an iron ring on one of my wrists and another
on one of my ankles which were connected to chains anchored
on a bed with a straw mattress without a sheet. . . . [To give
you] an idea about my condition, the first impression I had
was that I was hearing my own screams. But as I returned to
reality I perceived that other persons like myself were victims
of that authentic hell.

Lawyer Affonso Celso Nogueira Monteiro, a former city councilman
and congressman, wrote a letter on 26 October 1975, in the third
person, describing the tortures he suffered in the place described
above. The site appeared to be a rural property with many refine-
ments. His letter was included in the military court proceedings:

A trip was begun that lasted something like an hour, about ten
minutes in the city, half an hour on a highway with intense
traffic, and twenty minutes on an uphill unpaved road, with
irregular soil, full of curves and that crossed a railroad, a fact
indicated by the coincidence of a train going by. . . . When
he arrived at his destination he was taken out of the car by
someone who called him by name and told him that he was a
captive of the "clandestine arm of government repression" from
which no one could rescue him and that his hour had come.
He was then taken over a lawn to a cemented sidewalk, after
which there [was] a staircase that goes down four steps at a
right angle to a room they called the "hole" where they placed
him facing a corner of the wall. . . . He felt that the cement
floor was muddy and slippery and that the walls were humid
with flaking plaster that fell apart as he tried to lean upon
them. He therefore imagined that this was an underground
place. . . . He was taken to a room with a wooden tile floor,
once again going over the cement sidewalk and the lawn and

entering into a building, going up stairs and through corridors that turned at right angles. . . . He was once again taken to [be] tortured, now in the open air without a parrot's perch but with a new method consisting in hanging the victim by his feet while maintaining his arms suspended. . . . After being let down, they asked him if he knew how to swim and informed him that he would take a bath under a waterfall and then in the river. The first bath consisted in being laid down and kept in that position on the bottom of a shallow creek whose waters suddenly increased in volume and force, causing imbalance and friction of his body on the rocks, thereby worsening the injuries and the pain. In the river the victim was tied by the waist and pushed into a deep well or small cemented swimming pool with a slick bottom where several men entertained themselves with laughter and "smart" commentaries while forcing him into successive submersions to the end of his presumed resistance. . . . After remaining in that place for a period of time which he cannot estimate precisely due to his isolation and lack of usual information, he was informed that he was going to be transferred to another place, handcuffed and blindfolded, which was done in a trip that took about an hour. When he came to the new place they put him in a room built with cement and lighted by electricity, without direct ventilation, since the small opening near the ceiling of the back wall, measuring approximately 30/30 centimeters, was constantly closed. . . . So that his status as prisoner should not be forgotten, however, chains once again held one of his legs permanently to his bed and, in one of the corners of the room, there were two cubic blocks of cement with rings. . . . Under these new conditions he was able to restructure himself in relationship to time and space. He then concluded that the place where he had been was in a rural area, located in the midst of the woods, where birds could be heard and, occasionally, the sound of rain or wind in the trees, and whose only reference to the city was a periodic arrival of cars almost always followed by the screams of those who were being tortured. In the present place, it was evident to him that it was in a suburban area, for he could hear cars and even buses going by regularly.

Later the press found out that that rural property was a small farm in the Emburra district of Parelheiros, in the Greater São Paulo area. The entrance was marked "Fazenda 31 de Março" (31st of March Farm).[2]

SIXTEEN

THE CONSEQUENCES OF TORTURE

WHAT TYPES of reaction does torture provoke in a person?

Although the study of legal proceedings handled by the Brazilian system of military courts allowed for the recording of many denunciations of torture, there are few descriptions of the effect upon victims. Yet torture has physical, psychological, and moral consequences. Many victims remained silent about their torture and torturers. Some did so on the advice of their lawyers, while others were inhibited by the fear that the tortures had produced.

The authorities, for their part, tried to ensure that, as often as possible, torture left no physical marks on political prisoners. Proof of this policy is provided in a document from the Second Army's DOI-CODI, found in a set of São Paulo military court proceedings: "Press hard *without* leaving marks."

At times, however, prisoners were victims of tortures so atrocious that they suffered permanent bodily damage. Among the numerous instances in which this occurred were the cases of lawyer Elenaldo Celso Teixeira and engineering student Luís Medeiros de Oliveira, detained and violently tortured in a Pernanbuco sugar mill that was, ironically, called "Freedom." Oliveira testified:

> After Petrônio arrived they started to hit us with iron bars, any piece of iron that they could find in the warehouse, and fan belts for a long period of time. They beat me and Elenaldo. Then they took us outside the sugar mill; they tied ropes around our ankles and threw the ropes over a beam between two and

three meters above the floor, and hung us up by our ankles; they continued to beat us and poured alcohol on us while threatening to ignite us; and they also put a pistol in our ears and pulled the trigger although there were no bullets. After a long period of beatings they cut the ropes and we fell to the floor on our heads. This falling on the head upon the floor caused terrible pain. Then they dragged us to the place where a jeep was . . . and . . . dumped us there. From that point I don't remember anything else. I only remember that we arrived in Recife, at some place, and when we got out of the jeep I saw, written on the front: Police Department of Caxangá. I was thrown into a clean room, and we remained on the cement floor. We stayed there until morning, groaning with pain and the floor all stained with blood; everybody was bloodied because of our injuries.

Luís Medeiros de Oliveira was taken later to the first aid department of the Oswaldo Cruz hospital. When he recovered, he was again taken to the public security department of the state of Pernambuco, although he continued to suffer enormous pain in his kidneys and to urinate blood. He pleaded for a doctor several times but was not seen by one. He was constantly interrogated and tortured:

I knew that I was in poor shape and that the injuries from the beatings had not healed; my clothes stuck to my body and I couldn't sleep. On 22 August Miranda and three other policemen whom I had seen came into the DOPS room. They then told me that they were going to take me in order to find out everything, to see who participated with me, and that they were going to burn me all over with cigarette butts. . . . At that moment I became terribly afraid of being tortured again, and to escape from there I jumped from the window of the Department, while Miranda was asking a police officer for a pack of cigarettes in order to burn me. . . . I ran from the office where I was, stepped on the window sill and jumped outside and remembered nothing more. I came to when I was at the hospital, with all kinds of doctors around me and taking care of me. Miranda was there also, laughing and poking fun at me.[1]

Luís Medeiros de Oliveira survived. Ever since his torture, however, he has been a tetraplegic, with all four limbs paralyzed. Nonetheless, he was convicted by military courts for having committed a crime against the National Security Law. His condition notwithstanding, he was sent to prison.

The councils of judges of the military courts, at the request of defendants and lawyers, ordered into the records the depositions of persons who had been indelibly marked by violent treatment suffered in police and military interrogation centers.

In a letter that military court judges ordered to be appended to court proceedings, Leovi Antonio Pinto Carísio, 23, wrote in 1970:

> There, in a room especially reserved for torture, they tied my wrists and ankles with separate ropes, and put me on the small table; the ropes were then passed under the crosspieces that united the two legs of the table at each end; they forced my torso with sudden jerks, in the opposite direction of my spine movement. The pain was atrocious, and I still feel it, once in a while, along my spine. . . . I want to add that on 31 January my companion Lucimar Brandão Guimarães, although broken up by tortures, did not yet have his spinal column broken. On that day the police of the PMMG took him and from that time we don't know what happened to him; and will never be told, because today he is paralyzed as a result of the fractures of his vertebrae.

Another letter included in the same legal proceedings was written by the father-in-law of teacher Lenira Machado Dantas, 30, detained in São Paulo. The letter is dated 1971.

> As father-in-law of Lenira Machado Dantas, who already testified in this military court . . . he affirms that his daughter-in-law suffered the threat of pneumonia toward the end of last year; that she is now suffering from hepatitis, and vomits constantly; that because of the injury to her spinal column her right leg is almost paralyzed and shows alarming physical weakness because of her prolonged period in prison.

Another case of paralysis was recounted to the Navy's Second Court in Rio, in 1972, in the testimony of student Lúcia Maria Murat Vasconcelos, 23:

> that when she was detained, the defendant was taken to the CODI on Barão de Mesquita Street, where she was submitted

to a series of physical and psychological tortures; that she suffered beatings all over her body, and also the application of electric shocks on her tongue, breasts, and vagina; that she was then taken to Bahia where it was ascertained that her right leg was paralyzed . . .

On other occasions, those who were beaten in the course of their torture suffered many broken bones and related ailments. This happened to student Alberto Vincius Melo do Nascimento, 23, during a torture session he underwent in the OBAN in São Paulo on 5 December 1970:

> that they also touched an electric cable to his buttocks causing burns that were treated later in Curitiba by a sergeant nurse; that in the same room the peronial bone of his left leg was broken, resulting in the appearance of liquid in his left heel; that this fracture was recorded in the General Army Hospital in Curitiba; that his leg was set in a cast only ten days after it was broken; that on the day after it was broken, that is to say, 6 December, he was tortured again . . . that while his left leg was still without a cast he received kicks from Captain Magela . . .

Cases of perforation of the eardrums were also common:

> that practically everything included in the deposition to the police cannot be believed because he was obliged to admit to . . . crimes under tortures which also resulted in the perforation of his right eardrum . . .
> [José Ivo Vannuchi, 21, civil servant, São Paulo, 1970.]

> that the right eardrum of the defendant was perforated by slaps over his ears by Dr. Porto, [in] a type of torture known as the "telephone" . . .
> [José Jerônimo de Oliveira, 26, student, Fortaleza, 1971.]

> that he has marks of tortures suffered in the PE [barracks], because it was there that they burst his left eardrum, in addition to the marks on his body that can be ascertained by a medical exam . . .
> [Júlio Antônio Bittencourt Almeida, 22, student, Rio, 1970.]

In a letter dated 1969, engineer Diógenes Arruda Câmara, 55, who was detained that same year, told about the impact of torture on his health:

> It was then that I had my first heart crisis. They left me in complete repose during the day, one night and another day, while medics of the Military Police and of the Second Army gave me injections. At that time I could hardly walk; two persons had to lift me up. I grabbed the walls with my hands and dragged my legs along slowly. . . . That was my physical state: I could not get up alone, nor could I walk; there were . . . enormous bruises from my shoulders and back all the way down to my toes, and also over my arms and hands which became almost black with liquid coming out from under my fingernails and from the lines of each hand; my ears were swollen; a left rib was broken; my right kidney hurt; several ligaments in my right upper leg were severed, including the kneecap, which left me semiparalyzed for more than two months.

Some victims not only recounted but were able to exhibit the marks of aggression that they had suffered during their depositions in military courts. In other cases, physical maltreatment was attested to in medical reports made to police authorities. *Corpus delicti* exams carried out by army doctors also verified evidence of torture. In some instances, making no effort to hide their cynicism, the authorities openly admitted to the torture of defendants charged with political crimes, such as the case reported by the father of José Olavo Leite Ribeiro, 23, in a letter written to the magistrate of São Paulo's military court in 1970:

> Several days later (not more than four or five) we learned that our son was being tortured in the OBAN. I went there and asked to talk to the same Captain Maurício who, once he had found the reasons for my concern, replied to me as follows, word by word: "Your son is only receiving fist punches and kicks; but this is of no importance because he would also receive them in a university fight. He is also receiving electric shocks, but don't worry about them because the effects are merely psychological."

The consequences of torture were of course psychological as well as physical. Journalist Helena Miranda de Figueiredo, 45, testified in 1973:

> that, in response to questions from the lieutenant-colonel, president of the council [of military court judges], she answered that she might be able to recognize her aggressors, but that she would rather not do it, because one of them threatened to kill her, saying that he would run her over with his car. She added that to this day she is terrified by what she saw and heard, and that she suffered threats at every moment, hearing dirty names and promises of further tortures, not only upon her own person, but upon her relatives also, including her son who is now 13 years old; that obscene gestures demonstrating how her body would be utilized by many of the individuals that were in the vicinity, led her to become panic-stricken about [the practice] of which she had been a victim, although they have not yet carried out their threats; she feels that many things might happen, and that is the reason why she prefers to remain silent about the names of those who tormented her for such a long time . . .

Other defendants, however, not only denounced the names of their tormentors but also described, before the military court, the reactions that they had had to the tortures. In Brasília, lawyer José Maria Pelúcio Pereira, 34, testified in 1975 that after receiving shocks, "he remained without sleeping, and even when awake he had visions." In Rio, student José Mendes Ribeiro, 24, in 1977, "even lost the notion of time" after receiving electric shocks and beatings and going through the "ice box." "In those circumstances a person loses the notion of time," testified Paulo Elisiário Nunes, 36, a publicity agent, in 1976, who had been tortured in Belo Horizonte. Journalist Nelson Luiz Lott de Morais Costa, 22, made a more detailed statement in Rio's military court in 1971, after a long period of tortures in the barracks of the army police:

> that, within approximately one month, he lost about 20 kilos; that the doctors believed that he was not in perfect psychological health, for he spoke to himself, in disconnected words; . . . that, after these facts, he felt morally and psychologically shaken; that, later, analyzing his behavior at that time

and talking with other prisoners some time later, and also with psychiatrists, they agreed with him that his behavior was psycho-manic-depressive, with total absence of feelings no longer able to think any more; even when he arrived at a collective cell at 8 o'clock P.M. he talked without stopping until 3 o'clock in the morning, saying disconnected words; . . . that, presently, he continues to be a victim of hallucinations, depressions, and feels a desire to die . . .

A more scientific appreciation of the consequences of torture was found in the medical report on patient Maria Regina Peixoto Pereira, 20, signed by Dr. Ronaldo Mendes de Oliveira Castro on 17 June 1970:

Hospitalized in the 1st [District Hospital of Brasília], room 519, coming from DOPS, where she had been detained since 29 May 1970.

• Reason for hospitalization: removed for presenting a confused state and impossibility of locomotion.

• Main complaint: headache and feeling of weakness. . . .

• During her first days of imprisonment she began to feel anguished, suffering panic and fear, accompanied by a migraine headache on the left frontal-lateral side, constantly throbbing. At the same time she noticed difficulties in the movements of her whole body.

• She presented, soon afterwards, an acute confused state, temporal disorientation, loss of the sense of reality, and ideas of self-extermination. She had the impression, during the night, that the interrogation to which she had been subjected continued without ceasing; she was unable to distinguish the real from the imaginary, and could not say precisely for how long she remained in that state.

• She says that she has suffered physical aggressions, such as beatings on her abdomen and electric shocks on her head. . . .

• She also complains of the lack of memory for recent facts.

• She says that she has been having, for days, contractions over her entire body, not knowing when they began, but that it was just a few days ago. . . .

- Mental exam: hyper-emotional, frequent weeping. Slow conversation with a whispering voice and punctuated by periods of silence. Difficult initial contact, getting better in the course of the interview. Depressive humor.

- "Attenuated memory" for recent facts. Perception, attention, and intelligence without alterations.

- Lack of orientation in time and still somewhat confused. Main course of thought: experiences of terror and panic.

- Suicidal ideas.

- Presents primitive reactions of regression and hysteria.

Another example is the mental examination given to sociologist Lúcio de Brito Castello Branco, signed by two air force doctors: Major Samuel Menezes Faro, and 1st Lieutenant Roberto Romero dos Santos:

> We had a quick interview with the [defendant's] wife. . . . She told us that, right after the detainment, he was in a profoundly shaken psychological state, unable to react to stimulation from those around him, standing still, weeping constantly, and showing, in addition, a tremor in his right foot. His wife also mentioned his agitated sleep, his nightmares and agoraphobia. . . .
>
> Urged to answer about his imprisonment, he tells, with a certain amount of emotion, that he had been abducted by terrorists, in the presence of a colleague. That he had suffered ill-treatments at the hands of those individuals . . . We noticed, while he talked, a certain tremor in his right foot. . . . He presents a partial lacunary amnesia regarding certain events during his imprisonment. We say partial because we do not consider it opportune to insist in the recall of same. . . .
>
> CONCLUSION: The patient shows a reactive depressive condition in progressive remission. From what his wife told us, the depression must have been severe. At the moment it is moderate, and requires some time for a total progressive remission.

The personalities of some prisoners were so affected by torture that they ended up accepting all the demands of their prison guards in order to survive, as bank worker Manoel Henrique Ferreira, 21, illustrates in a 1975 letter to the 1st Air Force Court:

Those tortures also had the effect of making me come apart psychologically. They even led me to the point of going to a television station to make a pronouncement against the struggle in which I had participated. I went to the TV station and made a pronouncement retracting my ideas, and I did this in a complete state of psychological confusion on account of all the tortures I had suffered, [and because] of all the threats and of the fear I had of being killed.

Later this same person gave his public testimony in a book about political prisoners, in which he told about the impact those torments had upon his personality:

The fact that I was not prepared for prison was demonstrated right from the beginning, when I was overcome by true panic. Facing tortures and torturers, my condition was one of intense terror, and this led me to . . . extremely individualistic behavior which was reflected directly in the level of collaboration I rendered to the torturers. So that those tortures might come to an end, I gave information that led to the detainment of other comrades. I quit thinking about all the comrades who were killed in the promotion of that struggle. My only thought was to free myself from those tortures and, in order to achieve this, I collaborated with the enemy who sought to take the maximum advantage of that situation. During the time I remained in CISA [Air Force Information and Security Center] I was completely terrified. When I was taken to interrogation sessions, my whole body trembled with such an intensity that I could not control it. I despaired whenever I saw the shock machine and, at times, just seeing it and before receiving the electric shocks, I would begin to talk. At times [I] even invented things, with the hopeful purpose of not receiving any shocks. After a few days, my terror reached such a point that just hearing a door being opened would make me tremble. I thought of nothing more than the possibility of getting out of that situation. What I cared about was individual salvation, and not political survival. . . . When the tortures lessened, my psychological state was deplorable. While having done everything to free myself from tortures, I was now beginning to feel remorse for all that and I remained with a tremendous contradiction: for while I had not hesitated in betraying [my comrades] in order to improve my own personal condition, I was begin-

ning to think about what that treason had meant, not only on
the political level, but on the personal as well.[2]

To some political prisoners, the idea of suicide appeared as a way
of escaping from their endless suffering. Suicide was also the extreme
recourse for those who sought to remain faithful to their own convictions in the face of an implacable enemy, invested with the authority of the state, who had time and the cruelty of torture in his
favor and who operated with impunity.

In his deposition, in Fortaleza in 1971, student Manuel Domingos
Neto, 22, told the council of military court judges:

> that, because of ill-treatments received, he entered into a state
> of despair, in which he even thought of suicide; that, from that
> point, the police began to take maximum care to keep him
> from taking any extreme attitude against his own person, for
> they ascertained the state of spirit in which he found him-
> self . . . that physical and mental exhaustion overcame him, to
> the point where he had to be hospitalized in the S.O.S. Hospital
> in this capital city, where he spent ten days unconscious; that
> he was later taken to the Military Hospital where he underwent
> psychiatric treatment during four months . . .

In 1977, student Luiz Arnaldo Dias Campos, 21, declared that "he
even asked that they kill him, so that the tortures might end and,
in reply, they told him that he would remain alive in order to suffer
even more."

Other prisoners went so far as to try to kill themselves, in the
extreme effort to free themselves from ceaseless tortures, as was
the case of draftsman Jurandir Rios Garçoni, 29:

> that he wants to put into the record at this opportunity that,
> when he was detained by OBAN, he received ill-treatments,
> that is, tortures, in such a way that he became disturbed phys-
> ically and mentally; that he even tried suicide, cutting his wrists
> with a plastic fork, but not succeeding in his purpose because
> of the insufficient lesion for the desired hemorrhage and also
> because he was helped in time . . .

Other similar cases are registered in the archives of military court
proceedings:

He was taken to the DOPS, where he suffered coercion and even a psychiatric depression, during which he attempted suicide . . .
[Jethero de Farias Cardoso, 48, engineer, São Paulo, 1970.]

that, in Curitiba, he was in prison with a person who seemed crazy and that, later, he found out that he was Teodoro Ghescov; that Teodoro, on a certain morning, tried to drive a nail into his own head, using a shoe as a hammer . . .
[Newton Cândido, 39, radio technician, São Paulo, 1977.]

that he wants to clarify the fact that the confession obtained by the police, although it is the truth, was obtained through tortures; that, in the face of this, he tried to commit suicide . . .
[Antônio Nahas Júnior, 19, student, Recife, 1971.]

Some prisoners tried to use suicide as a gesture of protest, as did bank employee Inês Etienne Romeu, 29, who had been held in a private prison in Petrópolis:

From conversations heard during the dawn hours between Pardal and Laurindo, I surmised that a trap was being prepared that would culminate with my death. Pardal told Laurindo that "as soon as she leaves the car to walk the 200 meters, my car will already be at high speed; she won't have the time to see what is going to happen to her." Zé Gomes also commented to me: "You'll faint when you find out what is in store for you." In the face of all this, and in order not to collaborate with the farce of "accidental death," I cut my wrists . . . I lost a lot of blood and, feeling that I was about to lose my senses, the certainty that I should struggle for my life occurred to me, because I had the hope of denouncing everything that had happened and, also, all the things that I had witnessed in the hell where I was held. I therefore screamed for Pardal who, together with those who were in the house, took care of the first aid.[3]

A similar case occurred with Brother Tito de Alencar Lima, a Dominican, who was detained and tortured in the DOI-CODI in São Paulo, as he revealed in an internationally publicized report:

In the cell, I was unable to sleep. The pain increased moment by moment. My head felt like it was ten times bigger than my body. It anguished me to think of the possibility that other religious personnel might suffer the same thing. It became necessary to put an end to all that. I felt that I would no longer be able to bear prolonged suffering. There was only one solution: to kill myself. I found an empty can in the jail cell that was strewn with trash. I began to sharpen its point on the cement floor. The prisoner next door surmised my decision and pleaded with me to calm down. He had suffered more than I (his testicles were crushed) and had not arrived at despair. But, in my case, [my suicide] was meant to keep others from being tortured and to denounce to public opinion and to the Church what was happening in Brazilian prisons. Only through the sacrifice of my life could this be possible, I thought. . . . I had marked on my wrists the place for the cuts. I continued to sharpen the can. At noon, they took me out to shave. They told me that I would be taken to the penitentiary. I shaved poorly and returned to my cell. A soldier went by. I asked him to loan me a razor blade so that I could finish shaving. The Portuguese man, next to me, was sleeping. I took the razor blade and cut strongly into the inside bend of my left elbow. The deep cut reached the artery. The jet of blood stained the floor of the cell. I got close to the toilet and squeezed the arm so that the blood might run faster. Later, I recovered my senses on a bed in the first-aid sector of the Hospital da Clínicas.[4]

Torture had profound psychological consequences for Brother Tito. In August 1974, while in exile in France, he hanged himself.

SEVENTEEN

DEATHS UNDER TORTURE

IN THE military court proceedings, the BNM project found numerous testimonies of persons who witnessed the death under torture of other political prisoners. It is possible that other deaths occurred in similar circumstances but the persons are considered "disappeared" or are said to have died in "shootouts" with government agents. In this study, however, only the reports of those death episodes denounced in military courts and officially registered in legal proceedings will be discussed. The question of the disappeared will be discussed in the following chapter.

CHAEL CHARLES SCHREIDER

While testifying in Rio in 1969, student Maria Auxiliadora Lara Barcelos, 25, reported:

> that the defendant heard the screams of Chael when he was beaten; . . . that Antonio Roberto and Chael were beaten from 10 P.M. to 4 o'clock in the morning; . . . that around 4 o'clock in the morning, Chael and Roberto left the room where they had been visibly bloodied, including their penises, ears and with cuts on their heads; . . . that she heard Chael screaming that he did not know anything; . . . that these tortures lasted until 7 o'clock in the morning, when Chael stopped screaming, [having] fallen on the floor; . . . that Chael was trampled; that it was a Friday and that Chael died on Saturday; . . . that Chael was desperately screaming in the Army Police headquarters

on Saturday morning; that only twenty days later did she hear that Chael had died; that Antonio Roberto saw Chael die; . . . CHARLES CHAEL, who was kicked like a dog, whose death certificate registers seven broken ribs, internal hemorrhage, punctiform brain hemorrhages, and ecchymoses over his whole body.

In his depositions in Rio and São Paulo, student Antônio Roberto Espinosa, 23, confirmed what Maria Auxiliadora Lara Barcelos had declared:

> that after those three hours of tortures, Chael was taken to a contiguous room where there was a shock machine; that on that occasion the defendant was placed in the corridor next to the room from which the defendant heard the screams of Maria Auxiliadora and Chael; . . . that the defendant, while suffering shocks, heard Chael's screams, until those screams stopped at 2 o'clock in the afternoon; that Chael had been assassinated by Captain José Luiz, by Captain Lauria and by DOPS police officers; that the defendant is able to recognize them . . .

The autopsy on Chael Charles Schreider was done on 24 November 1969 by the forensic medical service of the army's Central Hospital in Rio. It was signed by army doctors Major Oswaldo Cayammi Ferreira, head of that unit, and Captain Guilherme Achilles de Faria Mello and by civilian doctor Rubens Pedro Macuco Janini. The report concluded: "The cause of death having been ascertained, the autopsy is finalized with the conclusion that it resulted from abdominal contusion with ruptures of the tranverse mesocolon and mesentery, with internal hemorrhage."

JOÃO LUCAS ALVES AND SEVERINO VIANA CALÚ

The assassination of these two persons was denounced in 1970 during the military court interrogation in Juiz da Fora of student Afonso Celso Lana Leite, 25:

> that the interrogations of those accused, including those of the defendant, were done under the most atrocious tortures which provoked the death of two of his companions: João Lucas Alves and Viana Calú; that these two companions died because they

did not agree with the depositions that were imposed upon them by torturers Thacyr Menezes Sia, from the DOPS, Ariosvaldo, from the DOPS, and several others from the DOPS whose names he does not remember . . .

EDUARDO LEITE

The premeditated death of Eduardo Leite, in 1970, was denounced in Rio by student Ottoni Guimarães Fernandes Júnior, 24, who had been with him in a private prison in a residence in São Conrado:

> that the police presented to the defendant, while still at the São Conrado house, a citizen by name of Eduardo Leite, nicknamed Bacuri; that Bacuri was also being tortured in another room of that house; that when the police officers introduced Bacuri to the defendant they declared that he was going to be killed, as it really came to pass in November, in São Paulo . . .

In São Paulo, economist Vinicius José Nogueira Caldeira Brant, 30, also declared in military court that he had seen Eduardo Leite in an official São Paulo prison:

> that the threats upon his life had a concrete base when they were carried out on the person of another prisoner who was suffering together with the defendant; that it was Eduardo Leite who was detained in the solitary cell next to his in the DOPS; that Eduardo Leite was taken out of there before dawn on 27 October, three days after newspapers had published the news of his escape, and that it is public knowledge that Bacuri was assassinated with refinements of perversity . . .

The death certificate of Eduardo Leite, 25, telephone technician, was signed on 8 December 1970 by medical examiner Dr. Aloísio Fernandes. It gave as *causa mortis* "internal hemorrhage and skull fracture resulting from an injury caused by a bullet."

LUIZ EDUARDO DA ROCHA MERLINO

The judges of São Paulo's 1st Military Court ordered into the records, in 1972, the following declarations of physicist Laurindo Martins Junqueira Filho, 26:

that he also wants to affirm that in this torture process he saw
the beatings inflicted upon a companion of his organization
called Luiz Eduardo da Rocha Merlino, and that later, in the
interrogation phase, this companion was taken out of the OBAN
in a deplorable condition, and that he died as the result of the
tortures received . . .

Also in 1972, these declarations were reiterated in São Paulo in the
deposition of sociologist Eleonora de Oliveira Soares, 27:

that during her stay at the OBAN she suffered physical tortures,
all the way from electric shocks to beatings with a stick, threats
of torture against her daughter, one year and ten months old,
and witnessing the death of Luiz Eduardo da Rocha Merlino
in the OBAN premises, whose death was caused by tortures . . .

Defendant Ricardo Prata Soares also confirmed in court, in 1972,
that he had seen the tortures inflicted upon Luiz Eduardo da Rocha
Merlino:

that the police deposition was carried out under moral and
physical coercion, to which the defendant ceased to resist after
seeing the tortures inflicted upon Luiz Eduardo da Rocha Merlino which resulted in his death within a few days . . .

The autopsy of journalist Luiz Eduardo da Rocha Merlino, 23, was
done at the Forensic Medical Institute in São Paulo on 12 August
1971; the autopsy report was signed by medical examiners Isaac
Abramovitc and Abeylard de Queiroz Orsini:

HISTORY: According to what has been told to us, he was run
over by a vehicle.

JOAQUIM ALENCAR SEIXAS

While testifying in São Paulo in 1972, Fanny Akselrud Seixas, 54,
declared during the 2nd Military Court proceedings:

that the [illegible] of her interrogation on page 217 that affirms
that her husband died in a shootout with the police on the

street is not true, because the defendant saw him inside the OBAN being tortured and heard his voice and his screams; that the defendant saw when they put his body in a station wagon and that at that moment she heard someone ask whose body that was, and they answered that it was Joaquim Alencar Seixas . . .

The autopsy of Joaquim Alencar Seixas, 49, was done at São Paulo's Forensic Medical Institute on 19 April 1971 and signed by medical examiners Pérsio José R. Carneiro and Paulo Augusto de Q. Rocha. It noted several ecchymoses and hematomas, and reported that the victim was hit by seven bullets. The report also stated:

HISTORY: He died as a result of injuries received after an intense shootout with organs of the Security Department of the State of São Paulo, at 1 P.M. of 16 April 1971, on Cursino Avenue, Ipiranga, São Paulo.

CARLOS NICOLAU DANIELLI

The first denunciation of this death was made in São Paulo's 1st Military Court in 1973, in the testimony of teacher Maria Amélia de Almeida Telles, 28:

that after the three were taken to the OBAN, that is, Carlos Nicolau Danielli, the defendant, and her husband, they were taken to three different torture rooms; that she asked them not to torture her husband because he had tuberculosis, having recently come out of a sanatorium, and that he was a diabetic; that when her husband was detained he carried a diabetic card and a prescription; that her husband entered into a coma and only then did he receive insulin, otherwise he would have died then and there; that her husband fainted and [when he was] in a state of coma they called her to see him; that Carlos Danielli was intensely tortured during three days, for the defendant heard his screams until he died; . . . that they showed the defendant a newspaper with the news of the death of Carlos Nicolau Danielli in a shootout, exactly like the deaths that were in store for the defendant and her husband . . .

In 1973, also in São Paulo, driver César Augusto Telles, 29, confirmed the deposition of his wife:

After getting out of the vehicle we were taken to the Chevrolet Opala under the point of said guns, where I saw that my friend Carlos Danielli was already inside, handcuffed to another individual and showing that he had been beaten; . . . as soon as the car entered the inner court of that police department, they took Carlos Danielli out of the car and beat him in front of hundreds of persons that were there. . . . We were then taken into the building where I immediately heard harrowing screams which I recognized as being those of Carlos Danielli on the ground floor. . . . In the early morning hours and under constant death threats and constantly hearing the screams of Carlos Danielli, my wife entered into shock which made the efforts of her aggressors useless. . . . During this time and until the fourth day they continued to torture Nicolau Danielli barbarously and, as time went by, his screams were transformed into lamentations and, finally, we noticed his silence in spite of the fact that we could still hear the sound of beatings. On the fifth day they showed to me and my wife news items from the newspapers that announced the death of Carlos Danielli in a shootout with police agents. When we protested that he had been killed as the result and at the end of tortures that he suffered in the OBAN, we were threatened with the same fate.

The death certificate of Carlos Nicolau Danielli, 43, was dated 30 December 1972 and signed by Dr. Isaac Abramovitc. The *causa mortis* was given as "acute traumatic anemia." The autopsy was done at São Paulo's Forensic Medical Institute, and the report was signed by medical examiners Isaac Abramovitc and Paulo A. de Queiroz Rocha. There were no references to marks of torture. The conclusion was the following: "We conclude that the person examined died as the result of acute traumatic anemia produced by a bullet, whose direction was from the rear to the front, slightly upwards and on the sagittal plane."

ODIJAS CARVALHO DE SOUZA

The death under torture of political prisoner Odijas Carvalho de Souza, in Pernambuco, is recorded in two sets of military court proceedings. In the first, student Alberto Vinícios Melo de Nascimento was the defendant. He testified before the council of military court judges in 1971 in Recife:

that here in the DOPS he saw the torture, rather he heard the effects of torture suffered by a prisoner named Odijas; that after those tortures that prisoner died; . . . that the person responsible for those events is the head of the DOPS himself, Dr. Silvestre; that according to what Odijas told him while still alive there is an investigator responsible for tortures; that this investigator was one of Odijas' torturers; beating upon him until he got tired, according to what Odijas himself told him; that the name of this investigator is Miranda . . .

The defendant in the second set of legal proceedings was student Lylia da Silva Guedes, 18, interrogated in Recife in 1971:

that she saw . . . another prisoner being tortured, and that his name was Odijas Carvalho de Souza; that said person was seated naked and was being beaten by about fifteen persons; that the defendant would recognize about ten of those persons, among them: Miranda, Edmundo, Eusébio, Dr. Carlos de Brito, Oswaldo, Fausto, Rocha, Brito, and that [the] tortures were commanded by Dr. Silvestre, current director of the Recife DOPS; that as the result of tortures Odijas Carvalho died. . . . that the defendant was able to list the several individuals who tortured Odijas because she already knew them in the Recife DOPS and saw them daily, including the two days in which she was tortured; that the newspapers gave the news of the death of Odijas as having happened on the 8th of February, resulting from a "pulmonary embolism" . . .

On the death certificate of Odijas Carvalho de Souza, 25, issued on 8 February 1971 by the Hospital of the Military Police of the state of Pernambuco and signed by medical examiner Ednaldo Paz de Vasconcelos, there was the following statement: *"causa mortis—* Pulmonary embolism."

ALEXANDRE VANNUCCHI LEME

Alexandre Vannucchi Leme was a geology student at the University of São Paulo. All denunciations about his death were made in 1973 in the 1st Military Court of São Paulo, with the single exception of the following testimony given by engineer Marcus Costa Sampaio, 27, in Fortaleza's military court in 1973:

that when he was in that cell he heard screams and groans of a person that had been put in solitary confinement; that the person had been in that cell 15 days before the defendant arrived in that building; . . . he wants to explain also that during his stay in that building he always heard screams and groans during the day and also during the night; that, regarding that young man in solitary confinement, he observed that in the beginning his screams had a certain intensity which gradually diminished until they became weak; that that young man was called to testify, at which time he left his cell walking normally and soon afterwards he returned to the same cell in the arms of some soldiers who seemed to belong to the Military Police although he is not sure; that the defendant saw that when the prison guard opened the cell door where the young man was, he ran to call other persons; that the order was given for prisoners to remain in the back of their cells and not come to the doors that opened into the corridor; that soon afterwards an inspection was ordered in all cells and of all prisoners with the excuse that they were looking for cutting instruments, at which time the guard said that the young man in solitary confinement had attempted suicide by cutting his wrists; that the defendant found out later that the young man in solitary confinement was ALEXANDRE VANNUCCHI; that while in Fortaleza the defendant read the newspaper *O Estado de S. Paulo* and saw two news items; one about the death of Alexandre Vannucchi which had resulted from [Vannucchi] being run over while trying to escape from the police, according to the version furnished by police organs; that in the same edition there was another item stating that the president of the University of São Paulo, Miguel Reale, was trying to find that young man who was studying geology and was the student body representative on the governing board of the School of Geology . . .

In the military court proceedings of radio technician Carlos Victor Alves Delamônica, 27, in São Paulo in 1973, the defendant testified:

that during the time I was at the OBAN, and as irrefutable proof of tortures to which I and others were submitted, my neighbor in the next cell, Alexandre Vannucchi, a 4th-year geology student, died as a consequence of ill treatment and barbarities . . .

The same tragedy was witnessed by salesman Roberto Ribeiro Martins, 28:

> Those tortures were witnessed by many persons and I also saw many persons being tortured; among them I can name Luiz Vergatti, José Augusto Pereira, and the most serious case happened with a young man whose name was Alexandre Vannucchi. During two or three days I heard his screams and, at last, late in the afternoon of 19 March, if I'm not mistaken, I saw his corpse being taken out of the solitary cell, spreading blood over the entire inner court; and then I heard comments of prison guards who spoke about suicide and to justify it they made an inspection in all cells . . .

Teaching assistant Neide Richopo, 26, had a similar experience, according to her testimony:

> that in addition to being tortured and of witnessing tortures on other persons, she also saw the assassination of a young man in the DOI called Alexandre; that Alexandre's . . . screams were heard throughout the day and that on the second day he was dragged, already dead, from the cell where he was. And that after this his interrogators presented at least three versions about his death as suicide, and that the official version is totally different from the three previous ones, for it was that he had been run over by a vehicle; that he could never had been run over because he was already dead when he left the DOI. That she said all this about the death of Alexandre because she views this as psychological coercion. If the defendant did not sign her deposition the same thing that happened to Alexandre might happen to her also . . .

JOSÉ FERREIRA DE ALMEIDA

Charged in a penal action with other military men, José Ferreira de Almeida, 63, a lieutenant in the São Paulo military police, died as the result of tortures suffered, according to a deposition put into the records by the military court judges. In 1975, Captain Manoel Lopes, 68, of the military police, wrote to the court magistrate:

> On that day, when they took me to the cell, I found there Carlos Gomes Machado, Luiz Gonzaga Pereira, and José Fer-

reira de Almeida, who had gone to the DOPS but were now back in the DOI. José Ferreira de Almeida, who was lying on a filthy mattress on the floor, grabbed the hand that I extended to greet him and said to me: "Lopes, I can't stand it anymore. I unjustly accused you when they tortured me. Forgive me." And sobs came to his throat and he finally said: "I'm going to die."

Also in a letter to authorities, dated 1975, Colonel Carlos Gomes Machado of São Paulo's military police reaffirmed the denunciation:

In addition, although they knew I had heart trouble and could not endure strong emotions, they took me to see other colleagues of mine being tortured, as were the cases of Lieutenant Atílio Geromin who was left with indelible marks on his legs in view of the fact that he had been tied to an armchair called the "dragon's chair" by interrogators; and Lieutenant José Ferreira de Almeida who, in spite of his 63 years of age, was killed by the tortures he suffered, such as the parrot's perch, electric shocks, *palmatória*, etc., which were repeated daily . . .

Signed by doctors Harry Shibata and Marcos Almeida, the autopsy of José Ferreira de Almeida was done at São Paulo's Forensic Medical Institute on 12 August 1975. The report registered "HISTORY: According to what was told to us, he died by hanging in his cell, where he was detained."

WLADIMIR HERZOG

On 7 November 1975 journalist Rodolfo Osvaldo Konder, codefendant in the same proceedings with journalist Wladimir Herzog, gave sworn testimony in São Paulo:

On Saturday morning I perceived that Wladimir Herzog had arrived. . . . Wladimir Herzog was a good friend of mine and we bought shoes together, and I recognized him by his shoes. Some time later, Wladimir was taken out of the room. We remained seated on that bench, until one of the interrogators came and took me and Duque Estrada to an interrogation room on the ground floor, next to the room where we had been. Wladimir was there, seated on a chair, with a hood over his head, and already dressed in overalls. As we entered the room, the interrogator ordered us to take off our hoods, which is why we saw that he was Wladimir, and we also saw the interrogator, who was a man of thirty-three to thirty-five years of age, approximately one meter and seventy-five centimeters in height, weighing some 65 kilos, lean but muscular, light brown hair, narrow brown eyes, and a tattoo of an anchor on the internal part of his left forearm that practically covered the entire forearm. He asked us to tell Wladimir "that it would do no good to withhold information." Both myself and Duque Estrada did in fact advise Wladimir to tell what he knew, because the information that the interrogators wanted to confirm had already been given by persons who were detained before us. Wladimir said that he knew nothing and the two of us were taken out of the room and back to the wooden bench where we had been before, in the adjoining room. From there we could clearly hear the sceams, first of the interrogator and then of Wladimir, and we heard when the interrogator asked that they bring the "little pepper" to him and requested the help of a team of torturers. Someone turned on the radio and Wladimir's screams became mixed up with the radio sounds. I well remember that during that phase the radio gave the news that Franco had received the last rites, and that fact was recorded in my mind because at that very moment Wladimir was being tortured and was screaming. From a certain moment, the sound of Wladimir's voice changed, as if they had introduced something into his mouth; his voice became muffled, as if they had put a gag over his mouth. Later, the sounds ceased altogether. . . . The interrogator left the room again and soon came back to take me by the arm to the room where Wladimir was, allowing me once again to take off my hood. Wladimir was seated on the same chair, with the hood over his head, but he now appeared to be especially nervous, his hands were shaking a lot and his voice was weak. . . . On the following morning, a Sunday, we were summoned . . . to hear a lecture about Russian penetration in Brazil, delivered by a man who appeared to be the person mainly responsible for the analysis of information collected by the DOI. This person was accompanied by "Doctor Paulo," a Nisei of about forty years or so, lean, one meter and seventy centimeters in height, and by an interrogator around twenty-five years of age, blondish, lean and tall, about one meter and seventy-seven centimeters tall. The man who appeared to me to be the main one was dark-complexioned, round face, fat, medium height, and a beard framing his face. He first talked about the question of Russian spying in Brazil, and later informed us that Wladimir Herzog had committed suicide the day before, in order to conclude that Wladimir must have been a KGB agent and, at the same time, "the right arm of Governor Paulo Egydio." . . . Wladimir's interrogator wore a white turtleneck shirt with short sleeves, and trousers that looked like they were part of the army's uniform. . . . Wladimir's interrogator, who was described above as having an anchor tattooed on his arm, was white. That when Wladimir's torture was initiated, the person making this declaration, who was in the adjoining room, heard sounds of beatings that were inflicted upon Wladimir; and that he calculates Wladimir's torture lasted about two hours, less than that of the person making this declaration, which lasted about four hours. That Wladimir's torture to which he referred to above was that which he could hear, and that he does not know whether Wladimir suffered other tortures later in other premises of the DOI itself.

EIGHTEEN

THE DISAPPEARED

THE ARBITRARY detention or abduction followed by the disappearance of the victim became a common tactic of these security forces in all the Latin American countries governed under the Doctrine of National Security. The technique of "disappearance" is the highest stage of political repression, because it immediately hinders the application of legal codes established for the defense of personal freedom, physical integrity, human dignity, and life itself. For the repressive forces, the "disappearance" of a person was a convenient and frequently used method of terrorizing political opponents.

Threatened with political abduction at any moment, the persecuted individual was forced to live in clandestinity, far away from his community. He lost contact with his family and was only sporadically in touch with his political organization, itself persecuted and forced underground.

When a person "disappeared," this fact was not publicly known. The courts, family, friends, and lawyers of the prisoners were not informed. This was an obvious advantage for the security agents, who could then exercise total power over the prisoner, torturing or even eliminating him at will. In addition, by the time interested parties had obtained proof of a detention, the security organs could already have eliminated the victim and destroyed all traces of his whereabouts. Finally, the uncertainty for the prisoner's relatives in itself constituted a form of torture.

In Brazil, a few disappeared individuals were seen in official or secret interrogation centers by other prisoners who fared better.

Their testimonies regarding those disappeared persons were included in the legal proceedings analyzed by the BNM project. The project concluded with certainty that the disappeared were persons hunted down by repressive organs. Unfortunately, however, the legal proceedings rarely contained any information that could lead to the discovery of the whereabouts of the disappeared, due to the refusal of the government authorities to claim responsibility for these disappearances, on one hand, and from the almost total impunity with which the intelligence services operated, on the other. They brooked no interference from the judiciary, the press, relatives, or lawyers of the victims.

The only established fact about these disappeared persons is that they were detained by a security organization. It can be hypothesized, however, that the victims were almost certainly murdered, and buried, usually at night, in clandestine cemeteries as indigents, under false names. No security agents were punished for these crimes.

It is believed that approximately 125 individuals disappeared in Brazil under these circumstances. Their whereabouts are still unknown. In some other cases, amnesty groups and relatives have been able to locate victim's remains. All had been buried under false names by the police. The BNM project has chosen a few examples from the most significant cases.

MARIANO JOAQUIM DA SILVA

Mariano Joaquim da Silva, secretary of the Rural Labor Union of Timbaúba, Pernambuco, was a farm worker, cobbler, and member of the national board of the Peasant Leagues. He was detained on 1 May 1971 in Recife and accused of being a leader of VAR-Palmares. The organism that detained him was the DOI-CODI of the First Army, which took him to Rio.

Silva was later taken to a clandestine repression center in Petrópolis. Inês Etienne Romeu affirmed that she saw and talked with him there several times.

> When I was taken to the Petrópolis house, a peasant from the northeast was already there, Mariano Joaquim da Silva, also known as Loyola. We talked three times, twice in the presence of our guards and once alone. Mariano was detained on the

first or second of May, in Pernambuco. After his detention he remained twenty-four hours in Recife where he was barbarously tortured. His body was full of injuries. He was then taken to that place where he was interrogated during four days without interruption, without sleep, without food and without water. He remained in the house until 31 May, doing all the domestic labor including the cutting of wood for the fireplace. Dr. Teixeira told me in early July that Mariano had been executed because he belonged to the VAR-Palmares command and was considered unredeemable by government agents. When I talked alone with Mariano he mentioned the detention of Carlos Alberto Soares de Freitas.

Romeu testified that she had contacts with Silva until May 31st. In the early hours of that day, she heard strange noises and discovered that Silva was being taken away. Later she asked her guards about him and they told her that he had been transferred to the headquarters of the army in Rio de Janeiro. Nothing was heard about Silva after that time.

In the house that served as a clandestine torture center in Petrópolis Romeu saw and heard references to other persons now considered disappeared.

Dr. Pepe confirmed to me that his group had "executed" Carlos Alberto Soares de Freitas, for whose detention in February of this year he had been responsible. He told me that his group was not interested in having leaders in prison and that all the "heads" would be summarily killed after interrogations. He also said that Marilena Vilas Boas Pinto had also been in that house and that she, like Carlos Alberto Soares de Freitas, had been condemned to death and executed.

According to Dr. Pepe still, former congressman Rubens B. Paiva had the same fate, although it was not the intention of the group to kill him. They only wanted him to confess but, in the course of the tortures, Rubens Paiva died. The death of the former congressman was considered a "goof" by Dr. Pepe.

Aluísio Palhano, former leader of the Rio de Janeiro bank workers, was detained on 6 May 1971 and then taken to that house on the 13th of that same month. He stayed there until the following day. I did not see him personally but Mariano Joaquim da Silva told me that he saw him arrive in a deplorable physical shape. However, I did hear his voice several times when he was interrogated. I asked Dr. Pepe about him, and he replied: "He vanished."

Dr. Guilherme told me, before 15 May, that they were going to detain Ivan Mota Dias on that day. He later told me that Ivan had been executed by them; but Dr. Roberto told me that he was abroad. Other subordinate individuals, however, confirmed to me the death of Ivan Mota Dias.

During the month of July, two militants of the VPR and one of the ALN were in the house. I think the first one was Walter Ribeiro Novais, a former Copacabana lifeguard. Márcio assured me that they had killed him. At that time (8 to 14 July 1971) there was a loud celebration of his death. The second was a woman I believe to have been Heleni Guariba. She was terribly tortured during three days, including electric shocks in her vagina. The third one was Paulo de Tarso Celestino da Silva, who was tortured for forty-eight hours by Dr. Roberto, Laecato, Dr. Guilherme, Dr. Teixeira, Zé Gomes, and Camarão. They put him on the parrot's perch, gave him electric shocks, and made him swallow a large amount of salt. During many hours I heard him pleading for some water.

EDGAR DE AQUINO DUARTE

Edgar de Aquino Duarte was an active participant in the political activities of the Association of Navy and Marine Personnel of Brazil (AMFNB) before 1964, in Rio de Janeiro. Following the advent of the military regime, he lived in Cuba. He returned to Brazil in 1968, arriving in Porto Alegre and using documents in the name of Ivan Leite. He contacted his parents in Recife, and remained in Bom Jardim, Pernambuco, for two months. He then went to São Paulo, where he set up a real estate business with a partner named José Leme Ferreira. Involved in his work, he lost contact with his former companions. One day, by coincidence, Duarte ran across "Cabo Anselmo," a former AMFNB leader later suspected of being a government spy, who said he had just arrived from Cuba and was out of work with no place to live. Duarte took "Cabo Anselmo" to live in his apartment. On Christmas Day 1970, Duarte, Anselmo, and the latter's fiancée went to Rio de Janeiro. In March 1971, Duarte was abducted while walking on Boa Vista Street in the downtown financial center in São Paulo. He was taken to the Second Army's DOI-CODI, where he remained incommunicado. His family even received a letter of his from prison. With letter in hand, his father and other relatives went to São Paulo, to the DOI-CODI and the DOPS, where they were told that Duarte's name was not on the list of prisoners. Several political prisoners, however, stated that they had been with Duarte in the DOI-CODI and in the DOPS, in 1973. Ivan Akselrud Seixas and José Genoíno Neto both sent signed documents to the military court in which they affirmed that they had been with Duarte while in prison. These documents were ignored by the military court.

Duarte was also seen by mechanic Luiz Vergatti, 41, who testified in São Paulo's military court system in 1973:

> that Edgar de Aquino Duarte is detained in the DOPS, because "we saw him there during the sunning period"; that Edgar de Aquino Duarte is an unknown person to the defendant and he did not show him any identification card but that, nevertheless, the defendant believes that he is that person . . .

While testifying in São Paulo, in 1973, salesman Roberto Ribeiro Martins, 28, also referred to the same prisoner:

> I would like to add, as a duty of justice and to prove that there is much arbitrariness in today's Brazil, that I found out in the DOPS the existence of a young man named Edgar de Aquino, in prison two years without charges and incommunicado . . .

BERGSON GURJÃO DE FARIAS

The death of Bergson Gurjão de Farias was denounced in military court in 1972 and 1973 by defendants José Genoíno Neto and Dower Moraes Cavalcante, respectively:

> that on one of the days in which he was being interrogated they showed him the corpse of Bergson Gurjão de Farias, a young man 25 years old who was killed with a bayonet and who had malaria, according to the police, and could not therefore run or move if he were pursued . . .

> that when he was detained he was beaten and submitted to electric shocks and death threats; that together with the defendant the following persons suffered the same process: José

Genoíno Neto, Luiz Reis Medeiros, Dagoberto Alves da Costa, and Bergson Gurjão de Farias who was killed for resisting detention . . .

ARMANDO TEIXEIRA FRUTUOSO

Armando Teixeira Frutuoso was also considered a disappeared political prisoner. Frutuoso was seen in a Rio prison by radio technician Gildásio Westin Cosenza, 28, according to his 1976 testimony in military court:

> that he was then taken to a cubicle where the torturers, standing behind the defendant, took off his hood; that he then saw himself in front of a man who was seated on the floor against the wall and who, when he tried to get up, did not succeed; that this man must have been between 55 and 60 years old, largely bald, grey hair, light skin, large and hooked nose, whom he had never seen before but that he found out later, through the interrogators themselves, that it was Armando Frutuoso, former labor union leader who had been detained with identification documents in the name of Armando David de Oliveira . . .

ANTÔNIO JOAQUIM MACHADO AND CARLOS ALBERTO SOARES DE FREITAS

The detention and later disappearances of Antônio Joaquim Machado and Carlos Alberto Soares de Freitas were discussed in the interrogation of teacher Maria Clara Arantes Pêgo, 28, in Rio's military court system, in 1972:

> that she wants to clarify the fact that Dr. Antônio Joaquim Machado is a lawyer, detained on 15 February 1971 in Rio de Janeiro, in Ipanema near Joana Angélica Street, and that he was probably assassinated under torture at the Army Police [headquarters]; that the defendant lived with that person almost eight months; that the defendant knew the family since she was a child and knows that he was detained on that day, because Carlos Alberto Soares de Freitas and Emanoel Paiva were detained with him, and that from that date [Antônio Joaquim Machado and] Carlos Alberto de Freitas continue to be disappeared after all legal means were used to find them; that

of the three persons detained, the only one still alive is Emanoel who is in prison in accordance with legal proceedings . . .

PAULO STUART WRIGHT

Another disappearance victim seen on the premises of security organisms was Paulo Stuart Wright, one of the founders and leaders of Popular Action. A former congressman who was stripped of his office in 1964 by the legislative assembly of the state of Santa Catarina in deference to pressures from the state's navy commander, Wright was abducted by the Second Army, in September 1973 and taken to the DOI-CODI on Tutóia Street in São Paulo. He was seen in one of the DOI-CODI rooms by nurse Maria Diva de Faria. Wright had been a guest in her residence on the day of his disappearance.

After being released by the DOI-CODI, Maria Diva de Faria agreed to testify secretly before the Justice and Peace Committee of the São Paulo archdiocese. This testimony gave Wright's relatives the chance to present a petition to the Supreme Military Court. In an unprecedented secret session, the court heard the deposition. It voted, soon afterward, to solicit information from the Second Army, which replied in vague and evasive terms. The STM demanded information a second time, but the Second Army answered in the same kind of language as before, which led the court to make a formal complaint to the minister of the army. The embarrassing matter died there.

EREMIAS DELIZOIKOV

A disappearance case that involved an "error of legal identification" was that of Eremias Delizoikov, a university student from São Paulo who was killed in Rio de Janeiro on 15 October 1969 in Vila Cosmos, in a repressive operation against the Popular Revolutionary Vanguard (VPR). At the time of Delizoikov's death, the command of the First Army distributed the following notice:

> Proceeding in its actions of repression against subversion and terrorism, the First Army carried out this morning, in the Vila Cosmos region, an action that resulted in the confiscation of a large quantity of armaments, ammunition, homemade bombs,

false documents, money, etc. In the course of the operation its members were received with gunfire by the terrorists who resisted the authorities by force. In consequence of this, three military personnel were lightly wounded and one of the subversives was killed.

The person killed in that operation, Eremias Delizoikov, was buried under the name of army sergeant José de Araújo Nóbrega, a VPR militant who was sought by the security organs. Only later was the dead person revealed to be Delizoikov. Nóbrega's name appears on the death certificate. Nóbrega, however, is alive. Delizoikov's family was constrained by this painful situation for many years. Afraid of making an error, they had refused to believe Delizoikov was dead, and to this day they consider him legally "disappeared." The matter was at least partially resolved, however, when Nóbrega returned to Brazil from exile after the amnesty was declared in 1979.

JOSÉ MONTENEGRO DE LIMA

During the wave of repression that hit the Brazilian Communist Party (PCB) in 1975, several of its leaders were detained by security organs. To this day, however, those abductions have not been admitted by the government. The whereabouts of the detainees have not been determined. Among them was José Montenegro de Lima, a market researcher who was detained on 29 September 1975 in his residence in the Bela Vista section of São Paulo. Lima's abduction was carried out by four police agents and witnessed by neighbors and friends. His relatives denounced the abduction to the 2nd Military Court in São Paulo, which, in turn, requested information from the DOI-CODI and the DOPS. Both organs denied Lima's detention. The DOPS stated, however, that his name was on their list of wanted persons. Later, in a judicial interrogation, Genivaldo Matias da Silva, a defendant in penal proceedings against the PCB, affirmed that he had seen Lima in a cell at the Second Army's DOI-CODI. Based upon this deposition, the family tried to reopen the case, without success.

LUÍS EURICO TEJERA LISBOA

On 28 August 1979, the day the Brazilian Congress approved the amnesty law, the remains of Luís Eurico Tejera Lisboa were found in the Dom Bosco cemetery in Perus, on the outskirts of the city of São Paulo. He had been buried there as an indigent under the name of Nelson Bueno. This young man had been convicted by a military court in 1969 for student activities, and he had been living clandestinely as an ALN militant when he was detained in unknown circumstances during the first week of September 1972.

Lisboa's family, through a careful study of the cemetery burial registry, was able to locate records of a prior police inquest, which concluded that Lisboa had committed suicide. This was not consistent, however, with the testimonies of witnesses or the circumstances described in the legal proceedings which recorded the discovery of a corpse. For example, the boarding house where the alleged suicide occurred had several bullet holes. According to the police inquest, Lisboa had fired several shots at random before committing suicide. In view of these discrepancies, the family reopened Lisboa's case. Several exhumations were made, but nothing was proven. In addition, pressure not to testify was applied to potential witnesses after the body and the boarding house where the events had taken place were discovered. Although the case was not resolved, Lisboa was the first of the "disappeared" whose remains were found.

ANA ROSA KUCINSKI SILVA

The drama which affects the family of a disappeared person is evident in the case of Ana Rosa Kucinski Silva, a professor at the Chemical Institute of the University of São Paulo and a militant of the ALN. She disappeared on April 22, 1974, in São Paulo, together with her husband, Wilson Silva.

The families of Ana Rosa and Wilson attempted several judicial procedures for finding them, but they invariably received negative replies. As if the despair of searching was not enough, Ana Rosa's family fell victim to an extortion and blackmail plot concocted by Army officers connected with the São Paulo DOI-CODI. Several military personnel and informants planned to extort money in exchange for information regarding Ana Rosa's whereabouts. Later, a penal action convicted the blackmailers. This episode is not only an example of the despair of relatives of disappeared persons, but also a demonstration of the ignominious practices to which the security forces stooped.

Ana Rosa's family, after receiving no response from various security organizations, contacted a lawyer who had formerly been a DOPS investigator. They believed that his background would facilitate contacts with those responsible for her detention. The lawyer sought information regarding Ana Rosa's whereabouts from an army sergeant who worked as an orderly for the commander of the Second Army in São Paulo and also from a civilian informant of the DOI-CODI. The information he received was that Ana Rosa was detained and being held incommunicado in the DOI-CODI.

This information was given to the family, which immediately requested that permission be given for a visit. They also asked for a health report. The informants alleged that to do this they needed a lot of money. Since their requests were not being met, the family requested that they at least be allowed to receive correspondence from Ana Rosa as proof of the information they had been receiving about her.

The corrupt police officers agreed to this request and gave journalist Bernardo Kucinski, Ana Rosa's brother, a note allegedly written by her. Bernardo questioned the note's authenticity but was pressured by the officers to believe it was real. Bernardo then requested the officers to ask his sister what nickname she had given him when he was a boy. The officers agreed and hours later they returned with an incorrect answer. Suspicious that he was being deceived, Bernardo nonetheless accepted the "informants' " proposal to introduce him to a colonel who worked at the DOI-CODI and who could personally give him information about his sister's situation. This alleged colonel told him that his sister was well and that although she had not written the note, she had dictated it. He promised to arrange a family visit to Ana Rosa as soon as the other half of the required amount was paid. Bernardo paid and the military personnel vanished. To this day, both Ana Rosa Kucinski Silva and Wilson Silva remain "disappeared" persons.

MARIA AUGUSTA THOMÁZ AND MÁRCIO BECK MACHADO

On 17 May 1973 Maria Augusta Thomáz and Márcio Beck Machado were assassinated by gunshots while they were sleeping on the Rio Doce ranch in the state of Goiás. The Brazilian Amnesty Committee file on disappeared political prisoners states that they were militants of the Movement for Popular Liberation. Both had participated in the São Paulo student movement, he as a student of the School of

Economy at Mackenzie University and she as a student of psychology at the Sedes Sapientiae College. In August 1980, as a result of an investigation by journalist Antônio Carlos Fon and with data furnished by the Amnesty Committee, it was possible to discover the circumstances of their deaths and the place where they had been buried.

It was known that the assassinations were committed by several agents who were members of a joint operation of the Second Army DOI-CODI and the DOI-CODI of the Brasília Federal District, supported by the military police of the state of Goiás and by local civilian police. The agents carrying out the operation ordered the peasants who lived on the ranch to bury the corpses in hidden graves. The identities of the dead persons were also concealed. The two militants were condemned by default in the 2nd Military Court of São Paulo, even though security organs knew that they had been executed.

Seven years later, when the burial places were discovered and the transfer of the remains were being prepared, the tombs were violated by individuals who identified themselves as police officers and took the remains away. Because the operation was carried out in secret and with great haste, it went awry. Relatives of the victims requested a judicial examination of violated tombs. The report verified the presence of hair, teeth, and bones in the place where the criminal burial had occurred.

Today the identity of the police authorities who ordered the clandestine burial is known. A police inquiry is still under way in the Goiânia Federal Police Department with no concrete results to date. The dead persons are still officially considered to be disappeared. In the BNM study of legal proceedings, it was verified that the prosecutor requested the DOPS to issue a death certificate for Márcio Beck Machado, so that the sentence against him could be dropped. Not even that request was honored.

One conclusion of this case is that the relatives of the politically disappeared do not even have the right to a death certificate documenting the demise of their loved one.

RUBENS BEIRODT PAIVA

The disappearance of Rubens Beirodt Paiva reveals the extreme cynicism of the authorities.

Paiva was an active federal congressman. He was known for his pronationalist positions; he supported, for example, the creation of the Brazilian state petroleum producing and refining company, Petrobrás. Paiva was stripped of his congressional office when Institutional Act No. 1 was passed in 1964, because he had participated in a congressional investigation of the Brazilian Institute for Democratic Action—a front for the generals who led the military coup. The investigation had verified that pro-coup generals, operating through the Institute, had received large sums of dollars from the U.S. government in 1963.

On 20 January 1971 Rubens Paiva was detained in his Rio de Janeiro home in the presence of his wife and daughter. At 11:00 A.M. that day, someone had telephoned to request Paiva's address, alleging that he had to deliver a letter sent from Chile. Half an hour later, Paiva's home was invaded by six individuals in civilian clothes. All were armed, and they did not identify themselves. They forced Paiva, accompanied by two of the abductors, to drive his own car to army police headquarters on Barão de Mesquita Street. The First Army DOI-CODI operated at this site as well.

Four agents remained in Paiva's house. His family was not allowed to use the telephone. Visitors were detained and taken to the army headquarters. Although the agents searched the house, they found nothing incriminating. Nonetheless, all address books were confiscated.

On the following day, Paiva's wife, Maria Eunice Paiva, and her daughter, Eliana, age 15, were detained, hooded, and taken to the army's DOI-CODI, where they were photographed, identified, and separated from one another. Paiva's daughter, after having been interrogated three times, was released twenty-four hours later. Paiva's wife was detained for twelve days. She was held incommunicado during the entire period and was interrogated several times, sometimes at night.

When Maria Eunice was released, the DOI-CODI officials returned Paiva's car to the family. The car had been kept in the DOI-CODI inner court; a receipt was given when it was returned.

All these facts were submitted to the Supreme Military Court, which, in turn, requested information from the commander of the First Army. Despite the incontrovertible evidence that Paiva was detained in his home, that he drove his own car to prison in the company of two security agents, and that his automobile had been returned to his family, the First Army unabashedly maintained that Paiva was not in prison.

Accused of exchanging correspondence with Brazilian exiles in Chile, Rubens Paiva was never located. The circumstances of his presumed death remain unclear to this day.

THE "ARAGUAIA GUERRILLA" MOVEMENT

It is public knowledge that, as of 1966, members of the Communist Party of Brazil (PC do B) installed themselves on the left bank of the Araguaia River in northern Brazil. From 12 April 1972 to January 1975, in three separate campaigns, government armed forces tried to eliminate the "Araguaia Guerrilla" movement. Prolonged warfare resulted in deaths on both sides. Ultimately, the guerrillas were defeated. Some of them were taken prisoner and were charged, tried, and sentenced under the National Security Law. Approximately sixty militants of the PC do B were killed in combat. The location of their burial site is unknown to this day, despite the fact that their bodies were identified by government forces. The names of those who died are included in Appendix I as part of the list of political disappearances compiled by the BNM project.

It is a matter of justice that the circumstances of these "disappearances" be revealed. It is also particularly important that the location of victims' remains be made known to their families. This demand is not only politically defensible, but has precedents in classical literature and the Gospel as well. It is also expressly required by Article 120 of the Geneva Convention, which states that "the detaining authorities shall ensure that prisoners of war who have died in captivity are honorably buried . . ."[1] Now that the period of military rule has ended in Brazil, the lingering doubts left by these and other politically motivated "disappearances" should be resolved. It should finally be possible to answer the questions posed by the country's great Catholic thinker, Alceu Amoroso Lima:

> Until when will there be in Brazil women who do not know whether they are widows; sons who do not know whether they are orphans; human creatures who knock in vain on implacably locked doors of a Brazil that we naively thought to be free from such insane cruelties?[2]

My father told me;
I'm going to tell my son.
And when he dies?
He'll tell his son.
That's the way it is: nobody forgets.

—Kelé Maxacali,
Indian from Mikael Village, Minas
Gerais, Brazil. 1984

NOTES

INTRODUCTION TO THE ENGLISH-LANGUAGE EDITION

1. The Brazilian transition to democracy has been extensively analyzed in the academic literature. Scholars have paid particular attention to the evolution of the Brazilian political regime and its changing relations to various social groups, as well as to the role of political institutions and economic factors in the transition process. See, for example, Maria Helena Moreira Alves, *Estado e Oposição no Brasil: 1964–1984* (Petrópolis: Editora Vozes, 1984); Sebastião C. Velasco e Cruz and Carlos Estevam Martins, "De Castello a Figueiredo: Uma Incursão na préhistoria da 'Abertura,' " in Bernardo Sorj and Maria Hermínia Tavares de Almeida, orgs., *Sociedade e Política no Brasil Pós-64* (São Paulo: Editora Brasiliense, 1983); Bernardo Kucinski, *Abertura, a História de uma Crise* (São Paulo: Editora Brasil Debates, 1982); and Alfred C. Stepan, ed., *Democratizing Brazil* (Princeton: Princeton University Press, forthcoming).

A number of sources deal with the role of the military in Brazilian politics. Those that focus on the pre-abertura period include Alfred C. Stepan, *The Military in Politics: Changing Patterns in Brazil* (Princeton: Princeton University Press, 1971); Alexandre de Barros, *The Brazilian Military: Professional Socialization, Political Performance, and State Building*, Ph.D. dissertation, University of Chicago, 1978; Edmundo Campos Coelho, *Em Busca da Identidade: O Exército e a Política na Sociedade* (Rio de Janeiro: Forense-Universitária, 1976); Eurico de Lima Figueiredo, *Os Militares e a Democracia: Análise Estrutural da Ideologia do Presidente Castello Branco* (Rio de Janeiro: Graal, 1980); René Armand Dreifuss, *1964: A Conquista do Estado, Ação Política, Poder e Golpe de Classes* (Rio de Janeiro: Editora Vozes, 1981); and Alfred C. Stepan, "The New Professionalism of Internal Warfare and Military Role Expansion," in Alfred C. Stepan, ed., *Authoritarian Brazil: Origins, Policies, and Future* (New Haven: Yale University Press, 1973), pp. 47–65.

Works that present information on the military in the postabertura period include René Armand Dreifuss and Otávio Soares Dulci, "As Forças Armadas e a Política," in Bernardo Sorj and Maria Hermínia Tavares de Almeida, eds., *Sociedade e Política no Brasil Pós-1964* (São Paulo: Editora Brasiliense, 1983), pp. 87–117; Maria Helena Moreira Alves, *Estado e Oposição no Brasil (1964–1984)* (Petrópolis: Editora Vozes, 1984); Wlader do Góes, *O Brasil do General Geisel: Estudo do Processo de Tomada de Decisão no Regime Militar-Burocrático* (Rio de Janeiro: Editora Nova Fronteira, 1978); and André Gustavo Stumpf and Merval Pereira Filho, *A Segunda Guerra: Sucessão de Geisel* (São Paulo: Editora Brasiliense, 1979).

For an analysis of the security apparatus in the postabertura period, see Paulo Sérgio Pinheiro, "Polícia e a Crise Política: O Caso das Polícias Militares," in Roberto da Matta et al., *A Violência Brasileira* (São Paulo: Editora Brasiliense, 1982), pp. 57–91.

2. "Tortura, nunca mais," *Jornal do Brasil*, 21 de agosto de 1985.
3. "A torturante culpa da tortura," *Jornal do Brasil*, 4 de setembro de 1985.
4. An early account of torture of political prisoners in various Brazilian states was compiled by former congressman and journalist Márcio Moreira Alves in *Torturas e Torturados* (Rio de Janeiro: Editora Idade Nova, 1966). The book was based on Alves' own investigative reporting. Another work based on investigative journalism was Antônio Carlos Fon's *Tortura: A História da Repressão Política no Brasil* (São Paulo: Global Editora e Distribuidora, 1979). The Brazilian Committee for Amnesty also organized a number of reports on human rights abuses involving Brazilian political prisoners; see, for example, Reinaldo Cabral and Ronaldo Lapa, eds., *Os Desaparecidos Políticos: Prisões, Seqüestros, Assassinatos* (Edições Opção, 1979). Two collective reports presented by political prisoners also contain detailed information about the repressive apparatus. They are *A Esquerda Armada: Testemunho dos Presos Políticos do Presídio Milton Dias Moreira, no Rio de Janeiro* (Vitória, Espírito Santo: Edições do Leitor, 1979), and *Dos Presos Políticos Brasileiros: Acerca da Repressão Fascista no Brasil* (Lisboa: Edições Maria da Fonte, 1976).

Documentation on torture and political disappearances in Brazil can also be found in numerous reports of international organizations. See, for example, International Association of Democratic Jurists, *Dossier Brésil*, April 1971; Amnesty International, *Torture of Political Prisoners in Brazil*, Report No. 5, 13 March 1970; Amnesty International, *A Report on Allegations of Torture in Brazil*, op. cit., 1972; International Commission of Jurists, *Report on Police Repression and Tortures In-*

flicted upon Political Opponents and Prisoners in Brazil, 22 July 1970; Amnesty International, Document of Prisoners in the Presídio da Justiça Militar Federal, 28 October 1975; World Federation of Trade Unions, the Commission of Churches on International Affairs of the World Council of Churches and the International Commission of Jurists, A Study of the Situation in Brazil Which Reveals a Consistent Pattern of Violations of Human Rights; Official Version, 19 March 1971; The Bertrand Russell Tribunal Session in Brussels, Belgium, On Repression in Brazil, Chile and Latin America (Nottingham: The Bertrand Russell Peace Foundation, 1975).

Many articles appeared in U.S. publications. Among the most notable were Márcio Moreira Alves, "Brazil: What Terror is Like," The Nation, 15 March 1971, and Ralph della Cava, "Torture in Brazil," Commonweal, 24 April 1970, and "Brazil: The Sealed Coffin," The New York Review of Books, XXII 19, Nov. 27, 1975, p. 45. Information on torture in Brazil was also published in Terror in Brazil: A Dossier, published by the American Committee for Information on Brazil, 1970, and in the Brazilian Information Bulletin, compiled by the American Friends of Brazil in the early 1970s.

5. " 'Brasil: Nunca Mais': A dissecação dos porões da tortura," Feira Hoje, 9 de agosto de 1985.
6. Antonio Chagas, "Para que investigar o tempo da tortura?" Afinal, 13 de agosto de 1985, p. 21.
7. Chagas, ibid., p. 24.
8. Among the works that specifically treat the Doctrine of National Security in Brazil are Eliezer Rizzo de Oliveira, As Forças Armadas: Política e Ideologia no Brasil, 1964–1969 (Rio de Janeiro: Editora Vozes, 1976); Joseph Comblin, "The National Security Doctrine" in The Repressive State: The Brazilian National Security Doctrine in Latin America (Toronto: LARU Papers, 1976); Joseph Comblin, A Ideologia da Segurança Nacional: O Poder Militar na América Latina (Rio de Janeiro: Editora Civilização Brasileira, 1977); José Alfredo Amaral Gurgel, Segurança e Democracia, (Rio de Janeiro: Livraria José Olympio Editora, 1975); and Dom Cândido Padim, "A Doutrina da Segurança Nacional à Luz da Doutrina da Igreja," Serviço de Documentação (SEDOC), volume 1, 1969 (Rio de Janeiro: Editora Vozes.)

The most extensively documented work on the armed struggle and the national security state, which deals specifically with the resulting "dialectic of violence," is Maria Helena Moreira Alves, Estado e Oposição no Brasil (1964–1984) (Petrópolis: Editora Vozes, 1984). The book has been published in English under the title State and Opposition in Military Brazil (Austin: University of Texas Press, 1985).
9. American participation in the training of Brazilian police is recounted

in A. J. Langguth, *Hidden Terrors* (New York: Pantheon Books, 1978). The American role in the 1964 Brazilian military takeover is discussed in Phyllis R. Parker, *Brazil and the Quiet Intervention, 1964* (Austin: University of Texas Press, 1979). See also Jan Knippers Black, *United States Penetration of Brazil* (Manchester: Manchester University Press, 1977).

10. "História sem revanchismo," *Jornal do Brasil,* 23 de julho de 1985.
11. Notable among the many works produced along these lines are three volumes of political autobiography by Fernando Gabeira: *O que é isso, companheiro?* (Rio de Janeiro: Editora Codecri, 1979); *O Crepúsculo do Macho* (Rio de Janeiro: Editora Nova Fronteira, 1980); and *Entradas e Bandeiras* (Rio de Janeiro: Editora Codecri, 1981). See also Alfredo Syrkis, *Os Carbonários: Memórias da Guerrilha Perdida* (São Paulo: Global Editora e Distribuidora Ltda.,7a. Ed, 1980). Carlos Alberto Messeder Pereira and Heloísa Buarque de Hollanda's *Patrulhas Ideológicas: arte e engajamento em debate* (São Paulo: Brasiliense, 1980) contains rich interview material with former guerrillas.

    For a summation of this production, see Heloísa Buarque de Hollanda, "Brasil, 1964–1978: idas e vindas da cultura de resistência," and Joan Dassin, "Fear and the Political Text in Brazil: Memoirs of the Generation of '68," papers presented at a conference on "The Culture of Fear," sponsored by the Social Science Research Council in Buenos Aires in May 1985.

    For an analysis of censorship, see Joan Dassin, "Press Censorship and the Military State in Brazil," in Jane Curry and Joan Dassin, eds., *Press Control Around the World* (New York: Praeger Press, 1982), pp. 149–86.
12. Patricia Weiss-Fagen, "Summary of Discussion on the Role of the Agents of Fear," report presented to the Social Science Research Council, 1983.

ONE

1. A. J. Langguth, *Hidden Terrors* (New York: Pantheon Books, 1978).

THREE

1. *Pasquim,* Rio de Janeiro, 12 (607), 4–18 January 1981.

SEVEN

1. Quoted in *A Repressão Militar-Policial no Brasil* (Military Police Repression in Brazil), mimeo., São Paulo, 1975, p. 22.
2. Golbery do Couto e Silva, *Geopolítica do Brasil* (Rio de Janeiro: Livraria José Olympio Editora, 1967), p. 13.
3. Bishop Cândido Padim, *A Doutrina de Segurança Nacional à Luz da*

Doutrina da Igreja (The Doctrine of National Security in the Light of the Doctrine of the Church), mimeo., São Paulo, June 1968.

4. Joseph Comblin, *A Ideologia da Segurança Nacional* (The Ideology of National Security), (Rio de Janeiro: Editora Civilização Brasileira, 1978), p. 237.

THIRTEEN

1. Press statement, 1981, Rio de Janeiro.

FIFTEEN

1. *Pasquim*, Rio de Janeiro, 12 (607), 12–18 January 1981.
2. Antônio Carlos Fon, *Tortura: A História da Repressão Política no Brasil* (Torture: The History of Political Repression in Brazil) (São Paulo: Global Editora, 1979), p. 40.

SIXTEEN

1. Testimony given to the Brazilian Amnesty Committee, 1979.
2. Quoted in *Esquerda Armada: Testemunho dos Presos Políticos do Presídio Milton Dias Moreira, no Rio de Janeiro.* Selection by Luzimar Nogueira Dias. (Vitória, Espírito Santo: Edições do Leitor, 1979), pp. 32 ff.
3. Dossier distributed to the press, Rio de Janeiro, January 1981.
4. Quoted in Frei Betto, *Batismo de Sangue* (Baptism of Blood), 6a. edicão (Rio de Janeiro: Editora Civilização Brasileira, 1983), pp. 234–35.

EIGHTEEN

1. Quoted in *The Law of War: A Documentary History*, vol. 1, ed. Leon Friedman (New York: Random House, 1972).
2. *Jornal do Brasil*, 23 October 1974.

APPENDICES

GLOSSARY OF ACRONYMS

AI	Ato Institucional	Institutional Act
ALN	Ação Libertadora Nacional	National Action for Liberation
AMFNB	Associação dos Marinheiros e Fuzileiros Navais do Brasil	Association of Navy and Marine Personnel of Brazil
ANL	Aliança Nacional Libertadora	National Liberation Alliance
AP	Ação Popular	Popular Action
APML	Ação Popular Marxista-Leninista do Brasil	Marxist-Leninist Popular Action of Brazil
ARENA	Aliança Renovadora Nacional	National Alliance for Renewal
BC	Batalião de Caçadores	Battalion of Riflemen
BNM	*Brasil: Nunca Mais* (Portuguese edition of this book)	*Brazil: Never Again*
CGG	Comando Geral de Greve	General Strike Command
CGI	Comissão Geral de Investigações	General Committee for Investigations
CGT	Comando Geral dos Trabalhadores	General Workers' Command
CIA		Central Intelligence Agency
CIE	Centro de Informações do Exercito	Army Information Center

CISA	Centro de Informações e Segurança da Aeronáutica	Air Force Information and Security Center
CNBB	Conferência Nacional dos Bispos do Brasil	Brazilian National Bishops' Conference
COLINA	Comando de Libertação Nacional	National Liberation Command
CORRENTE	Corrente Revolucionária de Minas Gerais	Minas Gerais Revolutionary Movement
CPC	Centro Popular de Cultura	Popular Center for Culture
CPM	Código Penal Militar	Military Penal Code
CPPM	Código de Processo Penal Militar	Military Penal Procedure Code
CSN	Conselho de Segurança Nacional	National Security Council
DEOPS	Departamento Estadual de Ordem Política e Social	State Department for Political and Social Order
DL	Decreto-lei	Decree Law
DOI-CODI	Destacamento de Operações–Centro de Operações de Defesa Interna	Information Operations Detachment–Center for Internal Defense Operations
DOPS	Departamento de Ordem Política e Social (early name for DEOPS)	Department for Political and Social Order
DPPS	Delegacia de Policía Política e Social	Political and Social Police Precinct
DSN	Doutrina de Segurança Nacional	Doctrine of National Security
ESG	Escola Superior de Guerra	Higher War College
FALN	Forças Armadas de Libertação Nacional	Armed Forces for National Liberation
FBT	Fração Bolchevique Trotskista	Trotskyite Bolshevik Fraction
FEB	Força Expedicionária Brasileira	Brazilian Expeditionary Force
FLN	Frente de Libertação Nacional	National Liberation Front

IBAD	Instituto Brasileiro de Ação Democrática	Brazilian Institute for Democratic Action
IPES	Instituto de Pesquisa e Estudos Sociais	Brazilian Institute for Research and Social Studies
IPM	Inquérito Policial Militar	Military Police Inquest
LSN	Lei de Segurança Nacional	National Security Law
MAR	Movimento de Ação Revolucionária	Movement for Revolutionary Action
MCR	Movimento Comunista Revolucionário	Revolutionary Communist Movement
MDB	Movimento Democrático Brasileiro	Brazilian Democratic Movement
MEP	Movimento pela Emancipação do Proletariado	Movement for the Emancipation of the Proletariat
MNR	Movimento Nacional Revolucionário	National Revolutionary Movement
MOLIPO	Movimento de Libertação Popular	Movement for Popular Liberation
MR-8	Movimento Revolucionário 8 de Outubro	8th of October Revolutionary Movement
MR-21	Movimento Revolucionário 21 de Abril	21st of April Revolutionary Movement
MR-26	Movimento Revolucionário 26 de Março	26th of March Revolutionary Movement
MRM	Movimento Revolucionário Marxista	Marxist Revoutionary Movement
MRT	Movimento Revolucionário Tiradentes	Tiradentes Revolutionary Movement
M3G	Marx, Mao, Marighella e Guevara	Marx, Mao, Marighella, and Guevara
OBAN	Operação Bandeirantes	Operation Bandeirantes
OSI	Organização Socialista Internacionalista	Internationalist Socialist Organization
PCB	Partido Comunista Brasileiro	Brazilian Communist Party
PC do B	Partido Comunista do Brasil	Communist Party of Brazil
PCBR	Partido Comunista Brasileiro Revolucionário	Revolutionary Brazilian Communist Party

PCR	Partido Comunista Revolucionário	Revolutionary Communist Party
PDT	Partido Democrático Trabalhista	Democratic Workers' Party
PE	Polícia do Exército	Army Police
PIC	Pelotão de Investigações Criminais	Squad for Criminal Investigations
PM	Polícia Militar	Military Police
PMDB	Partido Movimento Democrático Brasileiro	Brazilian Democratic Movement Party
PMMG	Polícia Militar de Minas Gerais	Military Police of the State of Minas Gerais
POC	Partido Operário Comunista	Communist Workers' Party
POLOP	Organização Revolucionária Marxista–Política Operária	Marxist Revolutionary Organization–Workers' Politics
PORT	Partido Operário Revolucionário (Trotskista)	Trotskyite Revolutionary Workers' Party
PRT	Partido Revolucionário dos Trabalhadores	Workers' Revolutionary Party
PSD	Partido Social Democrático	Social Democratic Party
PT	Partido dos Trabalhadores	Workers' Party
PTB	Partido Trabalhista Brasileiro	Brazilian Labor Party
REDE	Resistência Democrática ou Resistência Nacionalista Democrática e Popular	Democratic Resistance or Nationalist Democratic and Popular Resistance
RI	Regimento de Infantaria	Infantry Regiment
SNI	Serviço Nacional de Informações	National Information Service
STF	Supremo Tribunal Federal	Supreme Federal Court
STM	Superior Tribunal Militar	Supreme Military Court
UNE	União Nacional dos Estudantes	National Student Union

VAR-Pal-mares	Vanguarda Armada Revolucionária–Palmares	Armed Revolutionary Vanguard–Palmares
VPR	Vanguarda Popular Revolucionária	Popular Revolutionary Vanguard
WCC		World Council of Churches

STATEMENT ON TORTURE
World Council of Churches Geneva, Switzerland, August 1977

". . . the emphasis of the Gospel is on the value of all human beings in the sight of God, on the atoning and redeeming work of Christ that has given to humanity true dignity, on love as the motive for action, and on love for one's neighbour as the practical expression of an active faith in Christ. We are members one of another, and when one suffers all are hurt." [Consultation on Human Rights and Christian Responsibility, St. Pölten, Austria, 1974.]

The thirtieth meeting of the World Council of Churches' Central Committee [Geneva, 28 July to 6 August 1977] has heard the words of its Moderator who, with deep sorrow, directed its attention to "a steady increase in reports of violation of human rights and in the use of torture in an increasing number of countries of the world." Then the General Secretary recommended "a style of thinking and of being which is a prerequisite for furthering the unity, witness and service of the people of God according to God's purpose." One essential element of this is a determination "to be true, and live in truth." "Being human," he said, "means to uncover things, to bring them to light, to disclose them, to deprive them of their hiddenness, to bring them into consciousness."

We are called to bear witness to the light which has come into the world through our Lord Jesus Christ. At the same time, we know "the judgment, that the light has come into the world, and men loved darkness more than light, because their deeds were evil. For eveyone who does evil hates the light, lest his deeds be exposed" (John 3:19–20).

Today, we stand under God's judgment, for in our generation the darkness, deceit and inhumanity of the torture chamber have become a more widespread and atrocious reality than at any other time in history.

No human practice is so abominable, nor so widely condemned. Yet physical and mental torture and other forms of cruel and inhuman treatment are now being applied systematically in many countries, and practically no nation can claim to be free of them.

Next year the world will be called upon to mark the thirtieth anniversary of the adoption on 10 December 1948, by the United National General Assembly, of the "Universal Declaration of Human Rights." The preamble to that Declaration states that "recognition of the inherent dignity and of the equal and inalienable rights of all members of the human family is the foundation of freedom, justice and peace in the world."

The WCC Nairobi Assembly (1975) has urged us to hold high this concern for justice, to work for the implementation of all the rights enunciated in the Universal Declaration, and the elimination of the causes of violations of human rights.

The struggle to abolish torture involves "work at the most basic level towards a society without unjust structures." Torture is most likely to occur in societies which are characterized by injustice, but it can also happen in situations where most rights are protected. While torture is sometimes applied to common prisoners, the victims are most likely persons who have become involved in the struggle for justice and human rights in their own societies, people who have had the courage to voice the needs of the people. In the face of political opposition, rulers of an increasing number of countries have decreed emergency laws in which the basic guarantee of "habeas corpus" is suspended. Detainees are forbidden contact with a defense lawyer, their families, religious leaders or others, creating conditions propitious for torture. Under the pretext of "national security," many states today subordinate human dignity to the selfish interests of those in power.

Given the tragic dimensions of torture in our world, we urge the churches to take this thirtieth anniversary year as a special occasion to lay bare the practice of, complicity in, and the propensity to torture which exist in our nations. Torture is endemic, breeds in the dark, in silence. We call upon the churches to bring its existence into the open, to break the silence, to reveal the persons and structures of our societies which are responsible for this most dehumanizing of all violations of human rights.

We recognize that there remain, even among the churches, certain differences of interpretation of human rights, and that sometimes different priorities are set for the implementation of human rights according to varying socio-economic, political and cultural contexts. But on the point of torture there can be no difference of opinion. The churches together can and must become major forces for the abolition of torture.

We therefore urge the churches to:

1. a) Intensify their efforts to inform their members and the people of their nations about the provisions of the "Universal Declaration of Human Rights," and especially of its Article 5, which reads:

   "No one shall be subjected to torture or to cruel, inhuman or degrading treatment or punishment";

   b) continue and intensify their efforts to cause their governments to ratify the international covenants on economic, social and cultural rights, and on civil and political rights adopted by the United Nations General Assembly, 16 December 1966; special efforts should be made to achieve the ratification of the "Optional Protocol" of the "Covenant on Social and Political Rights" by which states agree to allow to be considered communications from individuals subject to their jurisdiction who claim to be victims of a violation of the rights set out in that Covenant by their own state; similarly, attention of governments should be called to the importance of ratifying specifically Article 41 of the "Covenant on Civil and Political Rights," by which a state can express its willingness to allow other nations to raise questions, through a careful procedure, about its compliance with the provisions of this Covenant, including its Article 7 which prohibits torture or cruel, inhuman or degrading treatment or punishment;

   c) inform their members and the people of their nations of the contents of the "Declaration on the Protection of All Persons from Being Subjected to Torture and Other Cruel, Inhuman or Degrading Treatment or Punishment" unanimously adopted by the United Nations General Assembly on 9 December 1975;

d) study and seek the applications at all levels of governments of the "Standard Minimum Rules for the Treatment of Prisoners" adopted on 30 August 1955 by the First United Nations Congress on the Prevention of Crime and the Treatment of Offenders;

e) study and seek the application of the "Declaration of Tokyo: Guidelines for Medical Doctors concerning Torture and Other Cruel, Inhuman or Degrading Treatment or Punishment in Relation to Detention and Imprisonment" adopted by the twenty-ninth World Medical Assembly in Tokyo, October 1975;

2. Seek to ensure the compliance of their governments with the provisions of these important international instruments, recognizing that while the declarations are not legally binding, they do represent a large international consensus and carry very substantial moral weight;

3. Express their solidarity with churches and people elsewhere in their struggle to have these provisions strictly applied in their own countries;

4. Urge their governments to contribute positively to the current effort of the United Nations to develop a body of principles for the protection of all persons under any form of detention or imprisonment, and to strengthen the existing procedures for the implementation of the "Standard Minimum Rules"; and of the World Health Organization to develop a "Code of Medical Ethics Relevant to the Protection of Detained Persons against Torture and Other Cruel, Inhuman or Degrading Treatment or Punishment";

5. Work for the elaboration by the United Nations of a "Convention on the Protection of All Persons against Torture";

6. Encourage other initiatives to establish an international strategy to fight against torture and to create an efficient international machinery to ban torture;

7. Ensure that law enforcement officials, members of the military and of special security branches, members of the medical profession and others be informed of the above-mentioned international standards and to press for their non-participation

in torture, and their non-complicity with others directly involved;

8. Work against any further international commerce in torture techniques or equipment and against the development in the scientific community of even more sophisticated techniques of physical or mental torture;

9. Seek access to places of detention and interrogation centres in order to ensure that persons held there are not mistreated;

10. Be especially attentive to the fact that torture most often occurs after secret detention, abduction and subsequent disappearance of victims, and see to it that special rapid and appropriate measures be taken to locate them and to provide legal protection for such persons by the competent authorities.

APPENDIX III

"DISAPPEARED" POLITICAL PRISONERS

1. Adriano Fonseca Fernandes Filho	- 1973 [A]*
2. Aluízio Palhano Pedreira Ferreira	- 1971
3. Ana Rosa Kucinski Silva	- 1974
4. André Grabois	- 1973 [A]
5. Antônio "Alfaiate"	- 1974 [A]
6. Antônio Alfredo Campos	- 1973 [A]
7. Antônio Carlos Monteiro Teixeira	- 1972 [A]
8. Antônio Guilherme Ribeiro Ribas	- 1973 [A]
9. Antônio Joaquim Machado	- 1971
10. Antônio de Pádua Costa	- 1974 [A]
11. Antônio Teodoro de Castro	- 1973 [A]
12. Arildo Valadão	- 1973 [A]
13. Armando Teixeira Frutuoso	- 1975
14. Áurea Eliza Pereira Valadão	- 1974 [A]
15. Ayrton Adalberto Mortati	- 1971
16. Bergson Gurjão de Farias	- 1972 [A]
17. Caiuby Alves de Castro	- 1973
18. Carlos Alberto Soares de Freitas	- 1971
19. Celso Gilberto de Oliveira	- 1970
20. Cilon da Cunha Brun	- 1973 [A]
21. Ciro Flávio Oliveira Salazar	- 1972 [A]
22. Custódio Saraiva Neto	- 1974 [A]

*[A] indicates those who died in the "Araguaia Guerrilla" movement; see chapter 18.

23. Daniel José de Carvalho — 1973
24. Daniel Ribeiro Calado — 1973 [A]
25. David Capistrano da Costa — 1974
26. Denis Antônio Casemiro — 1971
27. Dermeval da Silva Pereira — 1974 [A]
28. Dinaelsa Soares Santana Coqueiro — 1973 [A]
29. Dinalva Oliveira Teixeira — 1973 [A]
30. Divino Ferreira de Souza — 1973 [A]
31. Durvalino de Souza — 1973
32. Edgar de Aquino Duarte — 1974
33. Eduardo Collier Filho — 1974
34. Elmo Corrêa — 1974 [A]
35. Elson Costa — 1975
36. Ezequias Bezerra da Rocha — 1973
37. Félix Escobar Sobrinho — 1971
38. Fernando Augusto de Santa Cruz Oliveira — 1974
39. Gilberto Olímpio Maria — 1973 [A]
40. Guilherme Gomes Lund — 1973 [A]
41. Heleni Pereira Teles Guariba — 1971
42. Helenira Rezende de Souza Nazareth — 1972 [A]
43. Hélio Luiz Navarro de Magalhães — 1974 [A]
44. Hiram de Lima Pereira — 1975
45. Honestino Monteiro Guimarães — 1973
46. Humberto Albuquerque Câmara Neto — 1973
47. Idalísio Soares Aranha Filho — 1972 [A]
48. Ieda Santos Delgado — 1974
49. Isis Dias de Oliveira — 1972
50. Issami Nakamura Okano — 1974
51. Itair José Veloso — 1975
52. Ivan Mota Dias — 1971
53. Jaime Petit da Silva — 1973 [A]
54. Jana Moroni Barroso — 1974 [A]
55. Jayme Amorim de Miranda — 1975
56. João Alfredo — 1964
57. João Batista Rita Pereda — 1973
58. João Carlos Haas Sobrinho — 1972 [A]
59. João Gualberto — 1973 [A]
60. João Massena Melo — 1974
61. Joaquim Pires Cerveira — 1973
62. Joel José de Carvalho — 1973

63.	Joel Vasconcelos dos Santos	- 1971
64.	Jorge Leal Gonçalves Pereira	- 1970
65.	José Francisco Chaves	- 1972 [A]
66.	José Humberto Bronca	- 1973 [A]
67.	José Lavechia	- 1973
68.	José Lima Piauhy Dourado	- 1973 [A]
69.	José Maurílio Patrício	- 1974 [A]
70.	José Montenegro de Lima	- 1975
71.	José Porfírio de Souza	- 1973
72.	José Romam	- 1974
73.	José Toledo de Oliveira	- 1972 [A]
74.	Kleber Lemos da Silva	- 1972 [A]
75.	Líbero Giancarlo Castiglia	- 1973 [A]
76.	Lúcia Maria de Souza	- 1973 [A]
77.	Lúcio Petit da Silva	- 1974 [A]
78.	Luís de Almeida Araújo	- 1971
79.	Luís Inácio Maranhão Filho	- 1974
80.	Luiz Renê Silveira e Silva	- 1974 [A]
81.	Luíza Augusta Garlippe	- 1973 [A]
82.	Lourival Paulino	- 1972 [A]
83.	Manuel José Murchis	- 1972 [A]
84.	Márcio Beck Machado	- 1973
85.	Marco Antônio Dias Batista	- 1970
86.	Maria Augusta Thomáz	- 1973
87.	Maria Célia Corrêa	- 1974 [A]
88.	Maria Lúcia Petit da Silva	- 1972 [A]
89.	Mariano Joaquim da Silva	- 1971
90.	Mário Alves de Souza Vieira	- 1970
91.	Maurício Grabois	- 1973 [A]
92.	Miguel Pereira dos Santos	- 1972 [A]
93.	Nélson de Lima Piauhy Dourado	- 1974 [A]
94.	Nestor Veras	- 1975
95.	Orlando Momente	- 1974 [A]
96.	Orlando Rosa Bonfim Júnior	- 1975
97.	Osvaldo Orlando da Costa	- 1974 [A]
98.	Paulo César Botelho Massa	- 1972
99.	Paulo Costa Ribeiro Bastos	- 1972
100.	Paulo Mendes Rodrigues	- 1973 [A]
101.	Paulo Roberto Pereira Marques	- 1973 [A]
102.	Paulo Stuart Wright	- 1973

103.	Paulo de Tarso Celestino da Silva	- 1971
104.	Pedro Alexandrino de Oliveira	- 1974 [A]
105.	Pedro Inácio de Araújo	- 1964
106.	Ramires Maranhão do Valle	- 1973
107.	Rodolfo de Carvalho Troiano	- 1974 [A]
108.	Rosalindo Souza	- 1973 [A]
109.	Rubens Beirodt Paiva	- 1971
110.	Rui Carlos Vieira Berbert	- 1971
111.	Rui Frazão Soares	- 1974
112.	Sérgio Landulfo Furtado	- 1972
113.	Stuart Edgar Angel Jones	- 1971
114.	Suely Yomiko Kanayama	- 1974 [A]
115.	Telma Regina Cordeiro Corrêa	- 1974 [A]
116.	Thomas Antônio da Silva Meirelles Netto	- 1974
117.	Tobias Pereira Júnior	- 1974 [A]
118.	Uirassu de Assis Batista	- 1974 [A]
119.	Vandick Reidner Pereira Coqueiro	- 1973 [A]
120.	Virgílio Gomes da Silva	- 1969
121.	Vitorino Alves Moitinho	- 1973
122.	Walquíria Afonso Costa	- 1974 [A]
123.	Walter Ribeiro Novais	- 1971
124.	Walter de Souza Ribeiro	- 1974
125.	Wilson Silva	- 1974

About the Translator and Editor

JAIME WRIGHT, D.D., D.H.L., is well known for his ecumenical work in the area of human rights. As a minister of the Presbyterian Church (U.S.A.), he collaborated full-time for eight years, starting in 1979, with Cardinal Paulo Evaristo Arns, Archbishop of São Paulo. Wright has served the church in Brazil for forty-three years as a school administrator, teacher, pastor, executive, journalist, and translator. A Brazilian citizen, he holds degrees from two U.S. institutions: the University of the Ozarks in Clarksville, Arkansas, and Princeton Theological Seminary. Prior to retirement in 1993, he served for six years as general secretary of the United Presbyterian Church of Brazil.

JOAN DASSIN, Ph.D., is a specialist on the politics and culture of contemporary Brazil. She has conducted research and published books and articles on state cultural policies, press censorship, and the arts under the military dictatorship, as well as on human rights questions. The holder since 1974 of a doctorate in Modern Thought and Literature from Stanford University, Dassin has taught at Amherst College, Columbia University, and Fordham University, and has been Fulbright Lecturer at several Brazilian universities. From 1989–1992, she was Representative for the Ford Foundation's Brazil office in Rio de Janeiro and, from 1992–1996, served as the Foundation's Regional Director for Latin America, based in New York. She now works as an independent consultant. A native of California, Dassin has periodically lived and worked in Brazil since 1971.

.

Lightning Source UK Ltd.
Milton Keynes UK
UKHW020639070922
408458UK00008B/179